In Spite of Us

A Love Story about Second Chances

Deb & Sandy Palmer

ISBN 978-1-64416-436-5 (paperback)
ISBN 978-1-64416-438-9 (hardcover)
ISBN 978-1-64416-437-2 (digital)

Christian Faith Publishing, Inc.
832 Park Avenue
Meadville, PA 16335
www.christianfaithpublishing.com

Printed in the United States of America

CHAPTER 1

Duel in the Sun
(Deb)

THE SCENT OF STALE SMOKE and gin follow me through the doors of Nordstrom. A gaggle of salesgirls with sprayed coiffures and portrait faces pointing polychrome nails, alerting the others to take note of my presence. I'm surrounded by mirrors like a carnival fun house, mocking, stalking. There's no escape. Images of hair askew with remnants of last night's lipstick and smeared mascara chase me around the cosmetic counters. Sweet fragrances war, nausea swirls. I swallow, when a voice from behind calls out to me.

"Deb? What's going on?"

It's Paula, my friend from college, the only person privy to the telltale truths of my messy life.

"Not again," she says, reading my face. "He's a jerk."

Two weeks ago, Paula and I were strangers, paired as debate partners by Professor King who felt our common forty-something student status suited a good team. We've proven him right, slam-dunking assertions, leaving the burden of proof to our twenty-something opponents, doomed by a prima facie case.

She's the type that skips the cordial stage, diving into friendship jackhammer-style.

"You'll know when you've had enough," she says, trading the *I told you so* for a big hug.

I return the hug, waving her back toward her antsy husband, Jim, who looks like a little boy being held prisoner in a lingerie shop.

"Don't worry. I'm done this time. Go on. I'll see you Monday in the hub."

They walk away, arms linked, Paula shaking her head while Jim quizzes her about the drama. Seeing them together on a Saturday afternoon feels good, hopeful. Last week, they moved back in together, not the duo they once were but a trio of man, wife, and forgiveness.

Monday arrives, feeling like it doesn't belong between Sunday and Tuesday. I drive the Ellensburg Canyon, convincing the river, the trees, a hovering eagle, and myself—I am happy.

"You okay?" asks Paula before I can sit down at the table.

"Yes, everything's fine."

Silence hangs in the air.

"No, you didn't. You took him back? Again?" she asks, cupping a hand over one eye as if she's embarrassed.

So it goes. Do I believe the alluring magician with the smoke and mirrors? Or my friend, a seasoned do-or-die type, recovering alcoholic? Chimera may be a mythological monster, but truth is, it's such a drag.

I consider the safer choice because I'm a mom, a title which serves as a parachute when making decisions. Haley and Jay, eleven and eight, keep me somewhat accountable. Still, my mothering style is bipolaresque at best. Weekdays and alternate weekends, I perform parental acrobatics, attempting to make up for the divorce, working full time, and maintaining a 4.0 GPA. However, when my little red-heads wave goodbye to mommy from the window of their dad's sedan, all power to be *good* gets zapped by kryptonite, and the super-mom cape falls off.

I'm rather like the child described in the Henry Wadsworth poem:

> There was a little girl
> Who had a little curl
> Right in the middle of her forehead.
> And when she was good
> She was very, very good
> But when she was bad
> She was horrid!

Exchange the curl for big-bar hair (it's the eighties), and here I am, struggling to be good with *me-generation* propaganda ringing in my ears. My routine escalates as follows: *desire to be good, stress to maintain goodness, drink to relieve stress, additional drink, guard to be good drowns, self-hate joins the party. And lastly, things I thought I'd never do happen.* Some actions hurt others deeply but can be forgiven like name-calling, gambling, or lying. Others hurt to the core like infidelity. If you step over that line, don't bother turning back.

Starting an affair with my married boss was like tossing a Molotov cocktail at hope. My children, Haley and Jay, were helpless rubble, shards too jagged to piece back together. And I, the terrorist, sopping in liquid justifications of vodka and gin.

As a single mom, slightly disheveled old patterns emerge. On the weekends when their dad is the designated parent, my bad girl trumps my good girl. When Sunday drags in, I tidy up and make grandiose self-promises that start with words like *next time* or *never again*. I welcome them home with the best good-mom smile I can muster, and we play the Game of Life, chomp popcorn, and lick Rocky Road ice-cream cones.

When Monday appears, accordingly, I pack healthy lunches with bags of carrot sticks, send them off to school, and drive the Ellensburg Canyon singing "Cry Me a River," my theme song. I smile and nod to Paula, faithfully waiting at our usual table in the hub. I consider lies I could tell while paying for my coffee. Why did I phone her Saturday night tanked up on vodka and rejection? She begged me to make a clean break with Wayne. I said I would. I promised as soon I hung up the phone. And I meant it. Then Wayne knocked on the door.

"It's okay this time, Paula. He wants to do the right thing. He loves me. Really, he does. He's telling his wife today."

I hear myself saying, "It's different this time," and I wonder how she can bear the sound of my voice. It must stem from her belief in a power greater than herself, a euphemism for God she picked up in one of her daily AA meetings. I'm surprised our friendship didn't end the day I said, "I respect your beliefs but don't share them with me. I prefer to go it alone without a crutch."

No debate or disdain followed, then nor now. She just smiles and says something annoying like "Well, do what you need to do."

I admire Paula. Sometimes I wish I *was* an alcoholic. I'd muster up a powerful God who'd fix all my messes. Alas, I'm not an alcoholic. My drinking may appear as mayhem, but I have it under control. I can stop anytime I choose.

Now if only I could just get control of this affair. I don't even like Wayne. He's just there like food you'd never choose, not a glazed doughnut or a bag of salty chips, no saltine crackers or rice cakes. They're joyless, unsatisfying, dry, yet you can't stop stuffing your face, all while asking, "Why am I eating this?"

When alone in a room lit by vodka and delusion, it's a grand love affair. Even in the aftermath of being dumped, I lap up the emotions like a starving cat. There's an old western flick that best describes this sick love affair, *Duel in the Sun*, starring Gregory Peck and Jennifer Jones. The finale takes place in the desert. Scorned lovers trapped, one behind a boulder, the other in a cave. Depleted of tolerance, they steady aiming their shotguns, blasting holes in one another. After a brief celebration for hitting the targets dead on, they panic at the thought of losing their true love. Covered in blood, sweat, and tears, they crawl toward each other professing remorse and love, sharing a final kiss and gasp of breath.

Paula's tired of this scene, as anyone would be. She wants me to meet some guy from AA. *Betcha* he's a lousy shot.

CHAPTER 2

It Ain't No Cakewalk (Sandy)

STYROFOAM CUP IN HAND, I nod to the roomful of like-minded, half-awake coffee slurpers, saying the words I've said every morning since June 10, 1986.

"My name's Sandy. I'm an alcoholic."

Sobriety swipes the rug out from under your life, leaving random pieces hanging midair—family, finances, jobs, sex, ego. Without the bogus safety net of drugs and alcohol, you're involuntarily awake to witness the crash. Juggling life sober isn't easy, but I've managed to stack up three years, one day at a time.

A sober life's worth living, but it *ain't no cakewalk.* You're left at ground zero, stacks of bodies strewn from your chaotic past, rubble needing to be cleared away. Cindy, the nursemaid/girlfriend who stood by me through my last drunks, remains standing in sobriety. I try ending the relationship but can't seem to get her zipped into the body bag. She wants and deserves more than I can give.

I surrender my AA spiel for the day, quoting my first sponsor.

"I can do anything I want as long as I can live with the consequences."

The meeting closes with prayer and hugs. I skip the informal *after meeting,* allowing ten minutes to reach Eisenhower High School where I'm completing a special ed practicum. The bad boy from Davis, the other high school across the tracks, voted most likely to be town drunk, is on his way to becoming a respected teacher. Hah! Even my cop buddies, the ones who called me Sandy while slapping on the cuffs, will soon entrust their children to my care.

It's Monday, so I'm not surprised when several students are missing. John has bloody knuckles again from some fight he seems to have no memory of. Kenny, known simply as K, appears to be off his meds, chattering in turbo while obsessively picking at his skin. Marilyn's lethargic, looking like I feel after a Thanksgiving food spree. I assume the poor girl lost the battle to junk food over the weekend, adding to her 300-pound frame instead of losing, as was the plan last week. No real surprises, just the typical aftermath from the weekend. By the time I wrestle the group to order, the day's exhausted. I'm relieved *and* disappointed that it's over.

Broke with no time for an eat and run at Mom's for homemade soup and bread, I scarf down a can of refried beans (fifty-nine cents for mucho protein) and head out the door. Three nights a week, I carpool to Ellensburg with Paula, my friend Jim's wife, for evening classes.

Paula's a hoot. When she opens the truck door, I do a double take, making sure it's really her. I think random strangers select her daily outfits. Today, she's wearing what looks like a candy-striper uniform with white anklets. Last week, she looked like a biker's old lady. Doesn't matter. She and my childhood drinking comrade, Jim, are sober. Hanging with other recovering drunks works like a shield.

She hops into my Courier pickup, politely ignores the squeaks from the rickety battered seat, raises her soft voice to excel over the engine, and asks a question, as if she's been holding it in all weekend.

"How are things with you and that gal Cindy? Is that her name?"

I don't want to discuss my personal life but haven't a clue how to evade the conversation for the forty-five-minute drive. I answer her questions as if she's an interrogator for the Russian mafia. She knows the answers anyway. I hate when people do that, ask questions they already have answers for. They seem to have a sick need to hear you say it out loud.

"I haven't severed the relationship with Cindy because she *should* be the perfect match for me," I spill to Paula. "She doesn't deserve to—."

"She has a history of aiding and abetting alcoholics and deserves a master's degree in codependency," she says.

"I'm in the process of breaking it off."

"I only ask because I have this friend, Deb. She's just getting out of a really sick relationship and—"

"*Ya* think jumping from one sick relationship into another is such a good idea, Paula?" I interrupt, laughing.

Realizing what she's said, she laughs too. Face changing from innocent oops to devilish grin, she holds up a photo of this gal in lingerie.

"This is Deb. She's my model in photography class."

She continues before I can counter that I need to work on me before taking on another relationship.

"She'll be at the AA Valentine's dance on Friday. Are you going to be there?"

"Yes, Paula. As you already know, I'm on the set-up committee."

CHAPTER 3

They Don't Serve Cocktails at an AA Dance? (Deb)

"OJ, COME ON, BOY," JAY says, slapping his knees. "It's time for Pavlov's dogs. Haley, bring the bell."

OJ's our black cockapoo shelter dog presented to Haley wearing a huge yellow bow on her second birthday. His rightful name should be *OJ We Didn't Name Him.* At the time, OJ Simpson was in good standing with the world. Even so, we would never have named him that.

"What does OJ mean?" asked Haley when we mistakenly revealed his shelter alias.

Jerry, her dad, is struck with sudden mute syndrome (SMS), so I take on the challenge of explaining political incorrectness to our wide-eyed toddler.

"Orange juice. OJ stands for orange juice."

Hence the dog dubbed for life; his owners cursed, forever apologizing, swearing, "We didn't do it."

Sharing Psychology 101 stories like Pavlov's dogs combines study with fun family time. A visual like OJ, head cocked, awaiting his treat stays with you even when taking a test. When the giggles, slobbers, and bell ringing get old, we move onto signing valentines for tomorrow's class party. I can tell Haley is up to something because she's helping her little brother with his he-man valentines.

"Who's Rita? Why are you giving her the biggest card?" she asks.

As I listen to nosey sister sleuth for details, my own stomach turns thinking of V-Day. Paula is insisting I go to an AA Valentine's dance Friday night. I've been using a guy named Jack like a dose of methadone, managing to white knuckle ten days, to go cold turkey without Wayne. I met Jack while drinking alone, incognito in a dark lounge with a bluesy piano player. He approached, a walking platitude, as the song "All by Myself" mocked my heart.

"You look like you could use a friend," he says, sitting on the barstool next to me.

Gee, what a nice guy, probably a social worker by day, spending his nights consoling lonely women in bars. Yes, I'm an idiot looking for some loser like myself who's got nothing better to do than drink himself stupid in this dank nest of drunken litter mates.

I may be powerless to control the man who dumped on me, but here stands fresh, helpless prey, begging for a heart slap. He may as well be wearing a T-shirt with the words, "Will lie through my teeth for sex."

Like her generational comrades, my mom preached abstinence. The sermon began as one of purity, virginity, innocence then turned into a hellish tale of manipulation, control, and power. According to Mom and Na-Na, whose nose crinkled at the mention of S-E-X, it's no fun at all. S-E-X is something you hold ransom for control over your husband after you've snagged one in your pure white net of virginity. Confused and way too young for experimentation, I tested the theories myself. Conclusion? Mom, who flitters eyelashes with a *yes* smile whenever near my blatantly sexual Dad, lied. Even so, I kept her manipulation tactics handy, in case I ever felt the urge to pull the wings off a fly. As far as Na-Na? Well, she just may have been telling the truth.

Before long, my victim from the piano lounge is bringing presents, mowing my lawn, even spouting poetry. He was just what I needed. My chance at playing the predator, never to be the pitiful prey again. But the trouble is, groveling quickly becomes tiresome, and Jack soon reminds me of my pesky little brother begging for my candy.

"Another beer, Jack? I don't want to show up too early."

"Sure," he says, leaning over, lighting my cigarette. "I've never been to an AA dance, have you?"

"Of course not. They don't serve cocktails at an AA dance."

Poor, clueless Jack. The only reason I'm going to this dance is to eyeball Sandy. There's no real threat to Jack, at least he knows how to drink. This other guy is a puritan with three years' sobriety and a nonsmoker. He goes to those meetings and believes in God. Paula flunks matchmaking 101. She's trying, knowing my veins itch for Wayne and that soon I'll tire of Jack, my human methadone fix.

When we arrive at the grange hall, the parking lot is packed, so we park down the block. Jack sticks by my side like dog hair on Velcro. The party's in huddles of six or so people, all laughing and yelling over Lionel Richie, the DJ's ignored choice.

"Are you looking for Paula? She's over there," Jack says, pointing.

"I see her. I'm just checking things out. Let's go. This is not my thing. Oh crap, she's waving us over."

Like contestants at a picnic sharing a potato sack, I involuntarily drag Jack along to meet Paula and her husband, Jim.

"Hi, Jack. I'm stealing Deb for a minute. This is Jim. We'll be back," Paula says, prying me loose and leading me across the grange hall. "C'mon, you're late."

For a moment, I thought she smelled the alcohol on my breath but shrugged it off as paranoia. Besides, I've told her I'm not an alcoholic, and she of all people should know that normal people drink at parties.

"Sandy, this is Deb," she says, pointing to me Vanna-White style.

We shake hands, exchanging empty niceties. My stomach does that thing, that flutter thing. I want the moment to last, floating with this stranger in a crowded dance hall decorated with tacky paper hearts and pink balloons. But, like all dreams, an alarm wakes you before the best part happens. A nagging stare on my left pierced through the moment. Turning toward the threat, I see a blonde woman three chairs to the left, eyes narrowed like a sniper waiting for clearance.

"What are you doing?" Jack says, breathing on my neck.

"Uh, nothing. Jack, this is Sandy. Sandy, Jack."

They exchange a glance and an *hmph* then Jack whispers in my ear, "Let's go have a drink," to which I oblige.

The encounter with Sandy lingers in my mind that night and throughout the next day. He's traditionally handsome. Usually that bores me. Yet I'm intrigued by his *brute meets teddy bear* nature. I push the thoughts away. Logic rules out a relationship with a sober guy who needs God for a crutch. I've no use for weak men.

No time to daydream, I gather books and head to the park. The warmth from the sun coupled with the spring breeze competes with the fluttering pages of my Spanish notebook. I'm about to win the concentration challenge when I sense Wayne nearby (dubbed *the jerk* by Paula). He's shown up here before, claiming telepathy for my location. I question my motive for choosing this park. Paula says I have an addiction, not unlike hers to drugs and alcohol. The feeling of being watched intensifies until I have to turn to look, hoping no one is there. And there he stands, leaning on an oak tree, looking like a battered puppy dog.

CHAPTER 4

Step Ten—Revised
(Sandy)

I TURN THE KEY IN the ignition, starting the motor, along with Cindy's topic for the drive home entitled "Who's the Redhead?"

"What redhead?"

"The one with Paula. How do you know her?"

"Oh, her. She's just some gal Paula's helping to get sober. I don't know her."

Cindy's gifted at sorting information. She aligns words in a conversation, selects what she likes, erases those that disclaim her delusions. I like this about her. It keeps things civil and easy. I was a practicing drunk when we met, so a pick-and-choose reality works. Even sober, I still cater to her denial. What's the harm in changing a word or two if it makes us both happy?

For example, take AA's Step 10 which reads, "Continued to take personal inventory and when we were wrong promptly admitted it." Just insert *partially* before *admitted,* and it's doable. Partial truths are kinder. I know she can handle hearing that I cheated while helplessly drunk but telling her I've cheated while stark sober? That's plain mean. Sobriety is no cure for cheating or lying. My defense? I don't know how to tell her the truth.

"Gee, Cindy, it's been great, but now that I'm sober, I don't need a caretaker and would like to pursue sex when it's convenient. You know, smorgasbord style."

I don't strive to cheat on her. It's more like a child whose favorite toy dims when a new shiny one flirts a challenge, someone like Ann. I was at a friend's three-year AA birthday party when she sideswipes me with a jazzy hello, tossing her head back to laugh without reason. Then she sets the hook with a look I recognize as "I *want* this toy." I mean, come on, it shouldn't count because it didn't last long. And I ended it honorably with the truth. "I have no time, money or energy for a relationship."

As for Cindy, it's not like I'm hiding that I want out. I've ignored her voicemails, morning, noon, and night for nearly two weeks. She's had it tough. I care about her. We met the weekend my friend and her ex-husband, Blake the Flake, re-upped his drinking career for the umpteenth time. She's a drunk caretaker, mopping up messes as naturally as a mother wipes snot from her little boy's nose. Now that I'm sober, she's uneasy. I haven't said the hurtful words, hoping she'll take the hint. I should've known better. Today I found her sitting on point in my driveway. As soon as I pulled onto my block, I felt like a red laser sight was blinking on my forehead. Too late to run, I approach her Camaro.

"I've been calling. Are you okay? Have you been sick?"

I body block her attempt to open the car door, and leaning into the open window, I say the two words I've leapfrogged but never spoken, "It's over."

She backs out of the driveway and leaves like she got what she came for. I'm shocked that I didn't need the justifications I had primed for my defense. With just enough time to pick up Paula in Naches, I race inside, grab my books, and leave. Feeling like a master communicator, I decide it's time to speak up to Paula, tell her I don't want to get involved with that crazy redhead right now.

"Wait 'til you see my new photos of Deb. I developed them this morning," she says, skipping hello. "Here's one in a hat. We want you to come to dinner this Saturday. It'll be fun, the four of us. No expensive first date, a barbecue. Can you make it?"

"Sure."

CHAPTER 5

Somebody's Knocking
(Deb)

I'M SLAPPED AWAKE BY HALEY'S voice.

"Mom! Mom! Jay answered the door again."

I grab my robe with one hand, finger comb my hair with the other, and weave down the hall.

"I forgot," says Jay, meeting me halfway. He knows he's in trouble for answering the door when I'm in bed.

Two clean-cut men dressed in white shirts and ties stand in the door, smiling at me like department-store mannequins. They appear to be a father-son tag team.

"Good morning. How are you on this sunny Saturday?" asks the dad. "I wonder if we might have a moment of your time to discuss—"

My hand extends like a crossing guard, signaling STOP as he offers me a *Watch Tower* leaflet.

"I don't believe in door-to-door religion."

"Jesus went door to door," he starts.

"Are you Jesus?"

"No," he says.

"Then get off my doorstep."

Face flushed, I push the door shut with my foot. The thud reminds me of the witnesses standing behind me. Wanting a do-over but knowing better, I meet their wide-eyed faces.

"Go watch your cartoons. People shouldn't push their beliefs on others. It's rude. Your dad's picking you up in an hour. How's French toast sound?"

Hoping their favorite breakfast would erase the door scene, I pack their weekend bags and send them off. Today's a big day. Wayne is moving in. Last week, I told him I was really done. I meant it. I even had a *moving-on* plan. Nothing he could say or do would change my mind. But I'd never known him to cry, weep.

This might be what I've wanted. Yet believing it would never happen, I've no script, no outline or how-to list. We plan on sitting Haley and Jay down Sunday night when they get home. They don't know him, but things will work out. Kids are versatile. At least that's what my therapist says. This is about me, not them. They'll understand. Besides, he's not exactly a kid kind of guy, so he won't bother with them much. After all, they *have* a dad. It's my turn to be happy. They'll be fine really.

Wayne is late. I refuse to call and nag, so I slip on headphones, playing a perpetual loop of Beethoven's *Moonlight Sonata* and Debussy's *Clair de Lune*. With the crescendo peaks, my mind pulses between belief and doubt. He's saying goodbye to his wife. That's what's taking forever. He meant it this time. I know he did. Why would she want him to stay? He loves me. He does. There's no way he would back out again. No one has ever loved me, not like he does.

The day we met, our future started rolling like a marble down a track. I'm a female with a pulse, so I'm used to men showing interest but not men like Wayne. I've never wanted to be the *hottie* with the luscious curves men salivate and act like idiots around. And I'm not. I want to be the intellectual, mysterious, soft-spoken woman attracting the mature man, the one too interesting to be on the prowl. I'm *so not* her either. But give me a few drinks, and I'll believe it for both of us. Typically, that pretense reaps a guy hanging around confused, wondering what happened. Wayne, being fourteen years older than me, is the first gray beard to look my way, excluding a couple of toothless old perverts.

Adding Rachmaninoff's *Piano Concerto No. 2* to the loop, my thoughts turn to last week's talk with Jane, the college psychologist. She threatened to call the authorities because I said something I should have kept to myself. "If I ever feel the need, the Ellensburg canyon road has a perfect place to drive off."

She doesn't get me. I like to be prepared. Jane also thinks Wayne represents my father. Yuck! She couldn't be further off the mark. Dad's a sloppy, horny man who stares at my friends' boobs. He's a man with three daughters that he knows nothing about. To him, we're the same girl, just different sizes and hair color. If one of us was interviewed on national TV for winning the Pulitzer Prize, he'd say, "Who's the blonde newscaster in the tight red sweater?"

Wayne's not like that. He *sees* me, *values* me.

As a child, I felt differently, longing to someday walk in my mom's stilettos, finding a husband to adore me. The image of Dad tracking her every move, grabbing a taste when in reach, patting her bottom, cupping her breasts was my childhood definition of love. Thing is, it's a lovely picture, but the album needs more than one photo.

Years later in my lifeless, insipid marriage, I longed for the sizzling portrayal of love I was shown as a child. More so, I craved what I had not been shown—sweet kisses, hand holding, hair smoothing, and words of respect. I wanted what my mother had plus what she didn't. I wanted it all.

Wayne is now five hours late. I've called seven times, and he's not answering. I drip Binaca on my tongue, masking the bottle of *Gewurztraminer* I finished an hour ago. I grab my keys, heading for the door as the phone rings.

"Where are you?" I answer.

"Deb, it's me, Paula. He didn't show?"

"No, not yet. He will."

"Okay. Um . . . I invited Sandy to dinner next Saturday. I thought you could get to know each other in a friendly setting. You know, with me and Jim."

"Paula, Wayne's moving in. You know that. We're telling Haley and Jay tomorrow night. He's with his wife right now. That's what's taking so long."

CHAPTER 6

The Cats Are Back
(Sandy)

THE PSEUDO BLIND DATE WITH the redhead at Paula and Jim's? Nuts! I spent most of the evening wondering why I agreed to it, jumping in, ignoring the flashing neon "Danger!" sign. However, three things made the evening worthwhile—the price, the crash, the hug.

I was grateful for an affordable date, meaning it costs nothing. I get by working for my friend Frank, installing floors. He pays piecework and lets me arrange hours around my school schedule. My basic living expenses get paid, but there's not a dime left for impressing a gal who hangs out with Paula who's known for extravagant taste.

As we sat pretending Deb was not thirty minutes late, my regrets of saying yes to the barbecue grew. Finally, she shows up, apologizing with excuses about her busy day cleaning the garage and going to the dump. I'm always at least fifteen minutes early and expect the same courtesy from others. Smiling at me, she follows Paula to the kitchen, dimming my punctuality requirements, walking away in tight white pants.

Later seated around the table, I try to focus on the pointless conversation but can't. Three incessant cats take turns weaving in and out of my legs under the table. Since Deb is no longer smiling at me, I assume the cats are bothering her as well. Knowing she'll understand, I lean in close, whispering my secret.

"I have nightmares about cats clawing my eyes out."

Abruptly, she stands, grabbing empty plates as if the servant's bell rang. Then Paula jumps up and follows her out. Did I miss the emergency order to clear the table and run from the room? I hear high-pitched voices in the kitchen but can't make out what's being said. When they return, Deb sits with her eyes glued on the wall opposite me. I want to ask what happened, but the hair-ball cats start weaving between my legs again.

"The cats are back."

This time, she jumps up, heading toward the bathroom. Paula looks at me like I did something wrong. I start to explain.

"Your cats are making me crazy."

Then it happened. A glorious crash, like a hundred cymbals, clangs from the next room. We all rush into the den, finding Deb twirling in slow motion, singing "I'm sorry" with shards of glass at her feet. She's walked into the four-foot round glass tabletop that Jim and I had tucked behind a chair under Paula's order with a warning we should all be careful.

Fireworks, thunder, explosions, race cars colliding— all my favorite sounds! Deb just nailed my mating call; I can't resist. It doesn't get better than this, well maybe if she wore eau de cologne of methanol.

Like trauma victims, Paula and Jim join Deb who's gathering glass sprigs. They counter her repeated apologies with "It's okay" and "Don't worry about it." Spellbound, charmed, and no longer bored or bothered by cats, I join the clean-up crew. Deb's blush returns to flesh color as the last dustpan is dumped in the trash.

A motorcycle ride to Wenas Lake is next on the agenda. I relax, thankful to be free from tormenting cats and table chitchat. Deb's on the back of my bike, fingers awkwardly placed on my shoulders. It takes one-and-a-half exaggerated bends to bring her skinny arms around my waist, squeezing cobra-style. The one flaw in this moment? We're riding Hondas.

It's been two years since I lost my Harley. That day I realized getting sober doesn't mean life can't still suck. I remember it all—the smell of burning paint and melting tires; the sting as I swatted the flames with my hands; the sound of my voice screaming for a fire extinguisher; the fear on the service-station attendant's face as she fled to move her car to safety, leaving me to find the extinguisher on my own; squeezing the nozzle, the last hope to save my bike; the puff of dust mocking me from the empty canister; the perfect timing of the fire trucks arriving with nothing left to do but check the temperature of my bike now nothing more than a frame. Just a few moments prior, I'd strutted into the minimart, the cool guy wearing a new leather jacket, to buy a soda pop and pay for the gas. You see, my Harley told the world what I wanted it to hear. I don't know why it happened. The backfire through the carburetor is common for old Harleys. It had happened before with no problem, but this time, I needed a little help, and it didn't happen. It hurts to think about it. Feeling Deb's head resting on my shoulder reminds me to stay in the day. Right now, the day is good, even at the Honda's rebuke.

As the evening closes, Paula and Jim say good night, leaving us outside, alone and awkward. Revved up, I grab her, squeezing until she seems to need air. Releasing the hug, we say our good nights. I want to tell her, "Thanks for making it a special evening with the glass explosion" but decide to wait. She nearly runs over one of the cats backing out of the driveway. Had she succeeded, the date would have been perfect.

CHAPTER 7

Like Wearing a Black Leather Jacket with Footed Pajamas
(Deb)

SOME PEOPLE CLAIM, "YOU CAN'T hate an inanimate object." They've never owned a 1976 Cordoba. It's known for a lean-burn engine with a sick carburetor problem causing it to choke and die, usually mid-intersection. I know this because the Cordoba has a faithful *motor-head* following. Just open the hood, high heel in hand, giving your best bubble-headed girl pose. They'll screech to a stop and race to rescue the esteemed car. The fix takes five minutes. If you want to skip the carburetor tale, you'd best shoot them a beauty-queen wave and step on the gas. In the era of *I am woman, hear me roar*, it wasn't my finest moment, but my children preferred the dumb-blonde impression over the angry horns honking for us to move out of the way!

Today marks the final battle with the Cordoba. Maintaining its evil character to the end, it spat green, bile-like liquid at me while guzzling gallons of water bottled for its premeditated demise. The two-hour, twenty-mile trek ended with a vile hiss from its engine, defeated and delivered to its final resting place—the wrecking yard.

"Take that! Ha ha ha!" I laugh, walking away, ignoring the stares from the junkyard workers.

Danny, my brother, used-car dealer, pulls up beside me in the getaway car, stirring up a cloud of dust.

"Ah, the evil laugh. You're scary," he says. "Let's celebrate."

We've never needed much reason to party, but this is legit. The wicked witch with the insatiable gas tank is dead. I'm now the proud owner of a 1982 Dodge Colt. With ten dollars, I can fill the gas tank and travel the yellow brick road across the state. Besides, another party-worthy accomplishment beckons—Danny's graduation from another six-week outpatient treatment center for alcoholism. Like me, he's not an alcoholic, just unlucky, getting caught with one too many DWIs. Our plan's simple and safe—a four-drink quota with a midnight curfew and no arrests.

You'd think the bickering and matching red hair would peg us as siblings, but when we're out together, people think we're a couple. I hate that. Add booze to my gawky little brother, he morphs into Dad, slurring charmless sex talk at the helpless cocktail waitresses. Still, the night's not without its rewards like uncontrolled laughter; raw, true confessions; and proclamations of sibling loyalty.

As usual, the party gods ignored our plans, leaving us to close the bar, staggering home in morning light. But we didn't get arrested. I drove home, I think. I must have because I'd never have let him drive with his DWI problem. I hate mornings after, visiting with uninvited guests like remorse. I remember the Pastime Tavern in Selah—the savage dancing, everyone's watching and clapping. I also remember falling into the drums—everyone's watching, no clapping.

It's a good day to clean up the garage, go to the dump and the recycling center. A clean, organized home makes me feel normal. *Crazies* live in messy houses. Tonight's the blind date with the nondrinking, purist, God-barking friend of Paula. I'd rather go on a drinking date with a blind pagan. She waited like a perched tiger until I agreed to this ridiculous date. I never should have told her about my weak moment of pitiful prayer.

"God, if you're real, send me someone who can love me like I can love them." A lame prayer considering I don't believe in God. It was a just-in-case-I'm-wrong prayer.

As I load my Colt with bags of smashed Miller and Dr. Pepper cans, that sense of being watched returns. I shake it off as a leftover crud from the days when Wayne and I took turns stalking each other. Those days are finally over. The car reeks of beer, so I pick up an air freshener on the drive home. I wouldn't want Sandy to get the wrong impression.

By evening, I'm sick of arguing with myself. Why should I bother trying to look nice? It's a one-time deal. Why not have a couple of beers before? I'm not an alcoholic; they are. Cursing and sober, I drive to Naches. I've no excuse for being a little late and don't care. I never should have agreed to this *peekaboo* blind-date façade. A motorcycle is in Paula's driveway, probably Sandy's. I like his bad-boy biker aura, but add God and sober to the picture and it's like wearing a black leather jacket with footed pajamas.

Paula meets me at the door, pulling me through the clumsy introductions. Jim and Sandy go back to talking AA and motorcycles while she gives me a tour through her ever-changing artistic home. We're comrades with a common quirk—redecorating our homes more often than most people vacuum. I relax, inspired by her latest changes. When we return to the dining room, Sandy and Jim are carrying a heavy round glass through the front door.

"Just tuck it behind the chair over there," says Paula. "It's for my oak dining table I had refinished. We'll have to remember to be careful because it sticks out."

Seated at the table, we eat barbecued burgers with a side of forced conversation and crisp green salad. Tired of one-word responses from myself and Sandy, they talk amongst themselves. I dab at some dripped mustard on my white pants with my napkin, thinking of what to say to Sandy. He has this tortured look on his face and can't seem to hold still. I wonder if he is back at the bottle. Finally, he speaks.

"Cats . . . I have terrible nightmares with cats scratching my eyes out."

"Let me help clear the plates," I say to Paula, motioning for her to follow me to the kitchen.

"What's wrong?" she asks.

"He's mad! A crazy lunatic, babbling about cats. I'm done. I'm sorry, Paula, but this will never work."

Shushing me, she shakes her head like I'm the whacko, grabs my arm, and drags me back to the table. Seconds later, Sandy jerks, throwing his head back as if tapped on the shoulder at a séance. Excusing myself, I leave the table, walking toward the bath with plans to grab my purse, chatter an excuse, and race out the front door. Suddenly, there's a crash like a semitruck driving through their picture window, shaking my memory to be careful of the glass sticking out from behind the chair. But it's too late. When twirling around like Dorothy in Oz doesn't make it go away, I pick up glass shards as if I can put it back together. The hosts are in shock while Sandy appears to have enjoyed the show. After we clean up the mess, I can hardly refuse Paula's pleas to finish this date from hell.

I agree to a motorcycle ride. Sliding on behind him, I realize I know nothing about proper biker etiquette. Where do I hold on? I place my hands on his wide, shelflike shoulders, but the first acceleration sends my arms flailing like a mad flagman. With reckless regard for manners, I grab him around his waist and squeeze.

Daylight savings in the northwest is a glorious season with sunsets teasing until after nine in the evening. The light plays in the trees accompanied by the rhythmic motor. I press my face into his leather jacket, nestling, savoring a rocking-chair moment. Watching the trees fly by, pressing farther in, molding to his back, I wonder why it feels so right when I know it's all wrong.

The date ends at my car. Before I can recite my too-busy-for-a-second-date speech, he grabs me. My face is smothered in his chest. I can't breathe, but I like it.

CHAPTER 8

Who is Ann?
(Sandy)

You know that moment at the top of the roller coaster when you want to change your mind, but it's too late? That's what it's like with Deb. I want to jump out of the cart, save myself from peril, but swoosh, down the track I sail, thrilled yet scared out of my mind. I'm used to gals that say and do predictable things. Deb slaps me around with wit and intelligence, making me work for her attention.

I do wonder why I put up with her. She's like the Peanuts character, Pig-pen, with the dust cloud; exchange the dust for a blue haze of cigarette smoke. If I want her company, I must suck it up, accept her lethal shadow as one of her charms. At least the chronic coughing pauses her constant chattering. She spins a conversation into a four-wheel drift, pulls a slide job, then announces a pop quiz. I always flunk. Along with the habitual coughing and chattering, she wears a scowl like a sign that reads, "Don't even think about complaining." Of course, *she* expresses *her* beefs freely, insisting *I keep AA and the God thing to myself.* I'd gladly comply, but she asks nonstop questions about both.

During one of her don't-talk, tell-all conversations, we discover that Deb's brother, Danny, and I went through treatment together in the summer of '86. I immediately regret blurting out, "He's a hot mess!" She attacks. It's ugly. I stand listening while she argues in a circle, concluding the trial with a confession of her brother's guilt, a closing statement convicting *me* to save him and redemption for herself as *no alcoholic.* I'm impressed and amused that by quietly standing in one spot, I survived. Mentioning now that I can't fix her brother would be like spending an extra night in the lion's den. Danny swears he has no use for AA, and he's determined to find an easier, softer way to get sober. Good luck with that, Danny.

Tonight, I'm taking Deb to an AA birthday party. Maybe hanging around sober people, she'll see life can still be fun. I need to save what little cash I have for this weekend since my girls will be here. When Nanette and Stephanie come to town, I'm off limits. They don't need extra mothering and neither do I. They're highly capable after surviving two alcoholic parents. In past relationships, I'd disappear, no need to explain myself. If I am upfront with Deb, she'll get it.

Deb's dog barks when I pull in the driveway. Normally, he doesn't stir from his nap. I get that weird sense someone's watching as I knock on the door. It's probably nosy neighbors, intrigued with the divorcee lifestyle.

The party is Frank's three-year sobriety birthday. He entered the program shortly after me. I work with him installing carpets which brings in fast cash and suits my school schedule. I'm eager to introduce Deb to my friends. That is, until we walk into the den and there stands Ann. I panic, leaving Deb alone with the hungry lionesses while I escape to the kitchen with the other lions. Ann is friends with Kim, Frank's girlfriend, but she never runs with this crowd and should not be here. The last thing I said to Ann was "I have no time for a relationship." Here I am, caught red-handed, obviously involved with someone. My mind races through all possible ways out of this mess. I pretend to listen to Frank talk about tomorrow's job while honing for sounds of an uprising in the other room. The quiet concerns me. Breathing deeply, I brave entry to the den.

Ann springs forward.

"Hi, Sandy."

I nod. It's the best I can do. All eyes are on me like fans waiting for me to fumble the ball. So like any good player, I pass.

"Kim, Deb lives right down the street from you. Have you met?"

Deb is seated in a chair off to the side, away from the others huddled around Ann. Reading my help signal, Kim suggests we have a piece of cake, directing us to the kitchen. All smiles and full of grace, I relax knowing Deb is unaware of the jagged fangs she escaped.

After cake, we say our goodbyes, exchange AA hugs, and pile into my pickup for the short drive home. In the driveway, after a hug, I share my plans.

"Nanette and Stephanie are with me this weekend. I won't see you. I never let my relationships interfere with my girls."

She interrupts, "I have plans this weekend anyway."

Surprised and threatened by the abruptness of her vague plans, I wait for further explanation. Instead, she moves on to another subject.

"Who is Ann?"

"What do you mean?"

"Is she someone you've dated?"

"Dated?"

"Yes, dated."

"She's just an AA acquaintance," I lie.

"Really? Because I felt some weird vibes from her and her friends."

"No, I don't know her that well," I lie again.

CHAPTER 9

Keep My Children Safe and I Will Change (Deb)

I NEED THE MUSIC CRANKED up, a reason to wear high heels, and someone to listen because talk is my sport. Sandy needs quiet and comfortable clothes, and he's a Jesus freak. We'll never make it. So why bother trying? It's not that I wouldn't like things to work out; it's that I know they won't.

One rainy afternoon cooped up in his truck on our way to a remote yard sale, I light a smoke off the one I just finished. Recently, I switched to menthol. It helps my cough, sort of like a vaporizer. Anyway, he looks over at me like I ripped a broccoli fart.

"I smoke, drink, and curse. And I've no plans to change. If that's not for you, it's your problem, not mine."

I know he heard me. He looked over, choosing to ignore me. I could be sitting here naked with a live chicken in my lap, pull out a grenade, release the pin, toss it his way, and he'd fall into his *la la la this-is-not-happening mode*.

We pull onto a dirt road with a handwritten sign reading: Yard Sale. Waiting at the end of the road stands a battered farmhouse with a screened porch surrounding the ground level. A yellow Lab runs to greet us. Holding hands, we walk through an iron gate as if it were the pearly gates of heaven. Sandy spots an apple crate full of greasy tools, digging in with one hand while scratching behind the dog's ear with the other. We trade smiles, holding up potential buys like pirates mad on rum. Our differences wait back in the truck cab, for now we're comrades, ready to fall on our sword for each other. Adrenaline pumping, I hold up my best find, a red plaid jacket.

"Twenty-five cents! Whatcha think?"

"Whoa, good job," he says, as I model it for him back in the truck.

He holds up yet another old hand drill.

"I spent a dollar."

"Big spender. Can't have enough of those, right?"

We laugh, triggering my cough. I light up another Salem Slim. Junking and laughing feels good. Since Wednesday night's party, my esteem for Sandy has been running on empty. He lied about Ann. I know it. I'd say it's a sixth sense or women's intuition, but it's more like "How stupid do you think I am?"

Fact: They've slept together. Everyone at the party knew it, staring at me like they had a secret. Why did Sandy lie? Then afterward he puffs up and starts lecturing me about not hanging on him when his daughters come for the weekend like I've given him any reason to think I'm a clinging vine kind of gal. I was so angry. Doesn't the Bible say something about a lie for a lie? Maybe that's an eye for an eye. No matter, it serves him right.

How dare he speak to me like I'm one of his bimbos vying for his presence? His love for his daughters is one of the things I admire about him. But he's talking to me like I'm his pet poodle wagging my tail at his feet while he tells me I must stay home and be good until my master returns. Just last week after telling him to stay away so I could tackle homework, I caught him riding his bike by my house like a boy in puppy love.

Saturday morning, I wake the kids with the news of a road trip, bags packed and loaded in our Colt. I'm grateful for its magical gas tank that, unlike its Cordoba forerunner, travels the world on a ten-dollar fill-up. That's good since a road trip was not in our budget. My motive began as a way to show Sandy what's what, but now I'm excited for the three of us to get away. Normally they suckle fun from Disney Daddy's treat while I'm left serving unappetizing words like NO!

It's a bright June day forecasting triple-digit heat. We begin the ninety-nine-mile trek to Soap Lake in perfect harmony. Ten minutes later, pulling onto the freeway ramp, the sibling bickering begins. Jay's moods just happen. There's no transition. Boredom strikes like a cold bucket of tedium thrown in his lap. Ever resourceful, he initiates his favorite pastime—pestering his sister.

"Jay, stop kicking my seat," Haley screams.

Their bickering is like elevator music, annoying and predictable but easily ignored. Besides, I'm focused on *not* worrying about money. I have a credit card. The trick is coming up with the money to pay the bill later. After four stops, one for soda, three to get rid of it, we reach our random map choice, Soap Lake. I'm relieved to see it does have a lake. We change into swimsuits in the car, taking turns being the human curtain. Jay's too old to go with us in the ladies' room and too young to use the men's room in a strange town. He doesn't agree but keeps quiet, wanting to avoid a replay of last time when I ran into the men's room screaming his name because he didn't answer my calls from the door.

We approach the beach, ready for a new experience. That is until we look around. I don't trust my eyes until I see that Haley, like me, is in shock. Jay appears at ease. If I'd had words of wisdom, I would have used them, but instead, I resort to my habit of popping a funny when uncomfortable.

"Look, the Weebles! Weebles wobble, but they don't fall down," I sing, pointing to a round couple moving toward us.

They're speaking in a thick Russian accent. Approaching, the woman says something to me then laughs. Smiling back, I pretend to understand. Jay looks to me for an explanation. The man appears nude, but I have faith there's a Speedo hiding under his belly. But that's not what's weird. They're caked in a gray mud, as are the rest of the participants at this aboriginal beach party. Haley stares at the only safe place, the ground, while little brother continues to search for the Speedo.

Tugging on a tired, stretched-out bikini strap, the woman responds for me.

"The mud is good. Is medicine. Dah? You try it. It's miracle. Dah! Try. It's good."

I nod yes to Jay who's standing with a fist full of mud ready to smear. Haley cringes, looking like she does when Jay eats an ice-cream cone, elbows dripping onto his sneakers. The mud smells like rotten eggs or like the Toni permanents my sisters and I suffered in childhood. Grabbing a handful of the smelly paste, I swipe it across my chest, down my arms and legs and lastly my face.

"When in Soap Lake? Right?" I say to Haley.

Before she can answer, Jay and I give her a loving mud bath.

As the name suggests, the lake is soapy, leaving a white film on the skin. Before long, we look like the others—bodies rolled in batter, baked at 104 degrees, blanched in the lake, and dusted in flour.

"Some people travel thousands of miles to get healed in our mud bath. Locals just enjoy the show. Where are you from?" asks a mudless man sitting on a nearby towel.

"Yakima," says Jay, giving me the oops-I-talked-to-a-stranger look. "We're going to the laser show tonight at Grand Coulee Dam."

Struck bored with the guy, Jay and Haley leave me to answer his questions while they stand behind him mouthing "bald spot," pointing and giggling.

I answer his question about where we will stay tonight with "Not sure yet." He insists we'll never find a vacancy because of some big stampede going on. He happens to live two blocks away and offers to take us in. According to him, he's the world's most trustworthy soul. No, thank you. I may not be the best mom, but there are a few rules I've yet to break, like subjecting them to a serial killer.

Tired of the argument, I take the address written on the back of his sandy business card.

"Just in case," he says. "You can come in the middle of the night. I don't sleep much anyway."

We leave the lake, going on to Grand Coulee for the laser show. Jay is upset because I made him shower in the women's bathroom. I don't blame him. It's just too dangerous sending him to the men's room alone. I picture the faces from my own childhood, the ones that look noble until they get you alone, cornered. Even when you escape unharmed, you don't forget when the guy in the white hat turned bad. It's like that moment when you gulp a glass of milk, then gag as the curdled lumps sour your expectations.

The laser show is lame in the best way. *Chariots of Fire* and *Equinox 5* boom from an outdoor megawatt-speaker system while beams of color dance across the dam's spillway, transforming into upscale 2-D stick figures like fish, covered wagons, and Indian chiefs. The show began at dark, sharp, about 9:30 p.m., ending at midnight. Earlier, pulling into town, I searched for a lit vacancy sign, trying to prove Mr. Good Guy wrong. Jay is asleep as soon as he's buckled in. Concerned, Haley searches with me for vacancy signs as we drive through both ends of town. Defeated, I drive the twenty-six miles back to Soap Lake, hoping they will have a vacant room. Haley has given up, leaning on the door pressed against the window asleep. Lighted neon nos flicker next to every vacancy sign in town. I park the car in front of the two-story house with the address on the business card, wondering if I could make the drive back home to Yakima.

There's no reason to believe the guy is not okay. Jay liked him. The porch light is on. I'm about to drive off when he comes out the front door, waving us in. I sit there wondering what to do. He comes to the car and helps steer the kids into the house and to a bedroom downstairs. We work together like a married couple, tucking them into bunk beds, kept ready for the weekends when his children visit. He motions for me to follow him upstairs to the kitchen.

"Thank you for your hospitality. You were right. No vacancies anywhere."

"Not a problem," he says, lighting a candle, grabbing stemware, and pouring TJ Swan, the tasty strawberry kind.

"I don't drink," I say, surprised by my words. "It's AA meetings and coffee for this gal."

He clears away the bottle and glasses, apologizing, as if he'd shown up dressed at a nudist colony or vice versa. I'd already heard about his ex-wife at the lake. She single-handedly ruined their marriage and, with the help of a lawyer, stole him blind. Not knowing what to do without his wine-and-candle script, he nods as I excuse myself to the makeshift bed on the sofa. Two hours later, unable to sleep for fear the serial killer would go near my children, I consider sneaking back to the kitchen for the wine. What would Sandy think of me now? What do I care? A good mom would never let her children sleep at a stranger's house. I've broken one of my mom rules from a short, lax list. Then for the second time in thirty days, I pray to a God I don't believe exists, asking that he let me get away with this just once.

"If you're really there, please keep my children safe, and I will change."

The first sign of light, prayer forgotten, I gather our things. Refusing breakfast, I thank our host as we speed out the door. We inched our way home, stopping for hikes, miniature golf, and ice cream. I kept going with no sleep, fueled by coffee and gratitude.

I swear I heard happy theme music coming from our house as we turned the corner, promising showers, safety, our own beds.

"Who's that with Sandy?" Haley asks.

On our small concrete-slab porch sat two young gals with Sandy behind them, smiling as if he'd been standing there all weekend.

CHAPTER 10

No More Convicts for Girlfriends (Sandy)

STABILITY AND FOOD—THAT'S MY FAMILY'S love language. No kisses, hugs, or gushy words needed. Just show up for biscuits and gravy and dig in. No *please pass* or *thank you* needed; we know all that.

Sober time like this with my girls, hanging at Mom and Dad's, is my way of making up for the precious years I chucked out like a bag of empty Rainier cans. I don't understand the whys, but thank God, my girls are not only okay but exceptional young ladies.

Mom tends to our needs at the table like a hummingbird, hovering, dangling offers for more biscuits, warm syrup, extra butter. She'll grab a biscuit, swipe it with gravy, as if running a quality test, but never sits or stops to eat herself. At the head of the table sits Dad like a king, grateful that our presence turns his daily oatmeal and toast to country gravy, sausage, and buttermilk biscuits. It's like we're hanging inside a Norman Rockwell painting. Bad things don't happen here. Moms don't get drunk; sons don't land in jail; brothers don't die in car crashes. If they do, we don't talk about it.

Deb's road trip to who knows where bothers me. She was acting strange. Nice enough words were being said, but it didn't feel right. She didn't say she was mad and even agreed that I should spend the time with my daughters alone. It might be good for my daughters to meet Deb; she's different than the others, proof that my life is better today.

Back at my house, snuggling with my girls, staring at the wood stove, I throw the topic out for grabs.

"I've been seeing someone new a couple of months now. Her name's Deb. Uh, don't worry, she's nothing like Debbie."

Swift clarification is needed, distinguishing Deb from Debbie, a former relationship. Otherwise, it would have been like saying, "Hey, remember the potato salad that gave us all food poisoning? Let's have some more!"

They don't ask questions about my relationships. Not sure why. I'm glad because I don't have answers, not even for simple questions like the *why* of former girlfriend, Debbie. We got along fine, as long as she was away at a treatment center in prison or if I was away on a long-haul trucking assignment. We only had problems when in the same town.

Visiting days at the treatment center, I was her knight in shining armor, bearing gifts of pot, rolled and concealed in a pack of Marlboro cigarettes. Next to her, I was friggin' Dudley Do-Right. Later, while she served time in prison, I cared for her eight-year-old son, Dustin. The kid even used my last name. I may have been a pot-smoking drunk, but to Dustin, I provided a monastery, at least in comparison to the hell he'd been living in.

Sometimes I miss the protective veil of being a drunk, like now, looking in the eyes of my girls knowing they don't trust me. They didn't have it easy either. I'd smoke pot around them, thinking they'd think I was a cool dad. What a stretch. Why would two A students, popular, athletic, and talented, want a zoned-out, beer-guzzling dad? They kept quiet through it all, watching me play hero trying to fix Debbie's life while ignoring my own messes. Debbie just needed to listen to me. After all, I had a job and took better care of her son than she ever did. You can't put the toothpaste back in the tube, as they say, but I'm determined to clean up my mess. Someday, I want my girls to know I am not who I used to be. Meanwhile, stick to the plan—stay sober, graduate, become a teacher, and no more convicts for girlfriends.

Sunday evening, we happen by Deb's house. The porch light is off like they haven't made it back. Stephanie and Nanette sit on the porch steps, talking baseball, waiting for me to decide what to do next. Where are they? Last week, she announced she was swearing off credit cards, and I know she is low on cash. We've spent every possible moment together from the start. Haley and Jay are great kids, easy to be around. Deb's mom style is easy, natural, and honest. She models the same parenting techniques I've studied in psychology books and lectures. I've seen her spin a testy situation around, using humor and love as easily as one uses a knife and fork. It also helps that their dad is active in their life. I've never been in a relationship where the dad was more than a passing thought.

I realize it looks weird hanging on Deb's front steps as her Colt turns the corner with Jay's skinny arms flapping out the window. Before the motor's off, he springs from the backseat like a pebble from a slingshot. Deb smiles like she's glad to see me.

"Come on in. It's so nice to meet you," she says, ushering us through the door. "Haley, Jay, this is Nanette and Stephanie, Sandy's daughters from Spokane."

We just nod, saying one-word responses like *hi, yes, fine* while Deb plays talk-show host, producer, and director.

"Nanette and Stephanie go to high school in Spokane. Jay and Haley both like sports too. Did you girls have a fun weekend with your Dad? Haley, tell them about Soap Lake. Who's hungry? Thirsty?"

We don't stay long because tomorrow we're leaving early to go back to Spokane. I want to ask questions about the trip but settle for knowing she's home. I say goodbye with a good-night kiss on the cheek. Next weekend, we'll be alone. It's been two months with no sex. I've never waited two days. She talks about sex a lot. It's all about waiting—blah blah—doing things differently than in the past—blah blah. It's not like I'm begging her. I've never brought the subject up. It's like telling a child they must wait for a cookie before they lift the lid on the cookie jar. Now they, I, *really* want a cookie! It always ends with me saying, "Yes, I agree, we need to take things slow." Well, time's up. I've climbed the Mount Everest of control, the memory of the lingerie photographs tagging along.

I spent the week on my hands and knees laying carpet with Frank. Deb is working as a public-relations intern at the Red Cross, along with some freelance writing jobs. One story for the local paper is about a group in AA starting a Unity, Recovery, and Service club. I'm glad her questions about the program will be put to good use. The week chugs along, taking its sweet time until Friday. When I pick Deb up for dinner, she's wearing what should be a required uniform for all attractive women: a miniskirt, high heels, and a blouse teasing to be see-through. I never hang with nonalcoholics, so it's weird watching her sip a beer. Like sex, she talks nonstop about drinking, not drinking, and certainly not having a drinking problem.

As I take my last bite of steak, she crosses her legs, flashing a peek at a garter, and asks, "Have you ever had a peach melba?"

I search the gutters of my mind, sorting through every sex term I've ever heard with no hits for peach melba. Remembering the box of fresh peaches I gave her yesterday, I realize she's talking about a dessert.

"Let's go back to the house, and I'll make us one," she says.

Seated at the kitchen counter, I watch as she slices peaches, scoops ice cream into bowls, and drizzles raspberry syrup over the top. The ice cream works like a pacifier, keeping me content momentarily. I wonder how she knew that.

Before the bowls have time to warm, we heat up the kitchen. I consider swiping the dishes onto the floor, clearing the kitchen counter. Instead, I carry her to the sofa. With the last teeny button on her blouse conquered, I nibble the concaves of her neck. Suddenly, she jumps to her feet, runs to the sliding glass door and yells, "What are you doing? Oh my god!"

I move in behind Deb to see what's going on. There's a man standing at the corner of the patio. He sees me, turns, and runs through the back gate. For a few moments, we watch the gate gently swinging in the breeze. After that, it was clear—the times we felt someone was watching, OJ's random barking episodes staring at what appeared to be nothing. I push pass Deb.

"It's him. Don't go out there! I mean it. He carries a pistol in his jacket pocket."

Her logic is good. I choose to ignore it, following the path through the gate where he slinked away. There's no car in sight. We would have heard it start up when he left. He must have parked down the street, creeping into the backyard. After circling the house, finding no sign of him, I return through the glass door.

"He's gone, sweetie."

"He's been watching us all along, hasn't he?"

"Yes, I think so."

We sit for an hour discussing every creepy feeling we'd both had but shoved aside as paranoia. Soon we were blaming Wayne for everything—the stolen chicken and beer from the garage refrigerator, the flat tire, the missing sock. Over the sounds of our laughter, we hear screeching tires jolt to a stop in the driveway. It's Wayne's honky big ole brown Plymouth. Deb pushes by me, screaming, "Get out of here. Go!"

He lowers his window. I step between Deb and the car. He flings a stack of papers at her, yelling, "Don't forget what we had!" Then he screeches back out of the driveway, nearly sideswiping the neighbor's truck.

The papers strung out on the yard are photographs, mostly of Deb, one or two of them looking happy and normal.

"I can't believe this guy? What were you thinking hooking up with him? How could you let him treat you like that? He so used you. I hope you know he never loved you."

Snatching the photos from my hands, she tosses them into the air, screaming, "Shut up! Shut up! He loves me. More than anyone ever has or ever will. He's the only person who's ever really loved me!"

"That's not love. It's sick. You're sick. I'm out of here!"

CHAPTER 11

A Slave to Ice Cream and Lingerie (Deb)

SOBER PEOPLE ALL CARRY A bag of stupid sayings around, ready to pitch at the slightest provocation, things like "If you hang around the barbershop long enough, you're *gonna* get a haircut."

If that's true, then might I end up sober if I hang around the dried-up well of AA? I'm already showing symptoms of drinking failure—sipping beer, saying no to another round. It's like the purpose of drinking has been washed down the sink. Drinking teetotaler-style, I scream, "Why bother?" I know people live normal lives sipping a drink or two after five o'clock, but I've never met one. Besides, I don't want to trigger Sandy's drunken madness or leave him to think I've been struck by the drunk bug.

Thoughts of subscribing to teetotalers anonymous or, worse yet, abstaining makes me uneasy. We're a proud Scotch-Irish family. Drinking is a rite of passage. We don't worry about how much we drink. Not drinking enough, now that might be a problem. You better be able to conduct yourself properly, or fingers will point, and you could end up with the family label of shame—*cannot hold their liquor*. My parents didn't care if I earned good grades at school (which I did not) or received the good-citizenship award (which I did not), but I better be able to handle myself properly under the influence. Soon, I will earn the first college degree in our family. You won't hear that story from my dad. But he'll find a way to tell you about the time he smuggled his thirteen-year-old daughter into the Red Rooster tavern for her first public beer.

"We spotted those sons of guns from the liquor-control board outside. Debbie had drunk two full beers on her own. But she kept her wits, slipping out the back. Once the party poopers left, I found her asleep, hiding in a refrigerator box, out in the back."

Later in life, I learned about the *others*, the nondrinkers from my mom's side of the family. They were well-thought-of, loved, admired, but their infrequent, unsolicited visits were not welcomed. Normally, we'd hide behind closed drapes, ignoring their Sunday door knocking, waiting for them to tire, get back in their cars, and drive away.

I may have led Sandy to believe I'm in the teetotaler category. I like the way he laughs when I order one drink or mix my beer with tomato juice. It seems to please him. Besides, I am not an alcoholic. I just like to party. There's nothing wrong with that. Who wants to be the person standing outside knocking on the door? Besides, Sandy is not going to put up with me getting drunk. Just the same, I've no plans to sip, smile, and spout stupid AA slogans. We're rather the cliché, time-bomb couple.

Friday night, you could hear the bomb ticking. The evening was near perfect—a romantic dinner, flirting, teasing of what's to come. Earlier in the week, Sandy dropped off a box of plump, juicy, fresh peaches. Knowing he's a slave to ice cream and lingerie, I planned the evening around the two temptations. We'd waited to indulge our passions because, this time around, it seemed like the right thing. Neither of us claim to know what *right* means, so our logic meant doing the opposite of what we've done in the past. If we don't repeat old behavior, the outcome should be, at the very least, less disastrous.

I want him. No doubt. And he wants me. I need that. The peaches with their juices and color seem to be in cahoots with my plans for seduction, as is the delectable raspberry drizzle and the creamy ice cream. Reaching the climactic moment when spoons are laid aside, Sandy lifts me in his arms, carrying me from the kitchen counter to the sofa.

Teasing stage expired. I open my eyes to help with the last button on my blouse. Out of the corner of my eye, I see a figure standing outside the sliding glass door. Instantly, I know who it is but have hope I'm wrong. I slip away from Sandy and run to the door. It's Wayne, standing with one hand in his jacket pocket. I cannot make out the words of his malevolent whisper, but hearing it provokes a shudder. I've felt it before, the day he wrapped his fingers around my throat, boasting how easily he could snap my neck. Sandy ignores my warnings, chasing after him.

He returns unharmed. We sit trading stories of unexplained noises, feelings, and warnings from OJ.

"If he's capable of this, what else might he do? I know he wants to hurt me. I see it in his eyes."

Just then, we hear tires screeching and see lights in the driveway. It's Wayne. I go out to make it clear I want him gone. When his window lowers, I freeze, expecting to see the pistol. Instead, he tosses papers out, yelling something at me. Sandy picks up the papers strewn in the drive. I don't hear what Wayne yells. Sandy tells me later it was, "Don't forget what we had."

Sandy turns toward me. I expect he's going to hold me, reassure that we're safe. Instead, he approaches, eyes narrowed, accusing, calling me sick, saying Wayne never loved me. We scream back and forth. He leaves with the last words, "Why don't you give him a call?"

I watch him pull away, weighing my options: get drunk, get drunk and call Wayne, call Sandy. Giving him ten minutes to get home, I call. After it rings a dozen times, he answers, sounding like he's giving a command.

"Hello!"

"Forget it, goodbye."

We listen to each other breathe.

"I know he never loved me. I'm sorry. Will you come back?"

Ten minutes later, I hand him a peach melba, and we finish what began earlier. Later, safely wrapped in his arms, my head on his broad shoulder, we fall asleep in my bed, trauma all but forgotten. Around 4:00 a.m., we awake to high beams lighting the room and the sound of a revving motor closing in on the window. We pull back the drape, blinded by the light.

"It's him. I caught sight of his car just as he pulled away," says Sandy.

"No way. Go back to sleep. It's just some drunk."

I fell back to sleep, believing it had to be a nonrelated incident. A few minutes later, I hear noises once again. This time, it's Sandy. I grab my robe, finding him in the front yard.

"Look what that idiot did," he says, pointing to deep tire tracks ending abruptly at the bedroom window.

"Do you really think he did that?"

"I saw his car. It was him."

Sandy's staring at me, waiting for words of assurance. I know what he wants to hear. That I am 100 percent sure I am done with Wayne. And I tell him so. But saying so didn't quiet the voice in the back of my mind, nagging *what if.* What if my love language is *acts of insanity* like stalking? Isn't this what I wanted? Passion? Mad, crazy love? Isn't this why I destroyed my marriage and family?

CHAPTER 12

No Words
(Sandy)

As I SIGN MY NAME on the letter addressed to Ray at the state penitentiary, two words flash like a warning beacon from the middle of the page: "She's nuts!"

I can tell him stuff like that. He gets it. Plus it'll give him a big laugh. He's not your average Joe kind of guy. Most drunks approach the 12-step program gingerly. Ray dives in headfirst before asking if there's water in the pool. No half measures for him. He's either in or out, yay or nay. Like now, he's serving two years in prison for a sentence he could have easily avoided. Instead, he chooses to take responsibility for his part, dues for step three: "Made a decision to turn our will and our lives over to the care of God as we understood Him."

Turning my will and life over to a higher power doesn't mean I get to skip the consequences for my actions and choices. It's tricky. The water gets murky, like the Deb deal. A couple of weeks before our first date, she's taking lithium prescribed by the college psychiatrist for manic depression. After a week, she stops the *meds* saying, "I don't want to live a monotone life. If you take away my highs, what's left?"

I can't argue with that, not really. Honestly, I enjoy riding along on her highs. It's what makes Deb, Deb. Just look at her job history. Most people bore you to tears with their job history. Hers reads like a Stephen King thriller where the antagonist is just a normal bloke. Like her job at a nonprofit recycling center for disabled adults, it should be simple—go to work, smash some cans, drive a forklift around. One day, she gets an idea, calls the elementary schools, invites them for tours, overloading the calendar beginning the next day. That's when the art of mania kicks in. She pulls an all-nighter, not only writing a complete presentation but also creating puppetlike characters made from cans, paper, and bottles, complete with full personalities and stories. Soon, word of the educational puppet show spread, resulting in calls to the Department of Ecology asking for the Garbage Lady, enough calls to spur a *deadbeat* government worker to go out and find her. It's a great story with one flaw; that's how she met the psychopath, Wayne. He hired her. Manic depression brings good and bad, high and low—a single mom, an entrepreneur having an affair with her boss, all while pulling straight As in college. I admit, it's scary.

But who's nuts? Me or her?

My plans are to graduate, land a job as an industrial special ed teacher, and stay sober, one day at a time. Note: There's no mention of a relationship in my plan. I didn't write Deb on my to-do list. She just happened. We haven't talked about getting serious, but we're comfortable together like socks in a drawer, albeit opposing styles. I haven't given a serious relationship much thought. I don't know what I want, just what I don't want—my first marriage. Life with Barney, known as Bonnie to everyone else, was great at the start—two kids playing house with one united interest of drinking a lot. The problem is drunk Barney and Sandy didn't like each other. We had a baby, Nanette. We both loved her a lot. Still, drunk Barney and Sandy didn't like each other. We had another baby, Stephanie. We both loved her a lot. And still, not liking each other prevailed.

Likewise, I don't want what my folks have. On the surface, they get along great. Beyond that, who knows because it never goes any deeper. One thing missing in our family is words. We are downright stingy with them, always have been. The day after Jim, our sixteen-year-old brother, was killed in a car crash, I tagged off to school with my sister and brother. No words were ever spoken. No questions answered. No hurts consoled. My family's consistent, stable, predictable, but you won't find words in our treasure chest. Not one word, good or bad, when Dad bailed me out of jail, when I dropped out of college three times, whenever I needed money, not even when I knocked up my girlfriend, Barney. Words weren't needed, not really. I knew they loved me and that they were proud of me. Of course, those words would have been welcomed. When making amends to my dad, I had hoped my sobriety would open his mind toward AA, help him see that Mom needs help, that she can't do it alone. I walked away with nods but no words. He didn't need to say much for me to know he didn't believe God or AA necessary for doing the right things in life. For men like Dad, you just take care of it.

I need to back off with Deb, concentrate on finals, get ready to be a student teacher at Davis High School where I graduated in 1968. *Stick to the plan.* Tomorrow, I'll tell her we need to back off.

CHAPTER 13

About Three Loads of Laundry
(Deb)

"DEB, YOU ALL RIGHT?"

Hearing Sandy's voice through the door, I realize I'm ranting in the shower again. The warm water rinses away my defenses, causing the words in my head to fly out of my mouth. I'm glad he couldn't make out the tirade; it's embarrassing, rambling to an audience of my past—parents, siblings, classmates, teachers, ex-husband, a haughty stranger I passed on the street—rubbing their judgmental noses in their puddles of wrong assumptions about the girl who partied, skipped school, and should have paid rent to the principal's office. The one cheerleaders gossip causing jocks to assume she was an easy mark—that girl, me, the one who barely passed high school, soon will be graduating college with honors. Maybe not the biggest accomplishment but good enough to stand naked, flaunting my middle finger while hosting a crowd of past tormentors in the shower.

"Sorry, Sandy, I didn't know I was talking to myself."

"You want this?" he asks, handing me the newspaper.

Dripping, wrapped in a towel, I grab the paper, looking over the meager list of jobs. This is a new game. I'm used to lay jobs where you knock on doors until someone says, "Yes, you're hired." Now résumé in hand, I must pretend I know something worthwhile while performing a proverbial song-and-dance routine for a panel of judges waiting to clang the gong.

It's not like I have a degree in brain surgery with a hint as to what job I should get. My degree is in communication. I nearly changed to journalism until fate placed a true journalist type in the desk in front of me. I wanted to slap the back of his calm head, typing away during timed story-writing sessions, *clickety-clack*, as easily as typing rote copy while I ripped paper from the typewriter's carriage release, cursing. Ken remained focused, clicking away. Although we both excelled in class, our professor spoke of us entirely different. Ken absorbed facts like a sponge, whereas I was creative and descriptive.

The employment section lists a journalist position in Prosser, a thirty-five-minute commute. I need a job now. I can't wait for a position that reads, "Wanted: Hard worker with no real skills. Descriptive ability, a plus." I circle the journalist ad, running to answer the ringing phone.

"Hello? Hi, Mom. Glad you called. There's something I want to ask you. I want to bring Sandy home to meet you this weekend. Is that okay? Uh-huh, okay . . . great. Virginia? Really? Murdered? Oh, Mom, that's terrible! Yes . . . yes . . . what? You taped the newscasts? Right. I understand, but I'm not sure Sandy will be interested.

Okay . . . okay . . . okay . . . yes . . . okay . . . love you too, Mom. See you Saturday."

"That was my mom," I say to Sandy who overheard my end of the conversation. "We're all set for this weekend."

"I'll tell you about it later. I'm off to Prosser to hand deliver my résumé. I don't know why. I'd make a lousy journalist."

"Wait, who got murdered?"

"Don't worry about it. See you later. Bye."

Prosser is a rural town with a population under 5,000, so finding the newspaper office meant circling three blocks. The receptionist looks up as I open the door. I hand her my résumé. Before I have a chance to give my pitch for the job, a woman, probably early forties, approaches from an open office to my left. After a thorough head-to-toe examination, she asks questions with no regard or patience for answers.

"Are you here for the journalist position?"

"Yes, I—"

"Do you have your portfolio with you?"

"Yes, and—"

"Come on back. I'll interview you now."

She points to the metal chair in front of her matching industrial gray desk. I hand her my portfolio in response to the open hand extending across the desk and sit. I might have felt less violated undergoing a strip search than watching her shuffle through my clips. I stare at a photo of two children on her desk, hoping to ease the agony of the cavity search as she reads my collection of stories accurately dubbed fluff by any serious journalist.

"How long does it take you to write a story, like this one?" she asks.

"About three loads of laundry," I said, knowing a woman with pictures of children on her desk would know exactly what that meant.

She laughs then offers me my first professional job or at least the first one I didn't invent on my own. Hours of study, the commute, the insatiable student loans, the worry, the nagging voice telling me I'll never make it, all for this moment. I want to leap and cheer, "Yes! Yes! Yes!" My future fast forwards—*a journalist, a title of respect, a career, a Pulitzer prize, a paycheck*. She interrupts my thoughts.

"There's one stipulation. You'll have to move to Prosser. I need you available at a moment's notice. And the job starts at minimum wage. Can you live on that?"

Gee, let me think about it. Hmmm, a single mother with two children and student loans up the kazoo? What do you think?

I answered, "Thank you, but I cannot uproot my family at this time."

With a carload of invisible mockers, I drive home, listening to their *told you so and should haves*. I had no argument for their accusations: "You're a loser, a screwup, a terrible person, a divorcee, a tramp. You deserve whatever bad comes your way." When I could hear no more, I threw my uninvited passengers out the window, finishing the drive, raging renewed promises. *I'll show them. I don't need anyone. I won't apologize for who I am or what I've done.*

By the time I reach home, I'm convinced my degree is an expensive lesson with a slap-in-the-face reward, paying less than I made as a child pouring coffee for the 2:00 a.m. drunks. Now I know why my ex-husband's lawyer wagged his finger at me telling the judge I was playing at college, dabbling in English courses with no intention of a practical career like teaching or nursing. Were they right? Am I some silly woman who should have stayed home with my children?

The house is empty and quiet. I start to light my last smoke in the pack opened this morning but choose instead to feed my gnarly stomach a hunk of cheese along with a half box of Ritz crackers. I must have fallen asleep, waking to the phone ringing. Not wanting to talk with anyone, I let it go to the answering machine. It's the receptionist from People for People wanting me to interview for some job I don't remember applying for.

"Hi, sweetie," says Sandy, walking through the door. "How'd it go today?"

"Marvelous! I got the job. I just need to pack up the kids and sign my life over to the Prosser Record, all for minimum wage."

"You don't want to be a reporter anyway."

"Well, maybe I do. Or at least I'd like to know I'm worthy of a bone with a scrap of meat on it."

"You just started looking."

"I know. There's a call on the machine asking me to interview next week. I don't even know who they are. They probably want me to volunteer to flip burgers or something."

The next morning on our way to Auburn, my anxiety switches from employment to Sandy meeting my parents. There's no way they will like him. He has one fatal flaw—sobriety. It would be easier to introduce him as my boyfriend the serial killer than say, "He's a recovering alcoholic."

"Don't worry, my parents will love you," I say as we pull in the driveway.

CHAPTER 14

Bet He's Never Seen Anything Like It (Sandy)

AFTER TEDIOUS HOURS OF PREP and quizzing by professor Deb, I'm ready to meet the parents. The door opens. I'm drawn into the land of the McFarlands, a place I believed existed mostly in Deb's exaggerated imagination. Dema greets us at the door with a hearty, genuine hug. I'm confused because she's dressed like we're going to a black-tie event, and my only instructions were to wear a real shirt with no funny saying on it. She's all sparkly with sequins and jewels, the infamous auburn hair and makeup done to perfection. I feel better seeing Mac stretched out on his recliner, dressed like a 1950s cowpoke.

The twelve-by-twelve-foot living room is furnished for a room three times its size, so you have to cross the room walking sideways. Greetings barely obliged, Dema presses start on a VHS tape she had paused and ready for us since we left Yakima. The sixty-inch projection television can only be seen from the two recliners placed directly in front where Mac and Dema sit, both armed with a stack of remotes. Deb and I sit on the orange velvet love seat, our knees sideways so we don't knock over the glass table in front.

For the next hour, we watch news clips recorded from all three major television networks. Deb warned me this might happen; to which my reply was, "No, they wouldn't do that." After this, I will not question Deb's facts. The newscasts escalate from a missing person to murder while Mac and Dema insert background information, sometimes pausing to make sure we are keeping up.

Hindered by the sideways view and the interruptions, this is my best translation of the drama: Virginia is Dema's cousin. No one agrees whether she was on husband six, seven, or eight. She has a son named Lynn, a sailor who visited once and made homemade pizza from a box. Virginia had lots of money because of her husbands that she spent on diamonds and high heels. Dema says Virginia was spoiled as a child. She should know since they took baths together. Virginia was missing four days, with her car mysteriously parked in the driveway. Husband number six, seven, or eight claimed she vanished. Lynn, the pizza-making son, flew to Spokane, hoping to help find his mother. Suspicions grew. The police brought search dogs, finding poor Virginia buried in the garden along with the carrots and potatoes. The last news clip shows the husband in handcuffs being carted off in a police car. An autopsy revealed she had been shot. Everyone is relieved that Aunt Myrt, Virginia's mom, is not around to see this.

I'm exhausted, and we've just begun. Again, Deb was right, insisting my intro to the McFarlands be brief, without Haley and Jay who might blab something we don't want known.

"I don't want them to know we're living together," said Deb. "If we stay overnight, we have two choices—separate rooms, pretending what we all know not to be true, or same room, knowing the rest of the family is *powwowing* outside the door chanting *tsk tsk tsk*."

Considering our options, a short day trip seemed best. When murder-and-mayhem conversation dies off, we move to the next dramatic scene.

"Have you shown Sandy the bar?" Mac asks, knowing we've not left the front room. "Bet he's never seen anything like it."

"You haven't, come on," Deb says, motioning for me to follow. She side winds through her childhood habitat like a snake crossing the desert while I, new to the obstacle course, bump knees and elbows, unskilled at walking sideways. Mac and Dema follow. She carries a sixteen-ounce tumbler of scotch and water, room to room, like a portable oxygen tank. The story from Deb is that her mom confesses to the doctor a two-drink habit, omitting the constant refreshing and topping off.

I've spent time in bars, all types—redneck, biker, highbrow (dives to swanky black-tie joints), home bars, makeshift bars, tailgate specials. Yet none prepared me for the *McFarland's bar*.

Deb's eyes are begging me for words, but I don't know what to say. When words fail me, she involuntarily covers for me, chattering nervously, cooing, and fidgeting, like a cross between a dove and a quail.

"We had the bar built. It's regulation. So are the dozen stools," Mac says.

There's a mirrored back bar with shelves stocked and ready to fill any drink order. And Elvis is in the room—rows of gold and silver Elvis bottles peering down from shelves installed around the ceiling. There's a black light, twenty beer signs, a booth-style table, and a life-size poster of Mac dressed as a woman, an extremely ugly, toothless woman with a huge nose. Just imagine if Popeye had a sister. What comment am I to make? Deb is trying to cover for my silence.

"Did you see the disco ball? Cool, huh? Did you know the poster is Dad? The ceiling is painted black for the strobe lights. You should really see what it looks like at night."

Any moment, Deb's going to shove me on her lap, cram her arm up my butt, and move my jaw up and down like Edgar Bergen and his Charlie McCarthy doll. I open my own mouth to comment but not fast enough to delay what's coming next.

Deb's classy, attractive, soft-spoken mom calls me over to the bar. She's lined up a collection of ceramic figurines. I obey her call, nearing the harmless-looking monks and frogs. Then she hands me a monk.

"Turn it around," she says. "Isn't that awful?"

As I turn the monk around, he transforms into a ceramic penis. Why is this happening? Dema keeps saying how awful it is. I want to agree. Then she hands me a frog, asking me to turn it over. *Do I have to?* Deb gives me a just-do-it look.

"Isn't that awful?" Dema asks again.

I manage a laugh at the anatomically enhanced frog. It's not that I can't handle the joke. I feel like I've been captured and thrown into someone's really bad X-rated home movie. Finally, I speak.

"Deb, where's the bathroom?"

The conversation turns from ceramic phallic symbols to towels as I follow Deb's finger pointing down the hall.

"I copied your idea to roll towels on the shelves. I really like it." I hear Dema say to Deb.

I try to open the door to the bathroom, but something is behind it. I slide through sideways, finding a huge hook on the back of the door holding a stack of robes. The door's heavy and hard to close on the carpet, but I manage. Standing at the toilet, staring at a tall shelf above it, I count fifty-six hand towels, forty-nine bath towels, and sixty-two washcloths, neatly rolled and stacked like cordwood stored for the winter. If a busload of people needing a bath arrive at the McFarland's, they're covered for towels.

"There are fifty-six hand towels," I say to Deb as I squeeze back through the door. She shushes me while peeking in.

"Oh, that looks great, Mom. Rolling the towels saves a lot of space."

Dinner, however late, is worth it. I'd been told to expect greatness, and my hopes were not denied. The table was set with US Navy flatware and individual platters, not plates, crowded with heaping plates of Southern fried chicken, mash potatoes, country gravy, biscuits, and corn. Seated in unspoken assigned seats, with Mac at the head of the table, I remember one of Deb's warnings: "Whatever you do, don't pass the food in the wrong direction. It drives Dad crazy."

He passes the procession of steaming bowls ceremoniously clockwise. I try, but curiosity wins, forcing my hand to pass the corn upstream, against the current. Dema accepts the bowl with a nervous grin. Deb and Mac place their forks on the table, staring me down as if I'm the one who buried Virginia under the carrots. Not wanting to delay indulging in this feast any longer, I retrieve the corn, sending it clockwise. I know what we'll be discussing on the ride home to Yakima.

CHAPTER 15

The Irish Intervention (Deb)

"HE CAN'T HAVE ONE WEAK drink?" asks Mom. "How about just a beer?"

I ignore the question this time since I've already answered politely three times. It's not as if they're concerned for Sandy like he's a flapping goldfish out of the bowl needing something wet to survive. No, it's that his not drinking points a self-accusing finger at them.

"I told the doctor I have one or two drinks a day. He says that's fine."

"Mom! He doesn't want one drink. He wants all you've got. If he starts, you better keep it coming, or he'll maim and plunder for more!"

"Fine, but why can't you have a drink? Does he expect you to stop having fun because he can't control himself?"

I manage an eye-roll response. I've already told her I *can* have a drink but choose not to because I don't think it's fair to Sandy. Truth is, I want a drink more than ever right now. I've forgotten what it was like as a child stuck in a boozed-up crowd, wondering why you are the only one who knows the jokes are not funny, the woman hanging on my dad is ugly, and that Uncle Eldon is a scary old pervert who bit my ear. Seriously, staying sober is no less painful than remaining awake through major surgery. You hear, see, feel it all.

Mom and I carry opposite drinking styles. I get sloshed, blitzed, hammered while she gets lit, juiced, tanked. She's impressive, capable of feeding thirty people on a 3:00 a.m. whim, breakfast complete with garnish. I humbly confess, drinking half her intake leaves me slouched and spinning on the sofa, a family disgrace.

We may hold the right to bear steins in high accord, but don't think we turn a blind eye to intoxication abuse. Here's a little-known fact: The Irish invented the art of alcohol intervention. Okay, maybe it's more of an educated suspicion than a fact. A normal intervention is led by a professional counselor with family members and friends confronting a problem drinker and encouraging them to seek help. The Irish intervention is the same deal, with a twist. It takes place at a bar with a jury of professionals, and alcohol consumption is not only welcome but required for credibility. The focus is not abstinence; that's ridiculous, like potato salad minus the spuds. Instead, the professionals give firsthand advice on proper drinking etiquette, simply how to hold your liquor.

Mom wants what's best for me. What loving mother would sentence her daughter to a life of doldrums surrounded by sticks-in-the-mud determined to bore each other to death? Honestly, it was never my plan either. My dollhouse had beer in the fridge. Barbie greeted Ken at the door with his favorite cocktail. I want to live the *good life,* minus the messy stuff like fistfights, name-calling, and fires. No moms with black eyes, no children with swollen faces, no lies, no tears. Truly minus that kind of stuff, our family is perfect—the stay-at-home mom applying red lipstick at midnight to serve her trucker husband a hearty meal after work, a 1950s wallet picture of four children staircasing down to the final accomplishment (a boy, red haired and freckled like me, the last on purpose attempt for a boy). Why does someone always add one drop too much rye, spoiling the Irish stew?

Sandy is on the back porch behind the Tiki bar, watching a spider build its web. I admire his ability to escape, but right now, I wish he'd act normal since my folks are looking at me for answers.

"Where'd you say he works?" asks Dad.

"I told you. He's completing his teacher's degree. Dad, he drove truck for years. He's a hard worker."

"But he can't drink?"

"No, Dad, he can't. Why don't we check the news for an update on Virginia's husband?"

CHAPTER 16

I Need a Hitman
(Sandy)

THREE WEEKS AGO, SOPPED IN sweat, stinking of asphalt, back aching from the jams and slams of the dump truck, I drove home, showered, stuffed an ice pack down my pants—a happy man. It was my last day working for Columbia Asphalt, paving roads in the triple-digit heat.

After two days' rest, back still aching, I walk through the doors of Davis High School, a student teacher smelling as sweet as a librarian, a suitable mate for Deb who clicks off each morning in nylon stockings and spike heels to counsel and train others how to get a job. She's disappointed in her job but jokes on the irony of *getting a degree to teach others to land the position of their dreams.*

I should be concerned that my supervisor is revered in the education arena as the Dragon Lady, but I'm not. Dee Moon, the teacher I worked under during my practicum, entrusted me with her students while she dealt with her mother's terminal illness. Based on that performance and knowing the class would be nearly all the same students, she recommended I fly solo once again.

By mid-September, sunny days clinging like the leaves on the trees, my future beams from the tunnel of my thoughts. I'm settled in with twenty-five students, building trust and respect daily. If things continue to go in this direction, I may ask Deb a certain question, one certain to get a yes.

Normally, my day starts with Joe and Anthony tagging along at my sides like bookends, reporting moment-by-moment details of all I'd missed since the last school bell tolled. Instead, today I'm forced to hand my students back to Dee. I'm scheduled to attend a student-teacher training with the Dragon Lady.

I'm first to show, eager to get it over, sick of time-sucking ordeals disguised as trainings. I just want to do my job. A woman shuffles files and writes notes on the whiteboard as the forty-some chairs slowly fill with student teachers. She's not unattractive but carries that pinched nose, rulemaking persona I tend to stereotype as the typical teacher.

She begins a sluggish introduction, packed with details of accomplishments her own mother would snooze through. My hope to get this over dwindles as she recounts grueling particulars of college, birthing children, a short-lived kindergarten teaching gig, and so on. My only question never gets addressed: "What miracle took place to land her this job?"

My frustration builds. My students need me to be in class, not here. I've earned a degree of respect with them, one moment at a time. It all counts. I read the lengthy outline written on the board, realizing this woman who's spent little time in a real-life classroom is holding me hostage, threatening to replay a training I've not only been through but have been practicing in an actual, live classroom. If she'd just put her whip down and shut up, I could go back to my class and do what she plans on teaching.

Finally, the saga of the Dragon Lady ends. Next, she leads the group through individual introductions, encouraging details. If they follow her model, I'll die an old man in this chair. Please, God, grant me patience. With no choice, I learn that most of the group is in their first practicum. With that in mind, they could benefit from the training outlined on the board known as Madeline Hunter's ITIP. Mother Madeline's theory, my nickname, is one of the better models. My professor and adviser, Sam Rust, stressed that models are just that, an ideal to base your personalized plan from. Each student brings a new dynamic to the classroom, leaving you to evaluate, assess, and adjust to their needs.

"I'm Sandy Palmer. I've completed a special ed practicum and a short pre-autumn practicum which I am continuing this quarter just down the hall where my class is waiting for my return. I've been practicing Madeline Hunter's ITIP for two weeks now. I don't feel I need this review."

Tugging at the edges of her jacket, the Dragon Lady responds, "Well, Sandy. It is Sandy, right?" Going on without waiting for my response, she states, "This training is mandatory."

"I understand, but I've been through this training already with Professor Rust. I need to be back in my classroom."

"You need to be here with all the student teachers. Now, who's next?"

I contemplate an unscholarly response punctuated with a vulgar hand gesture. Sobriety has taught me to be selective when going to war. This battle cannot be won. I sit quietly through Mother Madeline's rerun.

The next day, Dee meets me before class with a pleased grin saying, "Just keep doing what you're doing. It's going great."

I appreciate her encouragement, especially regarding my sixth-period math resource room. It's a crazy hodge-podge of ninth to twelfth graders with competency levels peaking and dipping off the chart. Students range from studious to academically challenged, angelic to ruthless, hyper to lethargic. My other classes, in comparison, are a breeze.

Ending the day with the resource room leaves me drained. Even so, life right now is promising, satisfying, even good. Seven days a week at 6:30 a.m., I'm drinking coffee with fellow drunks, sharing how it used to be with AA newbies who walk through the door as certain as flies at a picnic.

Living at Deb's house is intense. I don't understand her. If she came with controls, she'd have one big toggle switch marked EXTREME. There's no such thing as easy does it; everything is urgent. She stays late at the office, sometimes past midnight, scheming ways to transform her social-worker position into something more to her liking. At home? Same wired mode—*declaring game nights, family meetings, home renovations* like General Patton going to war. All battles have a redundant theme: prove to the world she's good enough.

If I manage to drag her off the battlefield, she decompresses like a Jake brake. My house sits vacant, waiting for Dad and me to make some renovations needed before renting it out. When possible, I abduct Deb, sneaking her away from Haley and Jay, work, and house chores. I build a fire, wrap her in a blanket, and listen to her busyness until she exhales, snuggling into a foreign land of rest.

Fishing works too. Born and raised in Yakima, I know where every creek bends, when the fish bite, and where to find a stash of rocks suitable for skipping across the water. My brother, sister, and I explored the Yakima and Kittitas counties more thoroughly than Lewis and Clark. The first time I hijack Deb off to the Nile, she brings a stack of files. On the way, we stop to purchase a fishing license. Against her wishes, I buy two. Since we both share the art of thriftiness, I had a hunch she wouldn't be able to let money spent go unused. I was right. Within fifteen minutes at my favorite fishing hole, she leaves the car, moseys up, and sits on a rock near me. Five minutes later, she brings me the fishing gear I'd packed and left in the car for her.

"It's not that I mind touching the worm. It's that I don't want to be the executioner. I need a hitman."

I fulfill the contract on the worm, lacing it through the hook while Deb looks away. My own gear is primed and ready to cast when I'm summoned to untangle her line from a bush behind her. I didn't ask how, but I couldn't do it on purpose, if I spent all day trying. I move, finding a spot where I can see her but farther upstream. It won't hurt Deb to practice patience, untangling her own mess.

I'm in my realm of comfort, the place where my mind is quiet and breaths are deep. I'm startled out of it by a series of yelps and yowls. I expect a hound has tackled a paddling of ducks, but it's Deb. She's leaping on a rock midstream, holding her rod in one hand, the line in the other with a dangling silver fish best suited for bait. I'm impressed with her balance and enthralled by the most joyful face I've ever seen.

I want to see that face more. I think I know how. I've attended the Skagit Valley Dirt Cup sprint car races for five years. This year, I'm taking Deb. She's snarling about it, but if she can get this excited over a guppy, how will she react when a sprint car does a triple flip and flies over the fence?

CHAPTER 17

A Catholic with Sensible Shoes (Deb)

I *GET* THE SILLY HAMSTER running on his wheel. He's safe as long as he's moving. If still, anxiety piles up like shavings in the cage. My wheel is a list of *to-dos* I chase after like a carrot. When it squeaks to a halt, like the nervous hamster, I scurry about my cage wondering, "Now what?"

Today, we're fishing. Oh joy. Sandy insists. I agree to go along for the ride as long as I can work on my PR project. I want to prove to my employers that they need a public-relations director. I am the person for the job. That means handling the job I was hired to do on weekdays while creating the new position in my free time. I don't want to be some PR mogul, but it's better than teaching classes on a subject I've yet to conquer myself—career building. I need to work with what I have, a talent for BS.

I told Sandy not to buy me a fishing license. He forgot. At the fishing hole, I delve into my work, prioritizing stacks of paper on the dashboard. Not wanting to be a jerk,

I keep an eye on Sandy, ready to applaud if he outsmarts a fish. Did you know there are television programs with two guys in a rowboat talking about fishing? They say things like "Yup" and "Well, looky there."

Concentrating on work is not happening. Maybe it's the way the sun has placed Sandy in a spotlight, appearing majestic, golden, surreal. I watch as he laces the line through the eyes of the rod, ties a knot, bites the line in two with his teeth.

Earlier in the *are-you-joking-it's-still-dark* morning hours, we drive to a house with a handwritten sign nailed to a tree reading, "Night crawlers." A man with a white beard answers the door, leading us to the kitchen. He opens the fridge, pulling out a Styrofoam container kept next to an uncovered bowl of red Jell-O. Gleaming a six-tooth grin of pride, he lifts the lid displaying the worms eagerly cooperating, wiggling their alluring charms. For a moment, they share admiration for the performing worms. Then well pleased, Sandy hands him a dollar.

Now in the sun's spotlight, he slides the Styrofoam container from his vest pocket, chooses victim one, threads it onto the hook. Broad shoulders swaying, he casts the line, hitting the mark—a shadowed pool next to an algae-covered rock. A breeze lifts and lowers the line. Bewitched, I study his solid-block build, dark unkempt beard, and taken-for-granted confidence. I've found my Grizzly Adams, a man who'll bash through the door, toss me over his shoulder, forge through fires and storms, defend my honor, and bring fish home for dinner. Okay, no fish for dinner. He's a catch-and-release guy, petting the fish before putting it back in the stream slightly maimed. I don't deserve a man like him and wonder when this gig is up. Soon, he'll catch on to the lies and portrayals of innocence, running away to catch, pet, and release a lower-maintenance damsel in distress.

Work is not happening. I decide to give fishing a shot. The sun-baked boulders and grassy patches look like prime snake territory to me. As per my humble request, he slays a worm, handing me the pole, ready and waiting. I cast the line then wait forever while he untangles it from the tree behind me. He overreacts to the fluke accident, sending me upstream with a fresh worm on my hook. I tiptoe back through the snake-infested grass, balance my pole on a rock, worm dangling in the stream, and light a smoke. While fumbling for matches, my pole rolls off the rock. I grab it, relieved to have saved it from sailing down the current. Lo and behold, there on the hook flaps a frantic fish. Just like that! "Yup, yup, well, looky there."

Driving home, I can tell he thinks he's got himself a new fishing convert. I should have hidden my exuberance over the fish. Strangely, in his head, my moment of fishing tolerance translates to the likelihood that I will love car racing. And he says my mind works in strange ways? For five years straight, he's made the Dirt Cup sprint car races in Skagit Valley. His selling pitch is pitifully off the mark—cars crashing, soaring into triple flips, and flying over fences. You wear safety goggles because you're sprayed with dirt (thus the charming name). If you're lucky, you could get hit on the head with a lump of track clay.

"It's super loud. You'll love it. After the race, we can hang out in the pit, if you want to."

I'm picturing dirt clumps in my hair, a dusty hotdog, sitting amongst blood-thirsty fans roaring for another crash.

I'm ready to confess that, although this sounds charmingly gladiatoresque, I must decline when he puts his arm around me saying, "I really want to share this with you."

At home, relaxed from fishing, I cozy up on the sofa next to Sandy. One of his talents is entering a full-snore nap in five seconds or less. As I listen to the comforting drone, my last waking thought is gratitude for a man I respect, admire, and like.

I wake with thirty minutes to shower and get ready for tonight. We're going to some AA event, a special one that allows non-alcoholic *riffraff* like me to attend. Tonight's speaker is Sister Bea. Nicknames are vogue in AA, the stupider, the better, like Ill Phil, Diamond Dick, Neal the Wheel.

Arriving early, by my standards, we search for a place to park near the church, settling for a makeshift angle squeeze about a block away. I stay with the smokers out front while Sandy attempts to score some seats inside. He's grumpy because I balked when he said we needed to be early or risk standing room only. How was I to know Yakima is the drunk hub of the universe? Finishing my smoke, I walk through the groups conversing in growly smoker voices, laughing, and stifling coughs. Inside, I see Sandy waving me over to a table where two chairs have been squeezed in.

The meeting begins with a reading from the Big Book (not really a *big* book) and the Serenity Prayer. It's kind of a nice prayer, if you like that sort of thing. Next is a countdown where each person stands when they hear their sobriety time called. They started with fifty years. At forty-one years, one guy stands to much applause. There's no takers again until thirty-four years, followed by a few, trickling down until the momentum builds from scatterings to bevies to a herd as they reach one year and then thirty days. At the one-day mark, one woman and two men stand with over-the-top applause.

When the room quiets, the speaker, Sister Bea, is introduced. I'm surprised that the Sister tag is no nickname; she's Catholic, wearing sensible shoes and looking like Corrie ten Boom's sister. I am fascinated. Her story of lies, deceit, brokenness, and hope keep me seated, suppressing the need to go have a smoke. I'm amused that a non-alcoholic like myself can relate to most of what she shares. But the one resonating thought bomb for me was, "If drinking causes problems and you continue to do it, that's the difference between the alcoholic and a normal person."

After that statement, my thoughts wandered to my drinking style. Does it cause me problems? Wait, isn't that kind of a stupid question? Like what came first the chicken or the egg? Obviously when not drinking, there's less chance of disaster, but fun is not banging on the door either. I know my relationship with Sandy has stalled my party life. Hanging on the outskirts of sobriety, I've witnessed some charming aspects of this dry lifestyle. For certain, it's a good option for others in my life like Danny. Sister Bea's *problem theory* fits my brother's pattern perfectly. He's like a top spinning, bouncing into arrests, accidents, evictions, and pink slips. Recently, my witty baby brother with his curly red hair was found in an alley after being brutally beaten by four black guys. Later, the bartender told Danny he must have a death wish. With no memory of what happened, he's left with the bartender's version, claiming he begged for it, frothing lewd racist remarks at one of the guy's girlfriend. That's a strong case for drinking causing someone problems. Even a droll sober life is better than being beaten to a pulp.

The meeting closes with everyone linking hands in a gigantic wavy circle, reciting the Lord's Prayer. With both hands held hostage on either side, I'm embarrassed when tears drip down my face.

CHAPTER 18

It's a Routine Day,
Excluding the Dragon in the Room
(Sandy)

As usual, I walk into my classroom, Joe and Anthony, like personal bookends, competing for my ear except today; there's an intruder in my castle.

"I'll be observing your class today," says the Dragon Lady, extending her hand. "Just pretend I'm not here."

Meeting her handshake, I hope my smile hides my annoyance. She drags a chair to the back of the room under the clock, sitting cross legged, holding a notebook. I hand her a copy of today's lesson plan, also written on the whiteboard. Surprisingly, I'm not nervous. I've nearly three weeks with these students, and although we're still working out some behavior issues, I'm pleased with their progress.

It's a routine day, excluding the dragon in the room. I begin the task of issuing the five levels of lessons as per the Mother Madeline model. It's a challenge teaching finger counters, begging continuous encouragement alongside high-level students needing constant challenge. I've learned to choose my battles carefully. Less than ten minutes after receiving their assignments, Clint, a Native American student needing the math credit to graduate, slams his book shut, stomping from the room. It's not a new experience. He'll return in a couple minutes, ready to take another stab at the lesson. He's a great kid who's super hard on himself because, unlike his other studies, math is not easy for him. As usual, he's back in less than two minutes, faster than Terry needs to sharpen his pencil again and before the Dragon Lady can finish the mad scribbling in her notebook. Terry uses pencils on paper as if carving initials in a tree, breaking the lead repeatedly. I stocked his backpack last week with a dozen sharpened pencils; two remain. Tina, a bedhead, stick of a girl with a permanent piss-off expression, spouts obscenities periodically. As said, it's a normal day, nothing remarkable, the stuff you learn to roll along with.

Normally, I hang around after class with a few students like my shadows Joe and Anthony. Today, a dragon with a notebook is waiting, tapping a subliminal message with her foot. I walk out the door with my chattering students, waving them down the hall. When I return, she's standing at the door.

"How do you feel the class went today?" she asks.

"Okay," I said.

"You have no control over the students. They're disruptive. They need to raise their hands before speaking or sharpening pencils, and you did nothing when the student left the room. What if he hadn't returned?"

"I knew he would. I've been through this with him."

She can't understand because she's never taught a class like this or any class really. I remain silent while she nit-picks my lack of control. Watching her lips move, questions gnaw at my thoughts. Did she choose my most challenging class to monitor on purpose? I have four other classes she could observe with moderated students, unlike this class with students from every nook and cranny of the behavior and intelligence spectrum. Is she on a vendetta? Could she be small enough to begrudge my attitude in the training two weeks ago?

"I'll be observing one day a week for the next ten weeks recording your progress," she says, stifling a tattletale grin.

At home, Deb reads my face asking, "Are you okay?"

I share the details of the surprise visit.

"I'm not worried. Once she spends more time in the class, she'll see I'm doing a good job."

"I agree. She'll see the Mr. Palmer the students all adore."

"So how'd your day go?"

"I talked with my brother today. He's not okay. I tried explaining what Sister Bea shared. He really hates AA. He accused me of having a drinking problem, pointing the finger at others, just like you've said alcoholics do."

After a quick breath, she continues.

"You can help him. I know you can. I'm scared for him. He's trying. Really he is. He even joined an expensive club that not only expects no drinking but also no smoking, meat, or sugar."

I laugh at the typical plight of the drunk, willing to pay a fortune rather than swallow the *I'm-an-alcoholic pill.*

"Deb, I can't fix him. He has to hit his own bottom."

She rises, like a puff of air blew her off the sofa.

"What's it going to take? If you don't do something, his bottom is going to be a grave!"

"It takes what it takes."

That was not what she wanted to hear. There's nothing I can say or do, just wait out the Tasmanian-devil fit, spinning, cursing, demanding action—a full-blown tantrum.

I only know what it took for me and what others have said it took for them. It's an event, the day, time, and outcome known by God alone. For me, the beginning of the end happened 5:00 p.m., Tuesday, closing time at the tire shop I managed. I'd taken an after-hours service call for an orchard thirty miles out Ahtanum. Nothing out of the ordinary, a day like any other.

"Boy St. George, let's go fix a tractor tire," I say to the new guy whose real name is Steve St. George. "We need to pick up an inner tube at the warehouse."

Hired less than a week ago, he's eager to please. After loading the service truck with our tools, I drive to the Lewisville Tavern, a block from the shop, for a six-pack. I regret asking what he drinks because now I'm stuck drinking Miller Lite. By the time we pick up the inner tube, our six-pack is gone, with me drinking four to his two. I pull into a convenience store en route to the orchard for six-pack number two. When I return, Boy St. George is behind the wheel. I hop in the passenger side, unscrew the top off a beer, handing it to my chauffeur. We claim victory over the tractor tire returning to the shop around 7:00 p.m. I finish my fifth beer of the pack, waiting for him to drink his.

He declines the offer to join me at the Lewisville, something about needing to get home. At the bar, I motion for Jane, a new bartender on my get-to-know list. She's a generic bartender, the type you could meet at Safeway or church and know she works in a bar. I pop open the first Rainier, the second, and a third.

My next memory is driving on the freeway, wondering why the exit sign reads Granger/Mabton. I know I don't want to go there, but I can't think where I was heading. At the exit waits a cop car. I drive by, watching in the rearview mirror as he follows me like toilet paper stuck to my shoe. And sure enough, the lights flash, and I know I'm screwed.

"What's the problem?" he asks as I get the window rolled down.

"I missed my exit."

"You were going thirty-five miles per hour. Have you been drinking, sir?"

"Yes."

"Step out of the vehicle, sir. Step behind the car for a field-sobriety test."

"Don't bother," I say.

There are blotches of memories like leaning on the car as the handcuffs clamped shut, laughing about the cuff key in my pocket, the flashing lights, the cop's hand on my head as he steers me into the back seat. The next memory clip is at the jail in Toppenish. When I see the guy issuing the Breathalyzer test, I'm relieved. This is a bad dream, that's all. It's my old friend Jack from high school. But I don't wake up during the routine paperwork, the fingerprinting, or when Jack helps me call for a ride after releasing me on my own recognizance.

We call Rick, the guy you file away for this kind of favor. Jack assures he's on his way from Yakima. I walk out the door onto the sidewalk, light a smoke, and it happens—a full-blown *déjà-vu* moment delivered by the streetlights casting a hazy blue light. An eerie light I'd met, felt, feared stood in awe of once before. I was driving home after the usual Lewisville pit stop; from behind came the flashing lights of a cop car, magnifying what I knew to be fact—*I was wasted*. That's when the streetlights turned the unearthly hue, and the world spun in slow motion. In a still-frame moment, I bowed my head asking, "When will it all be over?" Pulling to the side of the road, cradled in a surreal fog, I exhaled as the cop passed by, stopping behind a red truck just ahead. Now once again, the same blue haze fell over the scene, reminding me of the prayer.

The night I was arrested in Granger turned out to be my last drunk. It was the night *enough was enough*, when I thought, "Maybe it's over." Was it a sign from God? Deb knows my story. I've told her, plus answered the never-ending whys. It's like trying to explain why sticking your finger in a socket receiving a jolt of 220 volts of electricity is an okay practice until one day it's not. It doesn't make sense. I don't know why that arrest knocked over the first domino leading to the fall that would save my life. Why didn't it happen when I was suffering DTs, seeing rats? It wasn't DTs or nightmares, suicidal thoughts or an intense death wish. It was a strange hazy blue light.

"It takes what it takes, Deb. That's all I can tell you. When Danny is ready, not a moment before."

"But, Sandy, if you talk to him. Tell him your story."

CHAPTER 19

Roll Models
(Deb)

SANDY IGNORES MY EYEBALL DARTS shooting across the
dinner table. It's my first dinner with his family. Laurel,
the mom, stands over the table, rebounding orders like a
devoted bat boy, wanting nothing more than to serve and
please her team. Flavius, the dad; Mark, the brother; Robin,
the sister; and Sandy demand more gravy, rolls fresh from
the oven, and another glass of milk. The words *please* and
thank you are foreign to the masters of this slave, and no
one but me seems to hear her pleas for approval.

"Who wants more of this crap?" she asks.

Taking the bait, I *ooh* and *aah* like a fool, hoping someone, maybe Sandy, will join my chorus.

"Oh! Oh my, these are the best rolls ever. Mmm . . .
and this gravy! Sandy? Sandy! Don't you think the rolls are
amazing?"

Talking over my solo of compliments, they joke, asking who posed as the *roll* model, each insisting the oth-

er's buns match the rolls. I feel like I'm held hostage by The Three Stooges, plus one. Laurel ignores my orgasmic sounds of pleasure for potatoes and gravy, playing along with the roll-model gag.

Later, she tolerates my help with the dinner dishes, frequently suggesting I join the others lounging in the living room. She pours the last of the bottle of Thunderbird wine into her glass. When the twist cap hissed earlier, all eyes turned her way then diverted, as if long ago the family agreed to look away. I wanted to say yes when she offered me a glass, but I've realized I'd rather have none than a little. This is not the time nor the place to let loose. Besides, getting sloshed with boyfriend's mom is a dangerous game. I've walked that tightrope a time or two in the past.

Robin goes home, leaving the original Three Stooges in the living room, talking over a rerun of Bonanza on the television. I'm sitting at the kitchen table with Laurel. Her lovely, tall, and elegant frame is mismatched with an I'm-less-than demeanor. Waving away my rerun of *oohs* and *aahs* of the feast, she spills a story with the opening line, "I'm a bad person. You don't know the things I've done." I counter with "No, you're not a bad person."

Appointing me as judge and jury, she shares the details of her past like a vehement lawyer's burden to prove her lack of worth to me. The story rivals *Gone with the Wind*. It's a real page-turner, but I'd prefer to view it on the big screen or, better yet, read the book in private. Face to face with Scarlett in catharsis mode is beyond my comfort zone. In less than an hour, I learn that Sandy's oldest brother, Jim, who was killed in a car accident, was not the son of Flavius. He was the product of a one-night stand, occurring while

Flavius was away at sea in the navy. All through the story, she emphasizes what a good man Flavius is to have married her anyway.

I perform acrobatic feats in body language and facial expressions, hoping Sandy will come save me. Alas, the men are busy poking fun at each other, comparing stomach bloats, oblivious to the melodrama unraveling in the kitchen.

"I told you, I've done terrible things."

"No, no, it's okay. Don't say that."

My impersonation of Charles Manson in the morning before coffee finally grabs Sandy's attention. He gathers our coats as I sing a solo chorus of *thank you, dinner was amazing, truly wonderful, thanks again.*

"If you have any notion that I might be willing to live a life of hell like your mother, get over it," I say before the car door shuts.

"What the—what's wrong with you?"

"You treat your mother like dirt!"

He shakes his head like I'm out of my mind. I make a mental note: Do not marry this jerk.

The answering machine beeps as we walk through the door. It's Danny, saying he'll be swinging by tomorrow morning. I'm disappointed Haley and Jay are at their dads. They adore Uncle Danny. His teasing leaves them begging him to stop while asking for more. I suspect he wants to talk alone. Last week, he was in jail again. He needs help. I have to do something.

I don't know the how-tos of brothers and sisters. I just know our rule book. There have been times when I wanted the little sucker gone for good, like when he hid under my bed with a stuffed glove attached to a broom handle or when he'd pop out from behind the shower curtain just when I turn on the light or the time he knocked on my bedroom window at six in the morning with his pimply, yellow-toothed friends, pointing and giggling at my pink foam rollers. Still, he was, is, and will always be my pain in the butt, and when I'm not planning his demise, I love the idiot.

When I was thirteen and Danny, nine, a silent bond took place. Mom and Dad wanted to go to Esmeralda's, a bar in the skid-row section of Tacoma. They'd spent the day doing what they called *things for us* and wanted some *adult time*. In the spirit of parental multitasking, they handed us a handful of change, along with a couple of Archie and Casper comic books. Upon cautioning we should not to talk to strangers, they left us in the pool hall next door. Mom checked in every thirty minutes. It was fun. That is until around 1:00 a.m. when the seminormal-looking people left us alone with the remaining sour-smelling men whose chins dripped of snuff after swigs from paper bags. Tired, we huddled on the floor, reading our comics. We kept our backs to the wall so no one could sneak up from behind and our eyes downward. I felt a creepy stare coming from a guy with a spider tattoo on his hand. Danny felt it too, wiggling and pressing close to me. As the guy's pointed-toe boots shuffled toward us, my goofy little brother puffs up, placing an arm around my shoulder.

"She's with me," he said in a squeaky voice.

I looked up, expecting the guy to laugh. Surely, even a dedicated ax murderer would think he's too cute for slaughter. When my eyes met the man's, it felt like when you have one of those *naked-in-public* nightmares. What did he see in place of the pair of redheaded, freckled-faced, scared, dopey, ivory-skinned kids? Danny's skinny arm quivered atop my shoulder, his legs bent, preparing to stand and what? Fight? That's when I swore a silent oath to protect him all my days and to quit calling him names. As we stood up together, a voice boomed from the adjoining door to Esmeralda's. It was Dad.

"Let's go!"

With that, the pervert scattered like a cockroach in the light. My folks apologized for being late, explaining their helpless situation.

"Everyone kept buying us drinks. They wouldn't let us leave."

I've kept the vow, the best I can, except for the name-calling. When he was sixteen, smoking weed and failing school, he moved from Auburn to live with my husband, Jerry, and me in Yakima. Together, we shopped for the best high school, with me barely twenty-one, asking the school authorities questions like a mother of six. It's always been Danny and me. Right now, he needs some help. He was willing to stand up at and fight for me, and I'm willing to do the same for him.

When he shows in the morning, he's noticeably hungover. He refuses a bear claw, grabbing for a coffee cup like an old man reaching for his cane. I listen to the ongoing saga of court dates, car accidents, stalking collection agencies, and girlfriends who exaggerate about his temper. I want to mention AA, but he might as well be wearing a sign reading, "I will bite the head off anyone who mentions my drinking."

"I need to ask you something. You can't tell anyone," he says.

He tears up. We light smokes. Sobs take over as he chokes, swallowing words.

"I'm having problems. Sex problems. You know—"

"Like what?" I ask, buying time.

"I can't . . . I don't . . . you know. C'mon, you know!"

He's crying. I'd do anything to help. Desperate, I resort to my one true talent, telling lies. Say what you want, lying is a skill when used responsibly. It's saved me many times from a variety of threats like jail, rape, and getting fired.

"Sandy had the same problems. That is before he quit drinking. He told me all about it. He couldn't function. Now he has no problem at all."

"Really?" Danny asked, swiping the back of his hand on his cheek.

"Yes, really," I lied. "You know, he goes to AA meetings every day. You should talk with him."

"AA is bunk. I'm doing this other deal. It's not just the alcohol. The guy I'm seeing takes a holistic approach. No carcinogens, sugar, or white flour. I've already paid $1,200."

CHAPTER 20

Why Do I Have to be the Guy with the Limp?
(Sandy)

MY DAD PLAYS SAFE, KEEPING opinions to himself, even complimentary ones. I've never heard him tell mom "You look nice" or even notice a new hairdo or perfume. Once our neighbor, Dottie, painted her big toenail black, hoping to disguise the hole in her patent leather shoes. Later when she'd gone home, Dad said it looked *silly*. Other than that, he kept editorial comments quiet.

Saturday, when I walked through the door with Deb, I was taken aback by his reaction. Waiting until she walks into the kitchen with mom, he leans close to me, whispering, "Those legs go on forever."

What? My dad did not just say that! I've no reaction filed away. He would never say that, yet he just did. I've learned hanging with Deb means anything can happen; people approach, seek her out like a moth to a light bulb. I tease her, saying she's a magnet for crazies. Right now, she's wearing a WWII-era mink coat, a miniskirt, a pair of red high-top Converse, and her favorite plaid Elmer Fudd–style hat. The trick is, she rocks it, and it's not just me that thinks so. I've played witness to others clearly admiring her style, whether it's a hat some chicken gave its life for or this look—a schizophrenic bag-lady aristocrat. I'm not that surprised he's charmed by her style; it's the leg comment that threw me. I'm aware of his *man thoughts* by things never said but known: He's a leg man; the poster in the garage of Sophia Loren in a wet T-shirt is never coming down; Mom is hot stuff; daughter Robin is pure princess stock. I've never been told these things, but they're facts just the same.

Jeopardy's theme song returns the dad I know who sits in his recliner, never shouting out the answers before the contestant but letting us know afterward that he knew it all along. I'm enjoying watching Deb with mom in the kitchen until I remember the conversation we had in the car on our way here.

"Sandy, I told a little fib about you to my brother. Don't get upset. It's for a good cause."

"Okay. What?"

"Please understand it was one of those moments when, well, you just know it's okay to lie. It's natural. It just slides off your tongue like it's meant to be, true or not. You know, it's like that moment when you toss the ball with no doubt it will make the basket . . . or like—"

"What was the lie? Just tell me!"

"Well, Danny was so upset, crying because he's having sex problems."

"Okay. What kind of sex problems?"

100

"I don't know. I'm not a guy. You know, a performance deal. I didn't know what to say, but then a solution popped into my head, a way to bring him on board with sobriety. So I . . . I told him you had sex problems too."

"But I don't!"

"I know! I know! I said it was at the end of your drinking days. Can't you see how this could help him?"

"I have never had any problems with sex, not ever!"

"So what! If it helps Danny get sober, boo-hoo to your manhood threat. It's an innocent white lie, and I'm going for it."

"What if he asks me about it?"

"Just tell him everything works great now that you've quit drinking."

"This is not okay."

I get what she means by a moment when a lie lands on your tongue like a gift. The difference is, my lies were given to judges, cops, and girlfriends. She did this to get back at me because I wouldn't fix her brother. I dared to say no, so she jumps in with a whopper of a lie about my sex life. Good intentions or not, why do I have to be the guy with the limp in the story?

I'm still pissed but find it hard to stay that way. She has a big heart; even my mom is opening up to her. I don't remember her telling my other girlfriends her life story. I've shared some family secrets with Deb but not all. I don't mind leaving a few dust bunnies under the bed, unlike Deb who shoos them all out into the open. We're different in many ways, sharing family dysfunction in practice, not style.

Last month, I met Deb's grandma. Like the other family members, she comes with warning labels. I must call her

Na-Na, never Grandma, and *never ever* ask or mention her age. Born in the year 1900, it will be hard to forget how old she is, but I'm keeping my mouth shut. My granny, a wicked woman, who destroyed the souls of her children had rules too—rules I went out of my way to break, like calling her *Granny*. She hated that.

Na-Na and Granny are nothing alike. Walking up the painted stepping stones past the smiley-faced pansies to her white clapboard cottage was like entering a fairy tale. Then she opened the door, smiling.

"Sandy, bless your heart. It's good to meet you."

Spellbound, instantly in love, I enter the land of all things fuzzy and warm. Maybe too warm, like an incubator wrapped in knotty pine walls with a coal furnace blasting in the corner, owning half of the eight-by-ten-foot living room.

"Have a molasses cookie," she says, offering a plate with carefully stacked tiers of perfectly round cookies.

"Thanks."

"I hope they're okay. They might be stale," she says in time with my first bite. "I stored them with some apples and soda crackers. That should have kept them fresh."

I loosen a few buttons on my shirt and roll up my sleeves, looking around the 600-square-foot haven. On the nineteen-inch television is a picture of Deb with dark-brown hair in a white wedding dress. I laugh aloud, seeing that the groom, Jerry, is covered up with a sheet of paper. I remember Deb saying she'd dyed her hair the night before the wedding, something about thinking she'd be a better wife as a brunette than a redhead. I'm learning not to bother understanding all of her logic.

"Don't you think she looks good with dark hair?" asks Na-Na while holding her hand over the already-hidden groom.

We spent the afternoon with Na-Na like children in a safe cocoon of love, talking about poker, gin rummy, train rides, and black licorice. The grand tour of the cottage was like flipping through a photo album, pictures matching Deb's childhood stories—the claw-foot, cast-iron tub; the chenille bedspread; the 1930s black rotary phone; the rickety slat–style cupboards; props I've come to know from her tales of Na-Na.

I couldn't help but compare her to my drunken, foul-mouthed granny who grabbed any chance to say mean things. When it was time to leave, Na-Na starts to walk us to the car.

"Na-Na, I promised Mom I'd make you use your walker," Deb says. "You know you're still wobbly since you broke your hip."

Obeying, she gets it out of the closet, stored in the back along with other useless items. I'm already smitten, but what happens next secures this woman in my heart forever. Leading us along the stepping stones with her begrudged walker, she suddenly stops, lifts the walker over her head slams it down then again and again, yelling, "I hate those rotten slugs!"

Once again, demure and sweet, she uses the multipurpose walker to scrape the slug from the walk. As we pull away, she stands waving, walker at her side. I'm thoroughly charmed, madly in love with Elsie, the Na-Na of every kid's dreams.

CHAPTER 21

I'd Love to Give Up the Socks, but How Do You Go Back Undetected? (Deb)

I WAS A DISAPPOINTMENT TO Beulah, my first mother-in-law. After attempts to convince her son to look elsewhere failed, she surrenders, saving energy for a new cause—molding daughter-in-law to suit *the ladies who lunch*. She frowned at my sunset of favorite outfits, saying "That's bright" or naming the color in a question like "Orange?" She sent me lovely boxes with huge bows, always holding some-thing expensive and gray inside. Wearing drab suits with *desexified* flat shoes, I was displayed at luncheons alongside Beulah. When *the ladies who lunch* asked me questions, she held her breath. My waitress status evoked synchronized eye shifting under neatly tweezed, raised eyebrows. One question was repeatedly asked, as if I needed more chances to get it right.

"What is your family's name again?"

"McFarland."

"I don't know the name. Have you heard of them?" they'd ask around the table, waiting for someone to speak the name into existence.

Beulah's head hung low until the waitress presented her with the perfect granddaughter. By the time she could boast of two grandchildren, my sins of color choice were forgiven along with the *hasher* social position.

Sandy's folks may not give open-arm hugs or Hallmark-card proclamations of love, but they accept me, as is. For them, showing love means poking stupid jokes at each other. They're growing on me like slapstick comedy, causing groans, but dang if you can stop laughing or wanting more. Watching them play catch with old worn-out jokes makes me feel safe—the redundancy of it, like a child asking to play the same game over and over.

My Na-Na is similar, using repetition to knit a safety net for others to swing in like a hammock. You know what to expect—the scent of blue carnation toilet water, juicy-fruit gum, the phrase "Well, bless your heart." It's impossible not to love her. I knew she'd be sweet medicine for Sandy. Earlier this week, he received devastating news; his dream to be a teacher is over. Waiting like Jack the Ripper in a dark alley, she sprung the news, twisting the knife, savoring the blood of her kill. The reasons for the ax were weak—lack of control over the class and not following the teaching model. Her claims contradicted the facts; the students love him as do the teachers and staff, but she holds the authority card like an irrational queen with a sharp guillotine, screaming, "Off with his head!"

Sandy trusted her; no, that's not right. He believed God would reward him for changing his life and working hard. All that did was give her the advantage of surprise. That day he asked to be dismissed from her training, she set out to nail his balls to the wall. She's a petty woman with wounded pride. She sees him as an arrogant, angry, a woman hater, but she's wrong. He's like a turtle, hiding vulnerability under a hard shell. If she cared to know him, she'd see that he's a genuine, kind, caring man who treats women with respect as any good father of daughters, brother of sister, and son of mother would.

The day with Na-Na brought laughter, peace, hope. Back home, he returned to the sofa absorbed by scenes of Desert Storm unraveling on CNN. He won't talk or listen. He leaves the house before sun up for a daily meeting, returning, mood as dark as when he left. Our contradicting coping styles annoy each other. When I'm depressed, I take action, which can be dangerous and often destructive. Sandy rolls around in anger, paralyzed, waiting to self-destruct. I shoot suggestions like pellets; in turn, he crouches behind his shield.

I miss him.

Work is my relaxation. Sounds *oxymoronic* but my way to relieve stress is to get stuff done. Making check marks on my to-do list is better than popping a Valium. At work, my clients are disillusioned, believing my job title guarantee I know what I am talking about. Lucky for them, I'm experienced at pretending. One tool proving handy is the steps and principles of AA. Some creative tweaking and *voila,* the concepts work for whatever ails whomever. I also take liberties with Sandy's story; it's inspirational and has proven to encourage others to speak up. Anonymity is a big deal, but no one said I had to keep quiet. If it helps someone, I'm using it.

The backlash I suffer is guilt by association with a recovering alcoholic. I might as well have a scarlet P on my chest for *party pooper*. At the office, a hush drops in the chatty cubicles as I approach, stifling plans for after-work-party plans. They see a finger pointing and judging them, a finger I am not wagging. I thought once I proved myself with a college degree and a professional job that the less-than label would finally fall off. I thought I could stop being the *odd man out*.

It seems the harder I try, the worse it gets. Sitting at the table alongside coworkers and bosses for my first staff meeting, I felt like I was in the oval office. I was tossed a small bone—design a training class for the upcoming group of jobless guinea pigs. At the second staff meeting, I presented the class design as asked, along with twelve additional progressive classes, followed by a potential promotion layout. My bosses loved it. Coworkers? Not so much.

I've had this problem my entire life but upside down. I was the girl no one could count on, not the perky A student obsessively dotting the I's for not only my work but anyone who'd hold their paper still. It makes me think of my sixth-grade love, Mark Taylor. He was super smart, but he liked me anyway. I know he did. He laughed when I made faces behind the teachers back, and when Miss Truman had me on my knees in the hall, testing to see if my skirt was long enough to touch the floor, Mark would smile as he passed by. I loved him because he loved me, as is.

Besides his near-genius status, he proved to be a boy with integrity. On Friday, our class would cast votes for *student of the week*. The top three candidates would wait in the hall until the final vote declared a winner for the prize, usually a Milky Way bar. With the school year nearly over, I was the only student left to have never chewed the Milky Way trophy or even stood as a nominee in the hall. Having some integrity of my own, I was annoyed when Dawn Tutland raised her hand, naming me in a nomination of pity, followed by her clique of *yes girls*. Along with two others, I was sent to the hall to await the final vote. I used the time to adjust the socks in my bra, an uncomfortable practice I started a few weeks ago. I'd love to give up the socks, but how do you go back undetected? When beckoned back to class, I was told in a clumsy fashion that Margaret, once again, earned the blessed chocolate bar. Taking my seat, Dawn whispers to me that Mark Taylor held out, saying a girl who never does her homework should not win student of the week. I thought he was right on, but after that, he stopped looking my way, socks or not.

CHAPTER 22

This Will Not Stand
(Sandy)

GET OUT OF BED. SHOWER. Make coffee. Wake Deb. Start the procession of "Come on, get up" outside Haley's and Jay's doors. Kiss Deb goodbye; shoot out the door for a meeting before she asks, "Are you okay?" Return to empty house. Turn television to CNN. Lay on sofa.

"This will not stand," says President Bush from the television.

I feel like I've joined forces with Bush, spending my days stretched out on the sofa, immersed in the riveting details of Desert Storm. With 24/7 coverage, I can forget my own demise and concentrate on the threat of an Iraqi takeover of Saudi Arabia which would leave old Saddam holding one-fifth of the world's oil supply.

Every day, it's me and Bush, the rockets and Scud missiles bursting. It keeps thoughts away like "How did I end up living in a house once occupied by Deb and her first husband?" Sometimes I want to go home but can't since it's rented to my friend Gary. I sure don't want to live with him. I'm an insignificant character, one I don't even like in a story that no longer holds my interest. What happened? I was riding a magic carpet of high hopes then swish the rug was swiped out from under me. A few words sent my hopes crashing, mere words spoken by the head of student teaching, Sylvia, aka the Dragon Lady.

"Please hand over your keys."

Apparently, she'd sat, pinched nose and quiet, in the back of my classroom like a simmering pot waiting to boil, biding her time ever since the day I'd spoken out of turn in her training, waiting for her moment to wield her power.

"Gather your belongings and leave."

Emasculated, broken, stunned, "Why?" reeling between my ears. I obeyed the finger pointing to the door. Driving home, I came too like a stunned bee ready to attack the swatter. I call Sam Rust, my adviser, who schedules a meeting for the next day.

"I read the report. This is a rough deal, Sandy," he says, eyes diverted. "Of course, I can speak favorably on your behalf based on what I know as one of my students. Unfortunately, I don't have any pull or say in this. What can you tell me about the situation?"

"It's a personality clash, with nothing to do with my ability or performance. Look, I pissed her off. It's a vendetta. What can I do? What are my options?" I ask, swallowing to quiet the sound of my voice, surrendering.

He gives two options: accept the decision or schedule a protest hearing. Shaken but not without hope, I choose the hearing. Two weeks later, I walk into the hearing, ready to state my case to the head of the education department, three of my education professors, and Sam. God has my back. It will be straightened out. I didn't screw up this time. I'm the good guy, sober four years, deserving a gold star for perfect AA attendance. I'm not the man I once was, and I'm not going down for something I didn't do.

It was like walking the plank on a pirate ship as I approached the lonely chair, clearly mine. Front and center sat the department head, eyes defining me as the pariah in the room. My support team was seated at his sides. In the still before the storm, each one apologized, communicating with eyes only, "I need my job. My hands are tied. I know this is wrong. I want to help but—"

The department head summarizes the report, with persuasive enunciation, revealing his judgment on the case. When allowed to speak, I give an honest rebuttal to Sylvia's claims that I had not taught from the ITIP model and could not keep my students under control. I explain the misunderstanding that happened at the training, and as gracefully as possible, I tell them she had it in for me. I swap the words in my head for better choices like "She's a raving idiot with a vengeance" for "She misunderstood, and we had a personality conflict."

After my account, the professors spoke on my behalf. I listened as each roiled up nerve, speaking on my good character, commitment to the students, and various examples disputing claims I'm unsuited to teach. This is not a voting panel, I know that, as they do. I respect their attempts, a wild-ass shot at changing the headmaster's prejudiced views. When all had stated their pleas, he asked if anyone wished to say more.

Taking a breath of courage, my industrial-education professor speaks out.

"It should be known that Sandy Palmer is a recovering alcoholic who has worked hard to stay sober."

I've no doubt he spoke intending to help, but dropping the alcoholic label did not work in my favor. It was inside information, confidentially shared in a friendship moment, intended for his ears only. Sam's expression switched from brave advocate to one of regret.

It was awkward, all eyes on me, as if awaiting a scene from Reefer Madness. With all their scholarly accolades, they were ill-equipped, capable only to judge out of stirrings and stories taken from their personal experience. Judgments based on drunken uncles, neighbors, maybe a parent, drunken escapades, and chronic relapse exposed as a single definition for all alcoholics. And if statistics serve, maybe even judgment based on personal bourbon wars. The uneasy moment ended with my dismissal from the hearing.

"You'll hear from us by the end of the week."

It didn't look good, but I believed right would prevail. Four years ago, I became the guy in the white hat, no longer the badass in the black hat lying, stealing, cheating. I don't drink or hurt people. I do my job. There's no way the bitter words of a woman, whose coworkers call the Dragon Lady, will trump justice.

Two days later, the call came.

"Mr. Palmer, we are standing by the recommendation made by Sylvia Severn. She's the head of student teaching. Her authority stands."

When I heard the words, I felt calm. Maybe I knew the outcome all along. The game players were a support façade, knowing the decision fell to the head of the department who slammed the gavel before the hearing began. Speech slow and deliberate, I ask what can be done. I'm given two choices: accept the decision and kiss my years of effort goodbye or petition the Education Department for the opportunity to complete another student teaching.

This can't be happening. As a drunk, I attended four universities over fifteen years, crapping out five times, never graduating and not deserving to. This time, I worked hard, stayed sober, played nice. Why?

I write the petition, sending it off before I can think. For the next two weeks, I do a single daily task—wait. When the phone rings on a Monday morning, I know it's *the call*. The robotic voice on the line speaks the foreign word I had hoped for *yes*. I may apply for new student-teaching position as long as I enroll as a full-time student at CWU. The receptionist didn't bother masking the stench of the BS, stating, "It doesn't matter what classes you take, just make sure you have twelve credits."

I might as well have chosen my courses blindfolded using the finger-dart method. Instead of graduating and looking forward to my teaching career this fall, I'm enrolled in a recreation course on national parks and a marriage-and-counseling course. And it's my job to find a student-teaching position for fall quarter.

One day at a time—hell one minute at a time. It's the only way I'll make it through this. Just get through spring quarter and worry about the fall when it gets here. In the meantime, I've good things to cling to like Deb. Come June, I'm taking her to the races. She's leery, but what's not to love? Noise, dirt, crashes, the essence of methanol—she'll love it!

CHAPTER 23

What Do I Need to Do?
(Deb)

"You did what?"

"I volunteered us to sit on a panel for my Marriage and Relationship class."

"But why? Do you need the extra credit?"

"No. I think the students can learn from us. We have a great relationship."

"Sandy, what were you thinking? In case you've forgotten, we're not exactly characters out of a 1950s sitcom. Are we going to sit there and lie?"

"No, just answer truthfully."

The day of the panel, we're scheduled to be stoned second to the last. I listen as perky teens speak of undying love, the kind that would send a cupid running, tossing bow and arrow, choking and puking in the bushes. All three couples share of first love, forever love, only love, and none have lived away from home nor held a job. Oh, wait, I forgot. The eighteen-year-old philosophy major has babysat her *entire* life since she was sixteen, and Michael, her lifetime beau, works on cars with his Uncle Simon. They also agree to a list of *never woulds*, like never would divorce, never would argue, and a *never ever* would cheat on their spouse. Upon graduation, they'll marry and become marriage counselors, teaching others from a pool of lifetime wisdom summed up in the song lyrics: "Don't worry, be happy."

Too late to bail, I take my seat in front of the class next to Sandy. The professor introduces us, unaware the party just switched from Pablum to gin. Sandy shares tidbits of divorce, shacking up, and general drunken mayhem. I watch the student's manner change from safe and bored to uneasy and interested. The prepared list of questions lay abandoned on their desks while Sandy feeds them AA slogans like a zookeeper tossing slabs of meat to the lions.

They appear content, gnawing at his bones of infidelity, lies, and arrests. I can see by the looks of pity sent my way that they've concluded I'm the victim in this story. I'm good with that. I'll just sit here looking meek and clueless, like any saintly codependent partner would. It works until some curly blonde, probably named Buffy, calls me out from my safe place.

"What about you? Why did your first marriage end? Were you abused?"

I had two choices: slump and cower, telling them what they want to hear, a story painting my ex-husband as a monster who beat me daily with a big stick; or hike my skirt up and tell them the truth.

"No, my husband was not abusive."

"Why then did you divorce? You have children, right?"

"I had an affair."

She looked like Bambi when mommy deer took a bullet between the eyes and dropped dead. I look over at Sandy, hoping he sees they're reaching for stones in their pockets and we need to flee for our lives. He returns my look with kind brown eyes, encouraging me to continue.

"I single-handedly destroyed my marriage with no good reason. I had the affair because I wanted out of a dead marriage. I wanted to feel loved, experience passion."

Like wedding rice, *whys* came at me from all corners of the room. Unable to think, I confess details I would've chosen to conceal, if given a moment of thought.

"Yes, the man I had an affair with was also married."

The room stilled until a gangly guy in a basketball jersey spoke up.

"Did you ever think about the lives you were destroying?"

Hearing this sent me into a state of hyperawareness. With astute clarity, I could see and feel their broken hearts and dreams. Through eyes resembling my children, I saw myself—the cause of every broken home in human form; the woman responsible for hurting their parents, neighbors, friends, innocent children, and helpless animals; the wicked woman from their favorite television soap opera, the one everyone loves to hate, here in the flesh.

"I was needy and confused. I don't condone my actions. He groomed me for a year. He said every word I needed to hear."

The guy in the jersey forces a cease-fire on me, aligning Sandy in his crosshairs for his final question.

"If you both have a history of infidelity, how will you ever trust each other?"

"I trust Deb with all my heart, soul, and strength."

Those words may have saved Sandy's life. With no time for the last couple to restore life as it should be, the professor calls off the stoning, asking if we might come back for a second session that he could record.

No, thank you!

We drive the Canyon Road home from Ellensburg, stopping to talk under an oak tree, the Yakima river skimming over the silky rocks. Drained from the interrogation, Sandy is ripe to speak openly on the wounds, now open and scathing. I ask questions I've asked before, but now they come with answers.

He talks about his brother Jim, the one killed in a drunken car accident at age sixteen. The brother who relentlessly forced little brother Sandy to the ground, knees on chest, punching, ignoring pleas of "Get off, I can't breathe!" I learned it was a well-intended remark by an aunt that slammed the door shut on his childhood faith. Standing over Jim's casket, she turned to twelve-year-old Sandy saying, "Don't worry, Jim's sins are forgiven. He's going to heaven. We had a priest summoned, and he was baptized."

Turning away from me, gazing over the rolling river, he confesses.

"Some priest sprinkles water on his head, and now everything's okay? No, that's when I decided God and religion were man-made."

Flipping through the Palmer family albums, I had wondered why he never smiled, the old black-and-white snapshots with the angry little boy. The photos didn't match the man I know with the gentle soul and love of God.

"What got you back believing? Was it AA?"

"No, actually it was Nanette's baptism. Barney, aka Bonnie, dragged me to classes at the Lutheran church she attended. I guess after a while, my mind opened back up, and I let God back in."

I admit attraction to the God he speaks of. A God, whose name mentioned, transforms angry little boys from dark to light. I wish I had what it takes to believe all the malarkey, but I don't. I don't need a crutch. I can take care of myself. I learned a long time ago not to trust anyone with anything that matters. Besides, it's too late for me. I've done every worst thing imaginable, and what I've missed, I'll probably get to later. I do like listening to him talk of his God. Until Sandy, I've always wondered why only crazy people believe in God. You know, the ones hanging at the airport on hallucinogens, handing you flowers. Or the nutcase I met one day walking home from work. He nearly got to me, even with a ridiculous cliché approach.

"Jesus loves you. He wants me to tell you that."

I was eighteen years old, living in a fully furnished $85 a month studio apartment. The only resident under eighty years old. The guy's timing was right on. The night before, I'd washed down a handful of amphetamines called *Yellow Jackets* with a bottle of Mad Dog 20/20 strawberry wine. Gail, a homeless gal I'd invited to stay with me, showed up with two guys who brought the wine and the pills. I still wonder why I remember every detail of that night, having lost details of far less traumatic events. I can smell the English Leather aftershave, feel the calloused hands, hear his partner's voice egging him on. I remember feeling sad for the shame he would suffer later as I lay unable to speak or move a single limb. I imagined he would spend his life in regret, unable to forgive himself for what he was doing to me. It was my fault for letting them in my apartment.

The next morning, I'm a prime candidate for the Jesus freak, vulnerable, ready to listen. I let him buy me a never-empty, ten-cent coffee at Sambo's restaurant. Later, I let the Jesus musketeer come back to my apartment because I want to hear more. Sitting on my purple mohair sofa, he recites scripture about a God who sent his Son to earth so I could be forgiven. I made boxed macaroni and cheese, and we drank a quart of chocolate milk. He talked through the afternoon until dusk, when I wanted him to stop. I'd had enough. I was ready to purchase at any cost. Yes, please, my sins forgiven, my stains washed away, a new life, a God who promises love and forgiveness.

"Yes, I want to accept Christ. What do I need to do?"

He resembles my brother, light complexion, curly red hair, so I recognized the signs of tears on the way, blotchy red spots appearing on the cheeks, and pink eyelids. I'm expecting a prayer or that he might have me read aloud from his Bible. Instead, he starts apologizing, saying he's a horrible person. I didn't understand. What had I done to change his mind? Then he lit the fuse, sending the trust he'd earned to hell.

"I . . . I . . . I'm sorry. I just wanted to get in your pants. I should never have come here. I'm sorry."

"But I . . . wait I—"

He left.

Later as a young mom, shortly after Mount St. Helens blew its top and all Yakima turned pitch-black at noon, I returned to my childhood Presbyterian (very short) roots.

I wanted Haley and Jay baptized, just in case. A six-week membership course was required, and only members could be baptized. They may as well have taught it in Greek because I couldn't understand anything. With one class left before graduation, I raised my hand, confessing I needed help with the Bible. Since they liked theologizing amongst each other, as if competing for a prize, I thought they'd be willing to mentor me. The room fell silent for a few moments, and then as if I'd never spoken, they dismiss the class for the day.

I stand by my case. It's the crazies that believe in God. Sandy and his AA. God seem almost normal in comparison.

CHAPTER 24

Swerve Left For a U-turn (Sandy)

PRESOBRIETY LIFE IS IN THE moment. What mess needs covered up today? How do I get from A to my next drink? It's simple really. The good and bad thing about sobriety is that your past and future become reality.

I can sort through the destruction of my past, my memories crisp and fresh. August 9, 1963 is circled in red on the calendar of my mind, a taken for granted Yakima-summer day, hot, bright, easy. I'm hanging at the park with friends, shooting the bull around a picnic table. It's midmorning, and I've loads of preteen energy to burn. My friend Chet's silver bicycle leans on a tree, begging for a try. Snagging the shiny beauty, I take it for a spin down Lincoln Avenue. It's one of those moments we think about later as grown-ups, wishing we'd cherished instead of presuming all our days would be jazzed with energy, free to peddle away.

I swerve left for a U-turn.

There's a blip of a man standing over me then nothing. I awake seeing the horror of my triple-sized head in my mother's eyes. Barely a year after losing her eldest son in the same hospital, face held in both hands, swaying, she looks like a puppet sustained by strings.

My head feels like it's been hammered on, but that pain is nothing compared to what I felt hearing the doctor say, "No football or basketball for at least a year, young man." He blabs on about brain concussions then adds lightly, "Maybe next spring, you can play baseball."

He acted like he was suggesting I give up ketchup or mayo, not the very reason I jump out of bed every day. He didn't know squat. I wasn't just playing around. I was serious, the next Brooks Robinson, a future all-star. I knew it. My coaches knew it. Everyone but the stupid doctor knew it.

I obey the doctor's orders to remain in bed, my only hope that the *maybe baseball* will turn yes in the spring. I consume Mad magazines, Casper the Friendly Ghost comics, and Dad's Playboys until the first day of school finally arrives.

I come from a shoddy family, on the other side of the tracks with a built-in badass reputation handed down by my brother Jim. The teachers hate my guts, expecting me to fit into their preconceived box of bad boy. I met some of their criteria, being known for fighting and smart mouthing teachers, but unlike Jim, I score As and Bs and had coaches lusting after my natural athletic abilities.

Without sports occupying mind and body, I focused on girls. They've always been there, but now it's like they're backlit, impossible to ignore, beaming with boobs and pink lipstick. With no before-and-after-school sports, I hang out in the alley with ninth graders, smoking Lucky Strikes stolen from Dad's stash.

It was a year of dangerous firsts—a kiss, a copped feel, a beer, and the almighty shot of whiskey. My introduction to beer came on New Year's Eve at Aunt Joyce's house while eating true Italian pizza, masterfully made by the wife of a real Italian. I copied my older (by three years) cousin Jeannie, sneaking sips from neglected bottles. I suspect they knew of our mischief, pretending to be blind so we could have our fun. Soon Jeannie snagged us our own bottles, and by the time the adults moved the party to the house next door, she was giggling at her protégé's slurred attempts at speech.

Dragging a red metal stool over to the fridge, she climbs up, reaching the cupboard above, pulling out a bottle of Jim Beam. I knew the name but had no idea that we'd become best friends and later the worst of enemies. Wanting to earn back some respect for slurring my words, I lined up shot glasses like a bartender, only to slop it all over the table, giving Jeannie more laughs. We toasted the New Year, clicking shots, slamming the liquid to the back of our throats like a pair of sailors. My new best friend, Jim, warmed my innards, tingling, soothing over me like a shower of divinity. I wanted more. Three shots later, Jeannie held my head as I involuntarily gave up Jim to the porcelain bowl. The rest of the night, I spent in humiliation, laying on the sofa, head in Jeannie's lap, a helpless kid.

After that night, I visited Jim, along with other liquid comrades as often as an eight-grade lifestyle allowed. I kept the honor-roll status and won the election for student-body president to prove I'm not the bum from a loser family the teachers made me out to be. It really gets them that a smart mouth, disrespectful kid pulls good grades without much effort and, worse yet, is popular with all the students no matter what their social status.

When spring came, the doctor released me to play baseball, ordering the helmet stay on at all times. Hey, I didn't care. I would have worn a tutu to get back in the game. I was devastated to find my star quality had dimmed. My natural athletic abilities that once oozed from my pores as easy as sweat had become a challenge. That fall, they gave my starting quarterback position away, leaving me to fight hard to gain a spot as center. I blamed the accident for destroying my childhood dreams, but looking back, my buddy Jim Beam helped drown my abilities. Before long, interest in sports and academics sank into an ocean of booze.

It's easy to see the culprit of my past failures, but what about today? I'm sober, doing things right, yet I'm still losing in this game of life. Why is God doing this to me? What am I still doing wrong?

Fall quarter, I'll be commuting to Wenatchee for a *do-over* student-teaching position with troublemaker brand on my chest. Last week, I had a promising meeting with Naches High School staff and Daphne, my vocational counselor. I was told they had all enthusiastically agreed on hiring me for the student-teaching position. But when the decision came down to the Naches student-teaching supervisor, like the camaraderie of cops, he chose to back the decision made by the Dragon Lady. I was told he didn't want to put energy into someone who is a problem. I'm a problem?

Driving one hundred miles over Blewett Pass, spending weekdays away from Deb is not ideal, but it's one more shot at making things right, one day at a time.

CHAPTER 25

Duh—Icicle River
(Deb)

I FELL ASLEEP IN CRAZY love, waking not only before the earth switched on its lights but before Sandy, the "up and at 'em" guy. I slip out of our zipper-joined cocoon, pull on Sandy's day-old T-shirt, inside-out jeans, and flip flops. Digging through a nest of cookies, Richard Bach's book *One*, and crumpled M&M's wrappers, I grab the Benson & Hedges and Bic lighter. I roll onto my stomach, slide off the loft-style bed, and slowly open the noisy barn-style doors of the van. Sandy rolls onto his side as the door creaks, skipping two beats before returning to the snoring melody. I consider crawling back up for a rerun of last night, choosing time on my own instead.

I follow the path we walked last night, leading down to the Wenatchee River. There's a few faint lights inside trailers, but I appear to be the only one ready to seize the rising sun. There's a path of rocks leading to a large boulder midstream, beckoning. I attempt to stuff my cigarettes in my bra and find the pack floating at my feet. Retrieving the pack, I remember a bra is not one of the two items I'm wearing. With the pack in my jean pocket, I prance across rocks leading to the inviting boulder, knowing I can't fall—a rare moment of unexplained confidence, like when you toss a wad of paper knowing it will score the trash can or raise a hand without a doubt you'll catch the ball.

Lifting Sandy's T-shirt carrying his alluring scent, I retrieve the pack, lighting a first smoke. It's chilly; the nip to my face is welcome. It's an orchestra moment—the water rushing, swirling, cresting; the sky breaking open, pink and yellow. Even the quiet plays a part in the symphony. My thoughts wander to the God discussions of late. Is God here, now, watching me? I don't feel alone, not in a creepy sense like stalker Wayne, more like a child aware mom is on guard. *God, are you here?* Do you know I exist? As the sun persists breaking through the dark, I remember that time I prayed, asking for someone to love me, really love me. What if God answered that prayer with Sandy? It's a silly thought. A God, over everything and everyone, chooses me from among the other ants on the sidewalk, granting my wish for love. Nice thought, but it's not logical. I choose to face life *as is*, eyes open.

As other campers mosey down to the river, my solitude is threatened by splashing children, eyeballing and nearing my boulder. Today, we're off to the races, whatever that looks like. So far, I'm in. Sandy has it all planned: first night in Leavenworth, the next three in Skagit Valley. There's an early morning promise of another crackling hot June day. Snubbing out my fourth smoke, I surrender to the young pirates and head back to our camp. Sandy meets me on the path, showered and ready for the day.

By noon, the temperature is nearing one hundred degrees. We're heading west on Steven's Pass alongside the Icicle River. Bare feet on the dash of the van, dressed like Sandy in cutoffs and T-shirt, I'm in a foreign land of contentment.

"The river looks amazing. Is there someplace we can get down to it and stretch our legs?"

"I think after the next bend or so."

We park, climb down a steep, narrow path to a haven of celadon-green water spraying across glassy boulders, sparkling in the sun. The other six or so paradise seekers basking in the sun nod a welcome as we approach. Sandy guides me, just enough for balance as we maneuver the slippery rocks. Standing side by side on a boulder built for two, I take his hand, suggesting, "Let's jump in." He makes a funny wincing face then nods. Like Peter Pan and Tinker Bell, we leap into the air, free, happy, in love. With the splash, our lungs deflate, defining the river's name. Like a pair of plastic fishing bobbers, we pop to the top. Shivering, we race to the car while onlookers snicker with looks of "Duh, *Icicle* River."

The sun dries our clothes and thaws our bones quickly. We mosey on toward Skagit Valley, detouring whenever a yard-sale sign beckons, leading us down back roads, munching Windmill cookies and black licorice.

We arrive at our campsite in time to set up and catch a power nap before race time. Packing ice chest, blankets, and goggles, we walk through the gates as the announcer blasts, "Welcome to the 1990 Jim Raper Memorial Dirt Cup."

Sandy marches us down front to our reserved seats, the same ones he's occupied for six consecutive years, five while sober. I light a cigarette, relieved to see I'm surrounded by fellow smokers. The habit pacifies me if bored. The races don't start for an hour. I don't understand why we had to rush, but ads for homemade strawberry shortcake, donuts, and infamous sprint burgers console fears of a long night.

"I've tried sitting other places, but I think this row on the aisle is the best. You can see the action on all four turns. When the track dries out, you'll need these goggles to keep the dirt out of your eyes," he says, handing me a pair of bug-eyed goggles.

He offers to buy me a Dirt Cup T-shirt, a sweet gesture, but they're expensive. I already splurged on a pair of vintage English riding boots we found at an antique store in Sedro Wooley, size 8 AA narrow (my size) for $20. Besides that, we scored the perfect WWII-era flowered hat from the free box at an estate sale.

After choosing a 1990 memorial shirt for his collection, we settle into our seats. It's 95 degrees, an anomaly for this side of the mountains. The purple silk cabbage roses on my free-box hat droop from the heat as we deplete our supply of Dr. Pepper. The speakers blast '60s rock songs, for which I'm grateful; Yakima is a two-song town: "Jeremiah was a Bullfrog" and "Kansas City."

I sweep my cigarette butts into a pile with my foot, waiting for the drivers to get done patting each other on the butt. Finally, the race starts. I can't make any sense of it.

"Sandy? Sandy! Who's winning?"

"What? Nobody. It's hot laps."

He explains, in-depth, but I quit listening. Pretty much, they're pointless laps accompanied by a bunch of hoopla to rev up the crowd. After the last bunch of cars finish laps, the crowd is ready for racing, especially me. Instead, a snail-speed water truck enters the track.

"What's he doing?"

"Sprinkling the track to get some moisture, keeping the dust down."

Sensing my failing patience, he leaves, returning with two colossal-size strawberry shortcakes made from old-fashioned scones and fresh local berries. Content, I watch the cars line up to race. There's a hush as the winged sprint cars scrunch together in formation. A man dressed in white stands in a cage above the track holding three flags. When the yellow light turns green and the green flag waves, the fans inhale simultaneously. Sandy hands me goggles as the synced rumbling of the engines turns to a roar.

Three laps in, I'm blind from the dust and can't hear anything over the engine noise. Slipping on the goggles, I look where Sandy is pointing as an orange sprint car flips like a trapeze artist. I cover my head thinking it's heading our way. Bouncing off the fence, it lands upside down on the track. Fans rush the fence to see; pit crew men run to the car, and an ambulance moves in, lights flashing. The announcer is yelling something over the loudspeaker, but no one can hear over the crowds. The car is in crumpled pieces scattered across the track. I'm ready to leave.

"I hate this! It's barbarian!"

"Don't worry, he's okay. Sprint cars are made to do that."

The fans quiet to listen as they see the racer crawl out of the mangled car.

"He's out of the car folks. Give him a hand."

The driver is not only okay but ready to do it again. Knowing he's okay, I'm ready for more. The remaining twenty-five cars line up in formation. Exhilarated, I take a bite of my shortcake, spitting it out, tasting the black grit of the track. Sandy laughs, "That's part of the race, sweetie."

After several yellow and red light crashes with no one hurt, the adrenaline rush wins. I'm hooked on the dirt cup, peppered shortcake, and all.

CHAPTER 26

Hey, Rat's Butt! Your Shoe's Untied
(Sandy)

LIKE MOST MEN, I WANT speed, loud noises, sex, and a Playboy prototype on my arm. Deb is *not* the centerfold type with a staple through her belly button. I wonder if the fantasy dried up in the desert of sobriety.

My "slamdangit, I'm head over heels in love!" moment happened beneath the silliest flowered hat, sagging and weeping racetrack dirt. With a flower vicariously hanging in front of one eye, Deb smiles, dirt stuck in her teeth. That was it. I was a goner ready to be committed alongside this crazy redhead.

The gritty grin is a relief. It's my turn to introduce something new, payback for a list of *first times* she's given me. For example, yesterday we junked all day. Before I met Deb, I thought that meant hanging at the wrecking yard. No matter, the races had kept us up past 2:00 a.m. Deb is ready to tackle the sport at morning light. By 10:00 a.m., random stops at a dozen yard sales, scored a Victorian velvet jacket, a polka-dot bowl, a hundred-year-old wooden-screw furniture clamp, and an 1898 Audel's electricity book. After an ice-chest picnic of cheese and salami, I make points with Deb, stumbling upon the town of Bellingham, three blocks of side by side antiques and thrift stores. The first store we enter is named Eartha Kitty, after the cabaret star Eartha Kitt. Deb spent most of her time purring with the fattest cat I've ever seen. I hate cats. At least Eartha Kitty is employed, greeting cat-loving customers like Deb when not napping.

"Look at this! Look! It's the best ever! Right? Can't you see it in our bath? It makes me so happy. Don't you think it's fun?"

She's holding a framed black-and-white photograph of two gymnasts/contortionists demonstrating incredible upper and lower body strength. I'm learning what *fun* means in reference to inanimate objects from Deb. I admit, the funny pose and the 1920s tights are amusing. Pulling three crumpled dollars from the pocket of her red-and-blue plaid jacket, she digs deeper for the eight pennies needed for tax, glancing over her shoulder at me like she's buying an original Rembrandt oil painting. Priceless plunder in hand, she dances and purrs with Eartha Kitty, thanking her for the incredible find. When we walk out the door, I swear that damn cat winks at me. Two blocks down, I find my prize in a dilapidated store called *The Hobbit*. It didn't have a marketing cat, but the owner looked like Bilbo Baggin's twin from *The Lord of the Rings*.

"How do you inventory this at tax time?" I ask, amazed at the piles.

I wasn't being rude. I was impressed. There were towers of stuff, stacked and balanced from floor to ceiling. Magazines, books, toys, army jackets, pots, and pans. I'm taking it in, when I see it, hear it whisper "Psst, up here." Perched atop an upright Underwood typewriter sits a gray Stetson fedora, identical to mine. Snagging it, I slap it alongside my leg, creating a puff of dust before placing it on Deb's head. It's a perfect fit.

"Ya think this would be a good dirt-cup hat? There's no roses, but it might hold up a little better?"

And that's when I became the guy in that couple wearing matching hats. To think, I initiated it.

After treasure hunting, costing a combined total of $10, I announce we're leaving for the races on time tonight. Yesterday, she thought we arrived early, unaware we were two hours late. Having been part of a pit crew, hanging out in the pits is a close second to the race. Now that I'm sober, I don't want to miss out. Years past, I'd pass out in the parking lot, missing most of the race. Worse yet, I was the drunk no one trusted to drive the race car.

Had I been sober, well, no need thinking about that now. Today is good, better than good. Two gray fedoras, side by side, strolling into the racetrack on time, hanging in the pit, meeting the drivers, scoping the cars. This is one time I enjoy answering Deb's excessive questions.

"Sprint cars are unique, constructed with a nose and top wing to keep them planted on the track, 850 horsepower, lightweight, 1,300 pounds of tube frame built to crash at speeds up to 120 mph. They have a short open-throttle life span of a hundred miles, at which time the motor is replaced."

We talk with the drivers, kick a couple of tires, laugh at a band of muddy kids sliding down the track, and make mud balls of our own. Everything is perfect until time trials begin, proving Deb's attention span to be less than fifteen seconds. She gets wound up like one of those old tin monkeys with cymbals, chatting *rat-a-tat-tat*. I'm trying to record the track times in my program. She's oblivious to the pencil in my hand, the announcer, and the cars circling the track. But she knows what everyone is eating, and she's obsessed with the elderly woman's tattoos seated to our left.

"Do you ever wonder about tattoos?" she asks, talking over the announcer as he reveals Jimmy Sills' time.

"What if you get a tattoo when you're skinny, and then you get really fat? Will the tattoo stretch out? Or what if you get a tattoo of a flower on your breast, will it grow a long stem when your breasts droop down to your belly?"

"I really don't know," I answer, wishing I knew what time Sills made.

"Betcha' can't look without laughing," she says, nodding her head to the right.

I turn, seeing two guys wrapping Saran wrap over their billed caps, preparing for the inevitable upcoming race-inspired dust storm. They're the same duo we watched run for cover last night.

"Ya think they're newbies?" I ask, failing to stifle my laugh. "There won't be a dust problem tonight because it's rained all day. We're in for an ideal track for racing."

With time trials complete, the announcer begins all the prerace particulars.

"We invite you to enjoy our beer garden located at the southeast corner of the racetrack. Please remember, there's a three-stamp limit. Those caught washing or licking off the stamp will be escorted out of the track."

We're howling at the idea when I hear a familiar voice behind me.

"Hey, rat's butt! Your shoe's untied."

A secret code known by me and one other. Before I can respond, she runs off, looking over her shoulder with an impish grin.

"Do you know that little girl?" Deb asks.

There's an awkward silence as I consider the plausibility of *the random kid calling me rat's butt story.*

"It might have been Cindy's daughter."

"Might have been? You wouldn't recognize the child you lived with for two years?"

"Yes, it is. It's Melissa."

Deb is a woman of many words, but her true powers show in silence.

Truth is, I don't have answers. This is really weird. I feel crowded, violated, intruded upon. This is my deal, not Cindy's. I didn't see this coming, not even yesterday when Deb said she thought she saw a woman that looked like Cindy waiting in line at the showers. I convinced us both it was only her imagination.

"She's here to make you jealous. To try and get you back."

"No, she just likes the races."

"That's bull!"

A voice booms over the loudspeaker, interrupting our brewing argument. The threat of rain canceling the race is over. A parade of trucks begins packing the track, preparing for the main events of the evening. Deb sits quietly smoking, staring to her right where Cindy, Melissa, and some guy are seated.

It hurts seeing Melissa, my little rat's-butt buddy. She must be eight years old now. I miss the kid. I didn't say goodbye or try to explain. I mean, what could I say? The first year in the relationship, not wanting a rerun of Dustin, I avoided her. My intentions with her mom, if ever serious, expired when I got sober, finding my attraction for codependent women had died. Meantime, my hopes to keep distant from little Melissa failed. At first, she was a convenient lab mouse for my special-education trainings. You don't have to be a special ed student to enjoy the benefits of M&M therapy. What started as easy access for case-study files developed into a friendship we both cherished.

The green flag waves, erasing thoughts of Cindy's intrusion. I embrace the welcome rush of adrenaline as the announcer shouts over the loudspeaker.

"Ladies and Gentlemen, stand and salute as the drivers make the final pass before the start of the 1990 Jim Raper Memorial Super Dirt Cup!"

Dirty Deb is down for the race, drinking soda pop without bothering to brush dirt from the lid. It's obvious she's into the race, no longer staring at the crowd or obsessing about Cindy. Two dirty fedoras dodging dirt clumps, dusting each other off between crashes—heaven.

Jimmy Sills, a personal favorite, wins the race. He stole my heart at the 1985 dirt cup, best race I've yet to experience—fifty laps from green flag to checkered, nonstop with Tim Green in the lead, Sills on his tail until the last quarter lap for a photo finish.

The patient clouds give way to the waiting rain, falling on the fans as we gather our belongings. Deb lacks skill in maneuvering through crowds, allowing people to push in front of her while she says "Excuse me" instead of aggressively weaving in and out. Because of this, we're slow getting to the van, having to wait an hour before getting out of the jammed parking lot. If Deb had been driving, we'd still be there, politely waving others by.

Back at the KOA en route to the restroom, I take a detour past the campsite I'd reserved for the past five years. I want to settle something nagging in my head. When I reach the camp, the guy that had been with Cindy at the races is sitting out front in a camp chair, stirring the campfire with a stick. Not only has she invaded on my trip, but she stole my campsite.

"Hi," she says, stepping out of the camper.

I nod, mumble hello, and walk on by. If she's trying to get to me, she succeeded. She took my spot! The rain is seeping through my hat, and the need for the restroom is urgent. When I get back to the van, Deb is tucked into the sleeping bag. Triggered by the door, she pops up.

"That must have been Cindy I saw in the shower line yesterday. Do you think she's staying here? You told me it was odd you couldn't get your usual spot."

"No. I don't think so. Well, maybe."

CHAPTER 27

Anna
(Deb)

JUST WHEN WE THINK THE relationship waters are safe, one
of the jagged-tooth sharks from our past floats to the surface. Wayne is like a dead body buried at sea, slipping free of
his cement shoes, popping up when least expected. I hang
up when he calls, turn and walk away when he appears in
the oddest places. He leaves his signature for us to find a
tri-petal flower drawn on a scrap of paper, a foggy wind-
shield or scratch in the dirt of our yard. He's like a rabid
scruffy dog, spraying the trees with his scent.

Sandy gets furious, threatening to call the police,
beat him to death, and worse. Now I understand. When
Cindy reared her head at the races, I felt violated, intruded
upon, and jealous. We were on a glorious yellow brick road
together, an adventure just for us, when the wicked witch
swoops in on her broom, tainting our land of Oz. Sandy
swears she's here because she loves the races. Yeah right,
Dorothy.

I won't let her spoil our trip. I'm okay as long as I don't picture her in my place alongside Sandy, picking fresh strawberries, junk shopping, or snuggling in our sleeping bag cocoon. Remarkably, I'm the one who loves the races. Comfortable, covered in dirt, adrenaline pumping as cars fly through the air performing double flips. One car got stuck in the fifteen-foot chain link fence like a fly on that sticky paper, hanging there with its wheels spinning.

Sunday morning, our day to go home, I lay next to Sandy, letting sleep come and go. The rain and wind gently rock the van, harmonizing with Sandy's snores—whoosh, growl, snort, whistle, whoosh, growl, snort, whistle. I press next to him like a sock fresh from the dryer, stuck on the back of a T-shirt. He lets out a lion-like purr, rolls over, leans in for a kiss and PLOP! SPLAT! The air vent above our heads gives way under the weight of built-up rain, dumping buckets of icy cold water atop our heads, sleeping bag, and mood. Desire drowned, we wring out the sleeping bags and pillows, sopping up puddles with towels and dirty laundry. Damp bedding hanging on the windows over the orange-and-brown drapes, we head home. Riding shotgun next to Sandy, sunshine flashing through the trees like an old movie reel, I'm content. There's some perks to the sober anomaly. This trip was the best time sober, I can recall. That doesn't mean I plan on taking up the sport. I'm just saying, I had a great time.

Since knowing Sandy, my alcohol consumption has nearly dried up. I have a red beer or a glass of wine because he thinks it's some great feat. It's uncomfortable for me. I drink for a good time, not to quench my thirst. As much as I enjoy each moment with Sandy, I miss the party life.

I love bars—loud music, crazy people, and dancing. The trick is knowing how to control your drinking. I had to learn the hard way to stay away from mixer. It's the real bad guy. It's hard on the gut, and you wake up with a nasty hangover. My optimal drinking regimen begins with vodka straight up with three olives. When the *whirlies* (room spinning) threatens, I switch to coffee and Kahlua. This supplies enough caffeine to perk me up, keep my words from slurring, and avoid sloppiness. When the *whirlies* subside, I go back to vodka mixed with Kahlua. If I get the timing right, no nasty side effects, blackouts, angry people, or new unwanted friends.

There are many disadvantages to what I call *sober by association*. At the office, party types treat me like a 1920s prohibition officer. Yet the depressed, slow-talking, long-winded types circle my cubicle like seagulls at McDonald's. Pete Anderson, the peskiest office gull, corners me at least once a day. I don't know what church he attends, but it most likely has a sign that states something like "Welcome, Christians! Hell, fire, and brimstone are us." Pete's segue to hell is not subtle. He jumps from casual weather chitchat to doom and gloom in one breath. While sharing horrific graphic details of *my* future, his face reddens, and the volume climbs. Eventually, I interrupt, squeezing through the cubicle exit, excusing myself, "Sorry, Pete, as long as it's not happening today, I've got work to do."

Even at home, the side effects of *sobriety by association* are not what I'd expect. Haley and Jay prefer to hang at their dad's where most weekends there's a party. I'm the *dud* parent. To compete with Dad's party nights, I schedule game nights and feasts. I follow advice in parent magazines, conducting family meetings and asking questions like "How do you feel about that?" It's just the four of us, no parties or big family gatherings. In the divorce, I gave Jerry custody of the fourteen-year friend list in exchange for a smaller dose of guilt. Besides, I don't think anyone would have forgiven me, being the harlot and all. Sandy's sober friends are okay but golly-gee guys. Can you talk about something besides *drunk-o-logues?* We also tried involving Haley and Jay in AA open functions, but seriously, if you're not one of them, the tennis match of slogans gets droll mighty fast. That life is not what I want for them—living a life where alcohol and drugs are the boogey man, believing you have no power or willpower. That's not how I've raised them.

Holidays break my heart. They travel back and forth between Dad's party and their new family of unknowns. Schedule splitting, awkward introductions, feeling left out of life-long family jokes and traditions are just a few of the repercussions you don't see coming when you decide willy-nilly to exit one family and enter another. The Palmer clan is great. It's not their fault we joined the club late. My children don't have it that easy at their dad's either, repeatedly answering the popular insincere question: "How's your mom?" They're just digging for dirt.

What's done is done. I couldn't put things back together if I wanted to, and the thought of going back to life before I met Sandy is frightening. I still wonder about that pitiful prayer, begging God to send someone to love me. I don't really believe it was answered, but I like thinking about it. If there is a God, would he answer a puny prayer from someone who only speaks to him when they're desperate. Besides forced rote prayers designed for public show, that's the only times I've ever prayed, usually when the pain of shame is unbearable and I don't have a better idea.

I don't know how Sandy would feel if he knew some of the things I've done in the past. Before I met him during the season with Wayne, I suffered shame. I couldn't get it off me. Like a dog rolling in dung, I kept adding more stench. At my lowest point, I packed a bag, fleeing to Spokane on a whim. It was after another ho-hum getting-dumped-by-Wayne episode and the same week the university psychologist prescribed Lithium. She insisted, stating she feared I might harm myself. I had to calm the woman down.

With Haley and Jay at their dad's for the weekend, I'd drank a little wine and a lot of vodka. I'd tired of circling Wayne's house, and I needed drastic. A geographic shift is the best I could do. I popped two breath mints, grabbed my credit card, the bag and headed for Spokane. I chose it because it's a big city with plenty of self-destruction potential. By the time I arrived, I was sobering up, doubting the plan, losing trust in the almighty Visa card. The quickest solution was a shopping-mall bar. After a lady-like white wine, I felt sluggish, so I visited the coffee shop next door for caffeine and my first food of the day, a sugary pastry. I studied the couple three booths down. The woman is my age but nothing like me. She's poised, soft-spoken, confident, and at ease with herself. The man next to her responds to her conversation with questions, uh-huhs, and nods. They'd look comfortable on the cover of a romance novel. Soon, maybe to avoid my stares, they get up to leave. He placed his arm on the small of her back, steering her gently out the door. As they passed my booth, I felt that familiar less-than jab in my gut. Then I saw it, sitting on the floor of the booth where they'd sat, a Nordstrom bag. I like to think most days I would have spoken out, returning the bag to them. But this day was not a day to be helpful or nice. I collected it from the booth, walk swiftly to the nearest ladies' room. In the bag was a white T-shirt made by Guess, a brand I look for in Goodwill but would never buy new. The receipt proves she paid full price of $40 with no sale discount. The bag is heavy. Stuck in the bottom corner is a men's leather billfold. It probably wouldn't fit in his back pocket because it was bulging with credit cards, membership cards, and a gold key to some fancy men's club, $300 cash, plus the normal stuff like a driver's license.

Trolling the shops, I spotted a high-end children's store, the type that moms on a budget who happily dig through piles of *three for $1* children's jeans on a blue tarp dare not enter. Knees weak, I selected my purchases without a glance at the price tag: one shirt, a pair of Dr. Martens boots for Haley, and a Levi's Jacket, pants, and shirt for Jay. I handed the salesclerk a Visa, nary a doubt, she'll trust the confidently scribbled made-up name, Anna Sequin. Channeling the poised woman from the booth at the coffee shop, I knew the clerk wouldn't check the signature, and she didn't.

By the time I strutted out the mall doors, I am Anna Sequin, the woman with the perfect complexion, well-kept hair, and doting rich husband. I drove to what I guessed to be the most expensive motel in town, Spokane's Inn at the Park. In case the cops were on my tail, I used the cash to pay for a room. As Anna would surely do, I stopped at the gift shop, purchasing a $5 pair of earrings for $42. I'm high with that "getting away with murder" feeling, signing this receipt, Minnie Mouse. The clerk takes it with a hand proudly weighted with diamonds, glances at the signature over the top of her reading glasses, and bids me a good evening. I'm not sure if I felt Anna could charm her way around the cops, if I didn't care or if I wanted locked up.

Entering the elevator, pushing the third-floor button, I decided Anna needs a real-life lesson. My room overlooks a street lined with sitting, standing, and reclining homeless men, rather a garden of bums. I'm ready to call the office to complain that my money should have a better view when I spotted an ice bucket holding a bottle of champagne, leaning artistically with a note dangling from its neck: "Compliments of The Inn at the Park. We hope your stay is pleasant." Must be a reward for good behavior. Thank you very much.

I showered, put the white T-shirt back on with the $42 earrings. I popped the cork, and not wanting to be gauche by drinking champagne from plastic stemware, I drank from the bottle. On the street below, there was a down-and-outer sprawled on the sidewalk, panhandler sign turned over as if closed for business. I thought about joining him, sharing my champagne and a few stories, but Anna is too chicken.

I finished the bottle, watching my friends below, and left for a night in the bars. I bet sweet Anna has never experienced the sick satisfaction, self-disgust, and assurance you can't sink any further one gains from a haphazard one-night stand. There's a one-cop car per block quota going on as I drove around town. It's too early to go to jail, so I returned to the inn's lounge. Normally, I sit at the bar. It gives a false sense of protection like you're not alone, just hanging with the bartender. When I entered the lounge, six frat boyish guys hail me over to their table. Anna would have stuck her nose in the air and walked away, but I drug her over. Looking back on the night, I wish I'd accepted the invitation to go across the border with them to a party in Couer D'Alene. They were fun, polite, promising to keep me safe. Stupid Anna in the white T-shirt said no, fearing they were a gang of serial killers disguised as nice guys.

Hours later at last call, I drug the last man standing, a nameless bald guy, back to my room. By 2:15 a.m., he's gotten laid and left. I puked all over my new T-shirt. Anna is gone. If I were an alcoholic, that would have been the bottom because there's nowhere lower to go.

CHAPTER 28

Chad?
(Sandy)

DEB'S AWAKE, HACKING IN THE bathroom. Soon she'll appear behind me, pull her cigarettes from her robe pocket, lighting smoke, one from her daily two-pack ration. I've accepted the habit, not because she ordered me to. I love her. I keep praying she'll be free of this addiction. It rules her life and attempts to govern mine, deciding where we'll go based on *smoker friendliness*. After fifteen or twenty minutes smoke-free, she's fidgeting for an escape. Speaking of denial, on hikes, she feigns interest in rocks, leaves, and flowers, stopping to comment between gasps for breath.

Mornings, I'm itching for her to leave so I can open windows and begin my single-task day: Get it over with. The simple routine takes place on the sofa in front of the TV in two modes, doze and zone. Wenatchee fell apart. I thought I could do it, start over one last time. Halfway through the twelve-week quarter, my drive to pretend like life didn't suck just got up and went.

Miss Hanson, the supervising teacher, pours her life into these young students. She is living her dream. Mine is to work with special ed high-school students, not elementary age *normies*. One day, I broke, confessing misery and the need to walk away. My feelings were no surprise to her. She commended my efforts, blessing the decision to quit trying to be something I'm not. I tried, but it felt like I lost an arm, so they tossed me a leg ordering, "Make it work." Living away from Deb hurts, but now I'm back living in her house. I can't stand being here or being away.

The bureaucratic bullies responsible for my demise tossed me a general pedagogical studies degree. Translation: a nonteaching, teaching degree. How's that supposed to work? Deb pushes me daily to apply for a job where she works or, worse, go through the program she teaches. We both know I don't need her class, but it could open doors leading to a decent job. I want what I worked for, a special ed position. If I can't have that, I'd just as soon go back to truck driving or stay here on the sofa.

I'm in good company. Our dog faithfully naps at my side. He's the ideal down-and-out friend with worse problems than me, i.e., his name. The odds for a respectable dog name were good, a 75 percent chance. The name game was Deb's idea, hoping it would eliminate fights for power of attorney. We each chose two names, wrote them on scraps of paper, and tossed them in a pile in the middle of the room. The dog, a six-week-old cocker-mix puppy, would unknowingly sniff out his fate by stepping on the winning name. Huddled like crap shooters, we watch the puppy swagger among the names. Haley and Jay canvas for their ballots. As hoped, the puppy stops, sniffs, and sits in front of the chosen scrap of paper.

"Okay, that's it," Deb says, picking it up. "Little pup is hereby named . . . Jay, is this yours? Chad? Chad. A dog named Chad."

After a group groan and a begrudged compromise, we agree on Jay's second choice. Certainly, it'll be better than Chad. Thus, the dog's destined label—Tubby. Besides a humiliating name, the poor dog is short on smarts. Deb's obsessive need to rearrange furniture leaves him confused. The first time it happened, I found him whimpering behind a chair, unable to find the door. I thought he'd gone blind! Add hygiene problems caused by plugged-up butt glands, a permanent bad-hair day, and a goofy flapping tongue, and the name fits him perfectly.

I relate to Tubby's disorientation for different reasons than furniture array. Haley and Jay have no use for me. They're like my girls, independent, not needy like most kids in single-parent homes. If there's a problem, Deb handles it. A few months ago, Haley introduced a new friend, Crystal, a female Eddie Haskell type, spouting *too-perfect* answers to our questions. We knew she was trouble, but Haley, a good student with no behavior problems, deserved a chance to prove us wrong. Last week, Deb got the call from the police summoning her presence at the Safeway store up the street from the house.

Shaken, Deb shared the details with me when she returned. She walked into the interrogation room in the middle of one of Crystal's whoppers. Flashing Crystal the stop-sign hand, she ordered Haley to spill the beans *now*. Deb said she could see the need to fess up on her face, and she did, all of it. She'd been lying to us about the makeup, jewelry, and random stuff, saying they were gifts or good buys purchased with saved babysitting money. We believed because we wanted it to be true. Haley had given us no reason to suspect she was part of an ongoing teenage heist.

I haven't earned the right to speak into Haley's life. We don't have a relationship. In my defense, Deb and I don't carry the same parent manual. She snarls and takes the mother-bear stance if she thinks I'm using *authoritarian* methods. We don't agree, so I let her handle things. It's not easy, sitting on the end of Haley's canopy bed, speaking to the mute, eye-rolling girl with Deb eavesdropping in the hall. I'm the man living with mom, no power or respect in that.

Later, when the shoplifting drama died down, Deb tells me she spoke with her bosses, and they think I'm a perfect candidate for their job program.

"They need success stories. They know you'll improve our statistics. They need you."

She's referring to the overload of clients who fail to complete the fully funded training. They skip the getting-a-job step, preferring the familiar, less troublesome mailbox employer. Attending my girlfriend's class as the poster boy for job success sounds awful, but how can I say no? Since CWU put the screws to me, I've applied for one bad joke of a job, a sales position at Harris Office Supply. It was the only job advertised that my back could survive. Waiting for the interview to begin, I pictured my future in a plaid suit, living life as Herb Tarlek from the TV show *WKRP*. How did I end up here? I rode the plastic horse round the education merry-go-round. I want to teach special ed, not sell office supplies.

"What do you think about riding to work with me tomorrow. They want you to come in for an assessment. It'll be fun. We can go to lunch after."

"Sure."

CHAPTER 29

Never Getting the Answers He Wants
(Deb)

I PUSH THROUGH THE SNAIL-PACED automatic doors at Safeway, drawing stares from startled customers.

"May I help you?" asks a cashier, looking up from her till.

"The police . . . I was told my daughter is here."

"Up there," she says, pointing to the stairway under the employees-only sign.

Haley's face eliminates any need for introductions, sending an officer my way as I enter the room. A silent mother-daughter conversation burns as I listen to fragments of the officer's story. "Charges . . . fines . . . criminal record . . . juvenile detention."

"Do you want to tell us how the merchandise we found in your possession got there?" asks another officer seated near the girls.

"I told you we didn't steal nothing. We lost our receipt and—"

Shooting Crystal *the look* known worldwide for *you'd best listen up,* I interrupt her lie fest.

"Haley, now is the time, your chance to fess up. I know you want to. If you lie now, things will get worse, not better. You have a choice."

Crystal exchanges her slouch for a straight-back position, shaking her head no at Haley. Her mouth opens to speak then closes, obeying the omnipotence of *mom in the room.* Likewise, the officers yield to the power of mom. Silence prevails. Just like an episode from a 1950s Perry Mason show, the witness spills it all.

"We . . . we did it! We stole the stuff. We've been doing it here and at Payless too. It's not the first time."

Relief smothers the sting of hearing my child confess to a crime. Confessing proves she's not a hardened criminal, that her conscience is alive and ticking. More so, the confession calmed my biggest fear—that my children would be like me. Unlike most parents, I never hoped for pint-sized clones. Like Crystal, I would have stuck to the lie. How did I end up with two conscience-active children? Like his sister, Jay cracks easily under pressure, showing no signs he inherited deviancy and deceit.

Sandy's lucky that way too. Nanette and Stephanie chose not to mimic the lawless, havoc-reeking model he held up for them. Instead, they strive to be better, different. I've overheard him thanking God for that very thing. I'm not eavesdropping on his prayers. It's just that his prayer schedule is catch-as-catch-can, in time and place. I catch him at it all the time, in the kitchen, bedroom, living room, and even outside. It breaks my heart watching him pray, never getting the answers he wants. He's unhappy, cursing, and complaining, at war with prayer and gratitude. His demeanor flips between turbulence and peace like a coin toss. I admit his faithfulness to pray keeps my interest in a God spurred. When God stomps all over his dreams, he keeps going to meetings and praying. One thing is clear, if he didn't have the God thing to cling to, he'd crash and burn. What I don't get is why God won't just give him what he wants. What could it hurt?

In the meantime, our relationship is uncomfortable. He's enrolled in the job-training program where I work, meaning participation in my class. It's challenging for us both. Knowing a certain success story when she sees one, his job counselor placed him in a six-month internship at Comprehensive Mental Health. Upon completion, it teases a full-time counselor position, working with troubled youth. But first, he must sit through my two-week class. My job is hard enough. Strip away the titles, I'm a sanitized circus barker, assigned to fill the heads of my students with visions of grandeur, of which only a few will succeed in landing a bland, unremarkable job.

Sandy is their gem hidden among the rest, the gold star representing the entire program. Unlike Sandy, the other clients have battered job histories or are welfare lifers with nothing to offer an employer but a big bag of worries. They are the ones the original heart of the program is for, but without a shiny success story, funding is fleeting at best. It's my job to build up their confidence, get them to believe they've got a chance to find a job that will pay the bills, change their lives. I want this for them, enough to believe my own hype. As the class progresses, it's my job to meet with the counselors, rather like a farmer reporting the progress of his potatoes and onions. If I sell them bad produce, they end up with a nonproducing caseload. Sadly, there was a time when they too believed in the down-and-outers, but after the hundredth warning to up the success numbers, the client is just that, a number.

With Sandy in my class, I feel more like a BS cheer-leader than normal. It's difficult for him, but he's making my job impossible. He could cut me a little slack, force a laugh, crack a smile. Does he think it's easy jumping around like Mary Poppins force-feeding motivation one spoonful of sugar at a time?

At home, we've added family meetings and more game nights along with cranking up security on Haley. Thankfully, her old friends are back, and Crystal is a mem-ory. Haley is not without consequences. She sees a juvenile probation officer once a month and will be working around the house to pay back the $500 fine. We were getting along fine until I insisted she write a letter of apology to Safeway and Payless to be delivered in person.

"I'm not going there! Why can't you mail it?"

"You're going!"

"No, I'm not!"

"Yes, you are!"

Sandy and Jay look like little boys gathering in the schoolyard, hands in pockets, pondering on whom to place their bet. With verbal threats, I move Haley into the garage. Standing next to the car, my power feigns.

"Get in the car!"

"No!"

"Yes!"

"I'm not going. It's stupid!"

"Yes, you are. Get in now or—"

Realizing I have no or what, I grab hold of her shoulders, gingerly attempting to coerce her into the car. She resists. We're suited to wrestle, being in the same weight division. We also are equal in not wanting to hurt the other, so the match ends comically in a dead heat. Laughing, we compromise, walking to Safeway and Payless, delivering the letters together.

CHAPTER 30

In a Rare Moment Inside Deb's Head (Sandy)

MAY 8, 1991, ON A dinner train headed to nowhere, I ask the question.

"Deb, will you marry me?"

I once thought stooping on one knee before a woman to be the ultimate groveling pose but not today. Placing myself below Deb, asking for her hand in marriage, is a place of honor. I love everything about her, even the things I hate.

I thought love meant finding someone who'd give me everything I want. That led me into relationships with women self-labeled as *pleasers*, more rightly named martyrs, forever unhappy with me for not following their script. Deb loves me for who I am, giving me freedom to do the same. There's no hidden agenda or secret expectations.

I take the one-knee pose, uninvited tears falling down my face.

"You don't have to do this, get up, honey, it's okay."

She wants to spare me from what she thinks is humiliation, as the other passengers hush and gather for the show. I want to stay on my knees, tell her I'm happy to be a public fool for her, but I have only the emotional energy to ask the question.

No plan for a *no* answer, I thank God for the *yes*. Crowd applauding, grateful for the entertainment, we hide in each other's arms. We're good at disregarding the bit players in our lives. High on the moment, we hobo jump the train cars, holding hands like kids whose parents should scold. Stopping at the caboose, we seal the deal with a wind-blown kiss.

A week later, Deb hijacks my van, and I find myself a helpless kidnap victim tortured by her driving, not even given a courtesy blindfold. If Deb had been with Lewis and Clark, they'd still be wandering around in circles. Not having bread crumbs to mark the trail, I note landmarks. Stopping at the north fork of Ahtanum creek, she orders me out of the vehicle, pointing while giving her best evil grin. As she leads me across the rocks to the stream, I fight to keep quiet, disagreeing with each slippery rock choice. She's on snake alert. I'd like to not fall down.

Letting go of my hand, she drops to one knee, wiping a tear from her cheek.

"Sandy, will you be my husband?"

Thinking we're officially engaged, I'm surprised at the proposal.

"Yes!"

I should have seen this coming. Following my proposal, she gave me one of her lectures. It had something to do with women needing to propose, that they shouldn't be the only ones pursued and conquered.

After a long hug, she traces back to the van, on alert for really dumb snakes. She returns with fishing gear, including night crawlers in a Styrofoam cup wrapped in half a box of foil inside a Ziploc bag. After baiting both our hooks, I pretend to fish. The only chance of snagging a fish would be if she'd planted a box of fish sticks. It's so shallow a fish would have to wade by. But I don't care. I'm a pursued and conquered happy man.

No fish sticks in sight, Deb bores, suggesting we move on to part B of the abduction. Once again, I'm the helpless victim to her aimless driving. Twice, she pulls into a private drive, and we keep circling back by the pretend fishing hole. I'm wondering how long I can keep quiet while we drive in circles when she speaks up.

"Okay, I give. I'm lost. I thought I could do this. I need help finding the Ahtanum Mission."

Disoriented and dizzy, I manage to find the mission, just as the park-keeper pulls a chain with a "closed" sign across the entrance.

"It's right here, but it's closed," I say, pointing at the sign. "And he's shutting off the lights."

Deb makes a face I've learned means *not acceptable.* Ignoring my pleas to drive on, she parks and gets out of the van, running after the man heading toward the ground-keeper's home. I could hear her calling "Excuse me, sir" and watched as the man stopped to listen. He shakes his head no then looks my way, nodding yes to Deb who races back to the van, wearing the look I've come to know means *I win!*

"I promised we'd close the gate when we leave. What a sweet man. Are you hungry?"

Grabbing a wooden picnic basket from the back of the van, she tilts her head with a silly grin, waving an arm like an usher in a theatre for me to follow. Choosing a picnic table close to the tiny log church, she spreads a yellow tablecloth with napkins, candles in crystal holders, and china plates, side by side. In the moonlight, candles flickering, we dined on home fried chicken, buttered bread, and baked beans, sipping Dr. Pepper from stemmed goblets. She's right; everyone should be pursued and conquered.

After our feast, I grab a candle, suggesting we explore the Ahtanum Pioneer Church built in 1873 when Yakima was a sagebrush wasteland and Washington state was a territory. The door is locked, but we can see through one window. We share an admiration for the simple charm, the history, the preserved quaintness of the 300-square-foot log cabin with its oak pews lending seats for about thirty people. Deb nearly knocks the candle out of my hand, jumping to get a better view. Handing her the candle so I have both hands, I lift her up to the window.

"This is it! Yes, right? This is the place."

In a rare moment inside Deb's head, I understood.

"Yes, this is the place. It has to be here. It's perfect."

Back at the table with the remaining stub of candlelight, we outlined our wedding plans. The place: Ahtanum Pioneer Mission Church. The date: September 6, 1991. The traditional wedding cake, "ex-nayed," replaced by our favorite homemade cheesecake with fresh strawberries. We'd write our vows and whoever officiated would be given one line: "I now pronounce you man and wife."

CHAPTER 31

Be the Best Person You Can Be
(Deb)

SEPTEMBER 6, 1991, WE PLEDGE our love before a triple-capacity crowd of family and friends inside the 120-year-old Ahtanum Mission log church. We're dressed in nineteenth-century attire: Sandy in a black derby, pocket watch, and vest; and I in a massive wide-brim hat, a Gibson-style gown, holding a bouquet of peacock feathers and black-eyed Susans. I profess my love for God, Sandy, and our collective family of Nanette, Stephanie, Haley, and Jay seated in the front row.

Speaking the words painstakingly written for this day, an accusing voice nags. Do I really believe in God, or am I pretending to believe what I'd like to be true? If I'm taking on another acting job like my first marriage, I'm in trouble. I love the idea of God—a big daddy in the sky who loves me. Who wouldn't want that? But I'm not buying the whole Christian hootenanny shenanigans. My mind won't accept a God with nothing better to do than peer down from heaven looking for those that are naughty, scratching names off his list with a divine red marker. I can hope in a power greater than myself, like Sandy and the others in AA speak of. That idea is comforting.

I'm willing to trust the God I've met in AA but not Liz Trumball, the pastor of the Unity Church. Giving any pastor too much reign over our wedding is risky. They might try to save everyone or sneak *Christianese* into the service. We agreed she'd have one line: "I now pronounce you man and wife."

Planning the wedding, we measured every decision by whether or not we liked it. After all, it's for us, not our guests. Do we like wedding cake? No, we like cheesecake with fresh strawberries. Wedding gowns and tuxedos? No way! A Victorian dress with a Merry Widow–style hat for me, a derby, vest, and walking stick for Sandy. White? Traditions? Pfft! Not for us.

On a sticky hot Friday evening inside the tiny mission church, we made promises to each other, our children, and God. Squished into pews, shoulder to shoulder, our sweaty friends and family are segregated into sides of *the sobers and not sobers*, a natural occurrence, without the aid of ushers. Most of the men are wearing Hawaiian shirts as a show of respect for Sandy, known for channeling Don Ho at formal gatherings. Women search for tissues while the men sniff back tears as Sandy recites his whole-hearted vows.

"I promise to encourage you to be the best person you can be, to always love you, to be at your side."

I search his eyes for signs of deception as he professes his love. He really seems to mean it. I'm scared, realizing I've waited until standing at the altar to ask myself the obvious questions. Can I do this? Be married again? Be the wife Sandy wants? Responsible? Good? I know I love him, but that doesn't mean I can be who he wants and needs. What have I done? Can I say, "Oops, I changed my mind?" I don't want to be one of those women who collects husbands like charms on a bracelet. And what about him? He probably wants to run out of here too. Which one of us will break first and fess up to this grand gaffe?

I glance over the crowd, all eyes longing for this romance to be true, dabbing tissues to smiling eyes. Stephanie and Nanette, high schoolers, soon to pursue dreams of their own, praying for a happy ending for their dad. Haley and Jay, wondering what this union means for them. My mom, dad, and brother, looking like victims of mutiny. I open my mouth to speak my vows, and the doubts float away.

"I will be at your side, support your dreams, love you through whatever life comes our way."

Rings slipped on fingers, promises made, Pastor Trumball recites her line, and it's a done deal. Moments later, outside the little church accepting hugs and best wishes, I see Na-Na holding onto to Sandy's arms, forcing eye contact like a mom laying down the law. Before I can get over by them, Sandy is swooped away by his sister, Robin. Sweet nearsighted Na-Na greets me with a hug.

"Sandy looks handsome in his hard hat."

"It's a bowler, Na-Na. You know, a derby. He's not wearing a construction helmet. Oh, never mind. He is very handsome."

I notice my dad is lifting up the tablecloths, snooping under the tables.

"Dad? What are you doing?"

"Since there's champagne, I thought you must have a beer around here."

"It's sparkling cider, not champagne. It's nonalcoholic."

"It's what?"

"There's no beer, Dad, sorry."

I light a smoke, pacifying myself and Dad who's happy to learn it's okay to smoke in the park.

Looking around, confused, assessing the crowd, he shakes his head.

"All these people are alcoholics?"

"No, not all, Dad."

I'm distracted by Paula, our photographer. She's madly snapping photos of a cute little boy. Sandy is behind me hugging his sponsor, Lew.

"Do you know that boy?" I ask.

"I thought you knew him. I haven't a clue."

We shrug in silent agreement not to tell Paula that her rampant shutter is wasted on a random kid in the park. After all, she's shooting our wedding for free, a huge gift, considering her talent and willingness to put up with our nontraditional guidelines. He's a cute kid. Someday, looking through our wedding album, we'll rack our brains trying to figure out his name.

My relationship with Paula seems stressed. It started when I called with the news of our engagement. I expected zeal, not questions like "Have you thought this through?" She means well. The lack of heartfelt blessing stems from a conversation we had a few months after she arranged our blind date.

"I'm scared for you," she said. "I feel responsible. You weren't supposed to get serious."

"The joke's on you. I'm surprised too," I laugh, waiting for her to join in the fun.

"I don't think he's a good choice for you. Jim says he's a womanizer. He's . . . he's not the one. He was meant to get you free of *the jerk*. That's all. I can't sit by and let this happen. I've seen how he looks at other women. He's lecherous."

The word *lecherous* felt like a punch in the stomach. Am I marrying a cardboard cutout of my dad? I know Sandy notices bulging cleavage and a peekaboo skirt flash. But who doesn't? To expect him not to notice, he'd need a truckload of drugs. I'm aware he stares at boobs when they're pushed up into a V-shaped valley. It's like trying not to look the way the arrow is pointing. That doesn't make him like my dad.

That day, seated across from each other, sipping tea, we agreed to disagree. I think she feels obligated to protect me because of one understandable flaw in judgment. Never mind the ninety-nine-thousand errors I did without her help. It happened near the end of the affair. I had told Wayne I was done, and for once, he believed me. He followed Paula to Ellensburg, cornering her at the door of the art studio. He promised he'd never hurt me again. Eventually, she caved, agreeing to persuade me to give him one more chance. Of course, he dumped on me shortly after. Now she worries my fate is once again in her hands. It's not. But my insecurities could have done without the lecher remark.

I've been known to be jealous. When it happens, I think about poor Mary Borton. It happened years ago in my parents' bar. My folks often invited friends and anyone still standing, home, along with the band after the bar closed. My bedroom is adjacent to the bar, and the drums, keyboard, and guitar resonate through the wall. I didn't mind. It was like getting to stay up late on a school night to watch TV. It was easy to sneak out and view the show undetected. This night, I'm particularly enjoying watching Mary and Howard Borton dance under the black light to the song "Stand by Me." They're beautiful, really old (probably fifty) and obviously madly in love. Not once did they break eye contact during the dance. That night, watching their love dance, I vowed never to settle for less. The next day, still dreamy from the memory, I shared my passion about them to Mom. She pats my head as if to say, "Oh Debbie, you are so naive."

"Last night, Howard told poor Mary he's leaving her, after twenty years. He's in love with some blonde gold digger half his age. The affair has been going on for seven years, behind poor Mary's back."

She continued on saying Howard should stay with Mary out of obligation. That's when I promised to never stay where I'm not loved, not even if I'm married with a pack of kids.

I've told Sandy that if he finds himself *staying out of obligation*, leave ASAP. Anyway, I've a tendency for jealousy, like the meltdown in aisle C at the Valu-mart. Sandy placed his leather jacket on my shoulders, shielding me from the air conditioning. I felt loved, dwarfed inside his coat. I lost him, somewhere between women's shoes and the garden center. After checking out a pair of polka-dot sneakers, I found him in the hardware department. He's standing next to a Madonna wannabe in a snakeskin skirt. I approached with expectations he'd stop midsentence, introduce me as the love of his life, peel the wench from his side, and walk off into the sunset with me. Instead, he ignored me. Is she *the blonde gold digger?* A dumb one, considering Sandy's empty gold pan. Feeling like a stranger intruding on their *tête-à-tête*, I walked away.

Moments later, one aisle away, Sandy sidled up behind me with a stupid look on his face.

"Where'd you go?"

The details of the scene that followed are not worth explaining. I wouldn't doubt if our pictures are posted in the Valu-mart employee handbook titled *Beware*. After the public brawl, Sandy's defense brought some comfort.

"I'm not a sociopath whoremaster. I'm just socially inept."

Still, hearing Paula label him a lecher stirs doubts. If she's right, it's too late now. The "I dos" are done and gone. It's dark. We wave goodbye to our guests, ready for the honeymoon. Looking back as we drive away, I swear our friends, family, and the random little boy are wagering bets on our union.

CHAPTER 32

Dab a Little Here and There
(Sandy)

AN HOUR BEFORE SUNUP, IN rubber boots and fedoras, we waltz with the tide, collecting sand dollars in red-and-purple plastic beach buckets. Besides counting each shell as a dollar earned, Deb's as off duty as I've ever witnessed.

Not wanting to drive all night after our wedding, we reserved a room at the Silver Beach Motel, forty-five minutes up Highway 12. The room works hard to give you an authentic log cabin experience. Lifting the curtain over the two-by-three-foot aluminum window expecting a *dive* motel scene of the parking lot, we find a picturesque snow-tipped mountain scene painted on a slab of plywood nailed over the window.

We putter our way to the secluded beach resort in Moclips, stopping whenever intrigued. At a roadside flea market, a perfume dealer next to a booth with unicorn and Elvis blankets waves us over. I ignore him. Deb walks his way. She always acts all enthused, even when she has no plans to buy because she *doesn't want to hurt their feelings.* He's one sad-looking *foo-foo* salesman—greasy hair, dirt jammed under his fingernails, and a tattoo of either a shark or a platypus on his wrist. Deb smiles at me as he goes into his sales pitch.

"Know what I do? When I don't have time to bathe? I dab a little here and there and even here."

I turn away as the dabs went from neck to pits and south. I don't know how Deb held it together, handing him a dollar bill, payment for the show rather than the fake Shalimar.

After a week of laughter, lovemaking, and rest, the Mazda packed to the roof with flea-market treasures, we inch our way back home. Some might say our decision to marry was like *putting the cart before the horse.* In our defense, there's hope the horse will catch up. We're banking on that old mare called *hope.* I am officially unemployed. With the internship at Comprehensive Mental Health completed, my career working with troubled youth may be over. It depends on the administrative decision: hire or not hire. If my supervisor, Joyce Delgado, has a say, the odds are in my favor.

I'm thankful for Joyce. She's been like a healing ointment for the burns on my confidence inflicted by the Dragon Lady and her loyal knights. She's openly enthusiastic about my work. At times, I'm embarrassed when she rubs the noses of the other staff members in my pile of billable hours and up-to-date caseload paperwork. Still, as we near Yakima, I wonder if I'll have a job. There's no reason to think I won't be hired, but then again, who'd have thought the other *for sures* would fall apart.

I need this win. Attending Deb's job-training class damaged our relationship. Every day, she'd spin confidence, pushing the class to believe in themselves. I watched, amused and sad, being the only one knowing she has less confidence than anyone in the room.

We kept our relationship a secret from the class until the announcement of our wedding on the last day. I made her job difficult, not purposely. Simply, I wasn't up to performing. My face could not look like it wanted to be there. Deb was entertaining and looked hot in her red business suit and heels, but I've better things to do than sit here. In class, she ignored my lackluster interest. At home, she'd accuse me of sabotaging her efforts to motivate the class.

"They probably think you're an ax murderer. And stop staring at my legs."

Our worst post-class fight happened when she thought I had fallen asleep. She switched on a cassette player with a pan flute and told us to lay our heads on the table.

"Relax, rest, picture your personal place of peace. Maybe at sea or deep in the forest. Rest."

I did exactly as instructed. When the exercise ended, she looked perturbed, and my fellow classmates were chuckling. Our fights suck. Although we battle various topics, the fight is always the same. Deb spins and screams. I shut down. She escalates, making demands.

"Say something, anything. Say something!"

Finally, I do.

"Shut the——"

Now, she's quiet, and I'm slinging ugly names and accusations, beginning with words I know better than to use like "you always" and "you never." Vulgarities fly out my mouth while my mind screams "stop!" I don't.

"Get out!"

"No! You, get out!"

After a primal orangutan-like discussion on territorial rights, Deb caves. She may throw the first banana, but in the end, she takes the fall, admitting fault, confessing over-reaction to hurt feelings. It's sick really, ending with both parties wanting to erase what's been said.

We arrived home from our honeymoon, greeted by four messages on the answering machine. The last is Joyce, my boss. I spend a sleepless night, wondering what's next if I don't get the job. The next morning, I'm sitting in her office as asked.

"Sandy, how was the honeymoon? Did you have good weather?"

"Great, perfect weather."

"What's the name of the place again? Near the Quinault reservation? Moclips?"

"Yes, Moclips."

"Well, Sandy, we'd like to offer you the position of case manager/therapist. Do you accept?"

I needed the words, the proof. God is looking out for me after all. The *happily ever after* can now begin.

CHAPTER 33

Nice Hats
(Deb)

SIDE BY SIDE, LOOKING INTO the mirror on the back of our bedroom door, I'm pleased with our understated costumes for the holiday costume party at Comprehensive Mental Health. Thanks to avid-junking habits, we have matching black derbies, tuxedo jackets, shirts with studs and cuf-flinks, and walking sticks. Next year, when Sandy's not the new guy, we can get bolder costumes.

We need a fun evening right now. All we do is fight about everything, from whether Jay should have Nikes like his friends to whose turn it is to take out the garbage. The stress of this season is not helping. We juggle family and work obligations, pushing to meet the expectations of each other, knowing we'll fail. It seems it's time to pay dues for our slaphappy choices of divorce and remarriage. We've created a world of *odd man out* for myself, Sandy, and our children.

It's not that we don't feel welcome, sitting at Christmas dinner with Sandy's family; it's just out of focus. A slight

twist of the lens, you see that Haley and Jay are bystand-
ers, extras thrown into this scene of lifelong relationships.
Having no insider information, they're left to ponder the
unspoken punch lines, verbal side jabs, and family innu-
endos. It's just the way of the scrambled nuclear family.
Holidays at my parents' house—same plot, different cast.
Sandy plays the part of the contagious sober alcoholic. I'm
the Benedict Arnold who married him. During our last
visit, my semisloshed brother, who stiffened when hugged,
later wagged his finger in my face, warning, "You're no better than us. And your marriage is doomed."

The worst events for me are the family shindigs held
at Sandy's ex-wife's house. There's Bonnie (aka Barney)
surrounded by a lifelong fleet of loyal friends and family
who've also known Sandy half his life, and me, the odd
peg with no hole that fits. It's not that I'm treated poorly,
quite the opposite. Bonnie is especially polite and gracious.
Nevertheless, I'm the mongrel in the pack.

Likewise, attending AA parties, open meetings, and
dances, I am the man (or woman) without a country, the
clashing, chartreuse M&M's, the wonky piano key, the
weirdo who doesn't drink but is not an alcoholic. Everyone
is polite, kind even, but confused how to interact.

In the elevator ride up to the makeshift ballroom, I dou-
ble-check our safe classic costumes, well pleased. Tonight, I
want to fit in, have fun. It's time to write my own character,
no preconceived ideas of who I am or am not. No one here
knows me, and I don't know them. No history, a fresh start.
The first thing I notice entering the room are the tables
with white linens, crystal, and fresh flowers. All eyes have
turned our way. The ladies in the ballroom are dressed in

long gowns of silk and crepe. The men are in tuxedos with shiny shoes. Not one is wearing a hat, carrying a pocket watch, or sporting a nineteenth-century walking stick. I realize that unless everyone conspired to dress as normal people attending a swanky employee-holiday celebration, this is *not* a costume party.

My face is pulsing, hot. I look over at Sandy. He appears to be having a marvelous time. He's eating a stuffed mushroom, tapping his foot, enjoying the music from the seven-piece orchestra. He is so happy in his little world of delusion, adding strawberries to his overloaded china plate, fiddling with his pocket-watch chain. I'm calm, thinking good thoughts like tackling him into the six-foot mermaid ice carving gleaming behind him. I approach just as a *normal* young man comes alongside him.

"Hi, Sandy. Good to see you here."

"Thanks. Mike, this is my wife, Deb."

"Hi. Very nice to meet you. Great hats, by the way."

I manage a nod.

"The costumes are Deb's idea. She's the creative one."

The rest of the evening is spent nodding to the "cute hats" remarks and answering questions about our suspenders and canes. When opportunity allowed, I asked several partygoers my one burning question.

"Did you see a flyer or hear anything about this being a costume party?"

Not one alibi, Sandy is the lone witness to the alleged flyer requiring costumes. Just him, standing by the food table, eating chocolate mousse with a silver spoon.

Driving home, I try to be a good sport, stay in the *someday-we-will-laugh-about-this* mode. Somewhere between his insistence that he was right and all the other well-dressed partygoers were wrong, a war started. Neither of us willing to toss the towel in the ring, I shout the last words.

"Get out! Get out! Get out now!"

Normally, he dawdles long enough for me to say "I'm sorry. Please, please don't go!"

This time, he's gone.

I don't know what to do. It's not what I meant to happen.

The ashes spill over in the ashtray as I snub out the last smoke in my pack. Tubby wants outside, probably needs air. My lungs feel tight opening the sliding glass door and hurt reaching for a pack of cigarettes in the cupboard. That means my signature chronic bronchitis is lurking. Bronchitis is the reason I smoke menthols. Smoking menthol is similar to using a vaporizer, and it stops the coughing temporarily. I empty the ashtray, setting up camp on the sofa in the front room where I can see if Sandy pulls into the drive. I just sent the man I love away, my husband. I cry out.

"I can't take this anymore. I want to change. I don't know how. Please, God, please. Help me."

I must have fallen asleep, surrounded by crumpled, tear-soaked Kleenex and an overflowing ashtray. Tubby is barking to come in. It's nearly eight o'clock. Sandy is awake by now, always up and showered by seven. He doesn't care about me. If he did, he wouldn't have abandoned me.

Tubby's wagging tail of gratitude makes me feel guilty. As I slide the door shut, my chest feels like it's squeezed in a vise. The bronchitis is taking hold; I can hardly catch my breath. I light a smoke, hoping the menthol opens my airways. It hurts to inhale. I snub it out.

Where is Sandy? I'm glad the kids are at their dad's this weekend. As much as we fight, we've been able to keep it hidden. Maybe if I go to bed, stop the window-watching obsession, Sandy will show. Walking the fifteen-foot hallway to the bedroom takes three heart-pounding, wall-leaning breaks. It's my worst case of bronchitis yet. Reaching the bed, I crawl under the covers, suspenders hanging.

Around noon, I wake to knocking at the door. Why doesn't he just use his key? It takes forever to get to the door, stopping every three steps to breathe. Sandy is pounding on the door. I can't get enough breath to yell for him to use his key. I make it, ready to fall into his arms, apologize, say whatever it takes for his forgiveness. I'm shocked, not seeing my hero, but a frail, blue-veined elderly man. He's blind to my gaunt, deathbed appearance and apparently impatient I took so long answering his door beating.

"I saw the for-sale sign. My bride to be and I live right there at Peach Tree," he says, pointing to the assisted-living complex. "Our families want us to remain at the home, but we want a place of our own. Could I take a look at your house?"

"Sure. Why not?" I say between short jabs of breath.

He's quite peppy. I explain I'm not feeling well and invite him to look around on his own. He's a talker. I slide onto the sofa, thankful for his distracting chatter.

"I was married sixty years, the first time. Here I am, in love again. Myrtle uses a walker, but we manage," he hollers from the bedroom. "They think we're too old. Not so, we've got plenty of living to do. I cared for Alice, my first love, the last ten years. She passed away six months ago."

He finishes his tour, asking if he can bring Myrtle back for a tour next Tuesday after the doctor removes the bunions from her feet. I nod yes, wishing I could brew some tea and visit. He winks, stepping out the door to walk back to the place Sandy respectfully calls the raisin ranch. Trudging back to bed, I wonder if someone will love me after my teeth, hair, and wits are gone.

I flop across the bed, face down, hoping this position might fix the problem. I wonder if it's something different than bronchitis. I can't even smoke a cigarette. I'm smothering on my stomach but can't roll over. I want to jump up when I hear the door and footsteps coming down the hall. I didn't lock the door. I bet he's brought Myrtle back to see the house. I feel the foot of the bed lower from weight. It's Sandy.

He's waiting for an apology.

"I need you to take me to the Medi-Center [long pause, catching breath]. I have bronchitis [long pause, catching breath] or maybe it's trapped gas. I can hardly breathe. Will you help me roll over? [Long pause, catching breath.] And would you bring me a beer? [Long pause, catching breath.] It might help the gas."

The mattress rises as he leaves. I hear the refrigerator door open and close and the "psst" of the can as he comes back into the room.

"Do you want a glass?"

"No. [Long pause to catch breath.] Where did you go? How could you just leave me here?"

"You told me to get out."

CHAPTER 34

She Will Never Quit Smoking (Sandy)

I'M TIRED OF BEING TOSSED out like a bad dog. I'm not going back. She can have her train wreck, solo. Last time she ordered me out, I stayed at my folks' house while they were at the beach. This time, they're at home. I don't feel like talking. I just need a place to crash.

My *sponsee* Delbert is a good choice. His second marriage just bit the dust, so he'll get it. Some understanding is worth the thirty-mile drive to the reservation town of White Swan. Delbert's a Native American, a self-made entrepreneur in the logging industry. There's always at least six kids living with him, so he'll be around. Our sponsor-sponsee relationship is an "I'll show you mine, you show me yours" deal. Simply said, we've exchanged dirty laundry.

It's past midnight when I pull onto his property holding both his home and business. It's like entering a Columbian drug cartel with the twelve-foot chain-link fence and flashing motion sensors. Delbert waves me in, recognizing my truck from the porch.

No explanations are needed. Showing up late at night told the story. A questionless greeting and a hug is what I expected and got. I need sleep. Tomorrow, I can figure things out. I eyeball the overstuffed sofa as my makeshift bed for the night. Delbert grabs his phone.

"Let me make a couple of calls," he says, dialing the phone. "Hey, Zeke, gotta friend here, my AA sponsor. You up for a sweat? Great, see ya. Oh, and call Joseph, okay? We'll get it fired up."

Ignoring my hand gestures waving "No . . . stop . . . no . . . no . . . no," he hangs up the phone, motioning for me to follow.

"C'mon, man, it'll be great. Trust me. Let's go."

Too tired to argue, I follow him outside. It's thirty degrees, but it feels like it's below zero! I gather firewood along with Delbert, placing it inside a hut made from tree limbs and covered with canvas. When the fire is glowing hot in the hut, we stack boulders on top, creating an oven suitable for Hansel and Gretel.

Zeke and Joe arrive, nod hello, strip naked, and along with Delbert, take turns mooning me as they crawl inside the hut. I'm left standing in the freezing-ass cold, fiddling with my shoes and socks. I'd heard stories about Indian sweathouses but never that it was done on a whim in the middle of an icy cold night. I did hear they smoke peyote and puke, thus purging all the sins they're hoarding. The other perk of smoking peyote? You get really stoned.

Toes and fingers numb, I slide out of my boxers, crawling in to join the others. The heat greets my face like a blowtorch. I'm relieved and disappointed that this is the AA sweathouse version with no cool peyote-pipe procession, just three naked Indians seated powwow-style in a pool of sweat and me.

I concentrate on the task of breathing in and out, listening best I can to Delbert explain the sweat-lodge process. This is round one: recognition of the spirit world, thanking the Creator for the elements, water, air, earth, and life. I am light-headed from the heat. I fight the urge to share my vision of Bugs Bunny in the boiling pot over the fire as Yosemite Sam adds carrots and onions to the water.

I fake it through the gratitude prayers, reciting whatever comes to mind that seems similar to their chanting. I want to delve into the spirit realm with the others, but I can't breathe, and fear of what's next is distracting. When Zeke lifts the door flap, I consider diving across the others to get out of the oven. I wait my turn. You know that old saying about stepping out of the frying pan into the fire? Well, stepping out of the oven into the icy cold is worse! I stepped out, heat met cold, disappearing before the door flapped shut behind me.

Delbert grabs a shovel, breaks ice formed on top of a metal horse trough, climbs the wooden steps, and falls headfirst into the trough. Moments later, he pops up, shakes grizzly-style, climbs out, and joins me at the bonfire. Zeke and Joe do the same, gathering at the fire, one on either side of me. I'm ready to scream "Hell no!" and run naked through the woods, if they pursue my turn. After a period of grace, the three naked wet Indians and I crawl back inside the hut. I welcome the 140-degree oven for about two minutes when the Bugs Bunny vision returns.

Round two is recognition of the Creator's wisdom, humbly asking for his help. When they'd spoken and the silence lingered, I ask for direction and solutions. Feeling clumsy, having never prayed out loud before, I wonder if they're laughing at the white guy. When they reiterate my words in prayer for me, I believe their sincerity. The heat is unbearable, and I'm ready to leap outside for another parts-shriveling session as the flap opens. One by one, they take the second plunge. When Joe pops out of the water, the smart side of my brain must have frozen. I climb the three wooden steps, diving in headfirst.

My lungs deflate; my manhood cringes. Automatically, I pray.

"Please, God, don't let me squeal like a little girl."

Prayer answered, I enter the hut for the third and final round, knowing that my first ice-water plunge is also my last. The final round centers on spiritual growth and healing through meditation and song. Delbert encourages me to ask for my song. Last month, I spent two days with Deb at the Toppenish Pow Wow while she ran an informational booth for work. The songs were beautiful, serene, haunting. I'm not asking God for the impossible. I nod like "Sure, hang on while I ask him now," but I didn't. I sat, marveling as Delbert, Zeke, and Joe lift guttural, spirit-led voices to the Creator. Song or not, I know something beyond my understanding and reach is present.

While they indulge in the final dip, I dress (blessed socks first) and stand next to the bonfire. They leisurely dress, say their good nights, giving me a sincere good-luck pat on the shoulder. At last, I'm horizontal under a

Pendleton blanket on the sofa. I've no worries that sleep will be sound.

I am wrong.

The remainder of the night, I ponder one question, "Why can't we get along?" Around 5:00 a.m., tired of battling, I get up, shower, and make a pot of coffee. An hour later, Delbert stumbles into the kitchen, pours a cup of coffee, joining me at the table. He's chained at home. A few months back, his wife left him with a herd of kids. Some are theirs, but most are informal adoptees from neglectful homes around his community. I'm grateful for the sweatlodge experience, but I'm not chancing a morning rerun of naked Indian guys over ice. And I need a meeting.

I make it back in time for the early AA meeting, but the serenity part doesn't take. I drive around, visit my folks, eat a bowl of Mom's beef-barley soup. I show up at our house, relieved my belongings are not strewn across the yard. That's the kind of crazy stuff she might do. The car is in the drive, and the porch light is on, as if she's still sleeping, but it's nearly three o'clock in the afternoon. Tubby barks when I unlock the door then runs down the hall to the bedroom. Deb is in bed, wearing last night's costume, lying on her stomach. She stirs when I sit on the edge of the bed, whispering. I can't make it all out.

"I'm not okay. I can't breathe."

I'm prepared for one of her fits but not this. I know this scene. My granny perfected it. She'd spoil everything, claiming one of her spells, demanding the world to stop turning while it catered to her ails. I didn't fall for Granny's act, and I'm not buying Deb's show either.

I get her a beer as requested—nice touch, Deb. She thinks she might have gas. I help her roll over. When a beer and a cigarette do not cure her, she asks me to drive her to the Medi-Center. I can't say no. No one ever said no to Granny, either for fear it would be the time she fell over and croaked.

Deb's playing the scene with all her heart, stopping, leaning against the wall, gasping for breath, holding her chest. I'm ready to toss her over my shoulder so we can get on with *Act Two* of this drama. At the clinic, she tells them she might have gas. *Now that's going to get them to hurry things up. There's a woman out here with killer gas. Get a gurney out here stat!*

We wait. We stare. No words. No looks. The others in the waiting room assume we're strangers. When Deb finally leaves with the nurse, I look for something to read besides parenting advice or senior-citizen propaganda. I settle on a People magazine with the headline "Sex and Politics." With the first flip of the pages, I realize it's another Anita Hill story. Bored, I hand it to a kid walking by. I feel a tap on my shoulder. I ignore it, thinking the kid wants to return the magazine. The presence remains. I open my eyes to the nurse in my face.

"Mr. Palmer? We need to call an ambulance for your wife. The doctor wants to talk with you."

Had I fallen into deep sleep, and this is a dream? The doctor greets me in the hall. Deb is gathering her purse and jacket. The doctor is speaking words I can't absorb.

"Her left lung is 80 percent deflated, a pneumothorax. She needs to go to the hospital now."

Deb slides off the table, leaning back on it for support. Waving her hand like she's shooing gnats, she orders.

"You're driving me to the hospital. I don't need an ambulance. I told them already."

She submits to a wheelchair, a favor to the nurse. Deb thanks her in the sweetest, sincerest, pure little voice. As soon as the door closes, the boot-camp sergeant voice returns.

"I'm having a cigarette on the way. Don't say a word! Who knows when I'll be able to have another."

I keep quiet.

An attendant with a wheelchair is waiting at the emergency entrance when we arrive. We are escorted straight to a doctor. For the first time since returning home from White Swan, I look at Deb. Her skin is yellow and drawn. Her body looks thin and frail. Why hadn't I noticed this before?

The doctor seems pleased for the adrenaline rush to his slow day. He smells my fear, knows I don't trust him with my wife's life. Holding the scalpel in one hand, he deadpans an explanation of the cause.

"A pneumothorax usually occurs as a result of a gunshot or knife wound in the lung or a fractured rib from a car accident. In some cases, it's caused by air blisters that break open, sending air into the space around the lung. That's usually a result from air-pressure changes from high altitudes or scuba diving . . . sometimes athletes, if they're really tall and thin suffering."

What? Deb hasn't been shot or run over by a bus. Nor has she been mountain climbing or scuba diving. She's *no* athlete. I want to scream, "Hey, Dr. Idiot, she smokes like the bowels of hell!"

Talking more to Deb now, he continues, "I'll be cutting a V-shape here [pointing to her left upper chest] to insert a tube into the lung. Try not to panic. As the air reaches capacity in the lung, you'll feel like you're drowning."

He turns to me. "You staying?"

"Of course, I'm staying."

But Deb has other ideas. Each word hurts, and she's getting riled up.

"Haley and Jay . . . talk to them. Don't call my folks. I'll tell them later. Go, please. I'm good. And please pack me a bag and grab my work files."

I pray on the run. I can't breathe. My affliction being the hand of guilt squeezing around my throat. Did I do this to her? How could I not see how weak and sick she's become?

I pack a bag for her. On my way out, I see her work files on the desk. When I reach Jerry's house, Jay is outside with his hacky sack. Haley must have heard the car. They approach, questions on their faces. I do my best to reassure it's all okay while dropping the news their mom is in the hospital having surgery.

Haley and I wait in the car while Jay tells his dad what's happening. Jerry nods consent at the door. We enter room 302, as directed by the desk clerk. Deb looks dead. I fight an impulse to protect them from seeing their mom like this. Tubes sprout from her like extra limbs, grabbing onto whooshing machines. She shifts a little in the bed, looking up at us, smiling.

"Hey, guys. Don't worry. I'm good. It's okay. Remember, I always look scary without makeup."

"Mom, are you going to quit smoking?" Haley asks.

"Well, I think it's the plan. Look, they gave me the nicotine patch," Deb answers, pointing to her shoulder.

Shortly, we're shooed out by nurses with rubber gloves. We walk down the hall, ride the elevator, drive home. We didn't say much, if anything. No need to say out loud what we knew to be fact. She will never quit smoking.

CHAPTER 35

Just Go to Your Room
(Deb)

THE GOOD NEWS: I DIDN'T smoke, not one puff. The bad
news: I got wasted at a work conference. I woke this morning in that dreadful state of bloodguilt. I don't know what
I did, just that I did something bad, the extent of which to
be learned soon.

Joining my coworkers for breakfast (a little late), there
are no good mornings, nods, or acknowledgments. All I
know is that somewhere between the voice in my head
warning not to order another drink, and waking up this
morning, I've been banished from the clan. The tables are
pushed together family-style. There's no chair, so I drag
one over, squeezing in at an angle.

Nauseous, I nibble on a sweet roll while staring at my
boss's back. Forcing memories, I recall faces—angry, disgusted, appalled. The images hurt. My mind rises to my
defense with musings of last night's laughter, dancing, and
joking. But then scattered words and phrases come back—

settle down, be quiet, you shouldn't have said that. I glance across the table, studying their vacant faces. I know Sandra, a coworker I'd wanted to befriend, sees me and feels the intensity of my stare.

I recall a sloppy, tearful scene from last night. Shame warms my face. What was I thinking? I knew she'd recently caught her husband cheating. I try dismissing the memory as wrong. Why would I confess my adulterous past to her? I used her to purge my sins like a catharsis-style catcher's mitt. In drunk mode, I was certain she'd understand. That she could see me (an adulteress) as human with hurts of my own. Now acutely sober, I know I wanted Sandra's forgiveness. Of course, she hates me.

Acid drips into my stomach. I wonder if I should race to the restroom. My boss, Renee, looks my way, quickly looking down when I try to meet her eyes. I remember her voice from last night.

"It's too late for an apology. Leave her alone . . . stop crying . . . just go to your room. Sleep it off."

Memory flash cards—pieces to a puzzle you don't want to complete, moments that felt right at the time, things said you can't take back. Normally, my party remorse is self-inflicted shame and embarrassment. This time, an innocent person is injured by shrapnel from my big mouth.

Although the details of the night are sketchy, the guilt is vivid. Could this be a blackout? If so, I've had them before. But like this time, I do remember a few things. It's not like I wake up in an unknown town, no inkling of why.

I don't know how to fix this. I can tell Sandra doesn't want to hear from me. On the drive home, I play along with the invisible game, like a carpool ghost. What will I tell Sandy? He calls me a *lightweight*, chuckling at my beer-and-tomato juice. I like how I look in his eyes. That's who I want to be, not a big-mouth barfly.

After the still two-hour ride home in the company van, I'm dropped at the curb in front of our house. I feel them exhale as I close the van door. Walking up our sidewalk, I notice that everything is beautiful—the grass, our front door, our porch. In contrast, I'm ugly, disheveled, and I stink. Vodka is odorless, so why do I reek of it? Opening the door, I regret choosing the silent breakfast over a shower.

"Hi, sweetie. How was your trip?"

"I don't want to talk about it. Okay?"

"Oh, no, you didn't—"

"No, I didn't smoke."

I go to the bedroom, closing the door. Tubby scratches, wanting in. Every time I show people who I really am, they're disgusted. So am I. Pretending to be someone I'm not is exhausting. I don't want to do it anymore. I want to be done, vanish, surrender. I'm angry that writing "The End" is not an option because I can't call the game without hurting my children. They don't deserve this. How did such beauty, innocence, and pure joy come from me? They're the reason I've tried to be someone better than I'm designed to be. I'm out of options. I weep.

"Please, God, do something. Change me. I can't do it. I've tried. Please help me."

I hear panting, meaning that Sandy is standing next to Tubby outside the door. I don't deserve the dog hanging at my door, let alone Sandy. I have to change, settle down, stop drinking, be the wife he deserves. Not drinking is good measure for the wife of a recovering alcoholic anyway. I'm not an alcoholic, but for him, I choose not to drink again.

"Sweetie? Can Tubby and I come in?"

CHAPTER 36

For My Sake
(Sandy)

IF I EVER HAD A polygamist fantasy, it died. I can't deal with the two wives I have now. One is smart, sound, sweet, kind, and loving. The other is irrational, unpredictable, nasty, and crazy. When I approach the one lovely lady they reside in, I never know which one she'll be.

Tonight, I walk in after work, welcomed by the smell of warm bread, music playing, and a come-take-me-now kiss. Somewhere between the dishes and kids going to bed, the other personality morphs onto the scene. I'm reading the paper, thinking about what's coming later, when a guttural cry wails down the hall from the bedroom. I race down the hall, expecting masked men, a gorilla, or at least a spider. Deb is hunched over her typewriter, sobbing.

"What the hell is wrong with you?"

"I can't do it! Tomorrow is deadline. I can't write any-more. I can't do anything!"

I sit on the bed amongst crumpled wads of paper and tear-sopped tissues. What does she want me to do? If writing the column for the newspaper causes this much grief, she should quit. They don't pay much anyway.

"Say something! You know I'd rather be slapped around than ignored. I hurt! Say something! Anything!"

"You're——! Nuts!"

A moment of chilling silence.

I'm hypnotized like a cobra victim. She lunges, grabs my shirt collar, pulls my face to hers, hissing the order, "Then you finish it!"

Deb curls into a fetal position on the bed while I read what she's written. As suspected, the column is great, needing only a closing sentence. It's the same problem—*not being good enough*, now heightened with nicotine withdrawal. I make something up, place a period at the end, and declare it finished.

I don't help because of her threats; those are comical, considering her size and lackluster for violence. No, I wrote the sentence because I know her suffering is real, the pain no less excruciating than a hand squeezed in a vise. Later, she thanks me, and we laugh at my first and last published sentence.

Every day is an urgent task for her, striving to accomplish the one thing that will prove she is *okay,* anything to erase her self-applied name tag reading, "Less than." If her obsession was food, she'd weigh 500 pounds. *Enough* is not in her vocabulary. I thought I could be *enough*.

It's not enough that all the department heads revere her work. She won't be satisfied until coworkers like her. I don't know why it matters what they think. But it does. She returned home from the conference in Seattle, devastated. Whatever happened, it was bad. She wouldn't talk about it (totally out of character). Prying, I learned one thing: She drank too much. In character, she does a 360 spin to *never drinking again*! It's the reason that bothers me—for my sake.

She's not an alcoholic. I mean, come on. Based on what I've seen and what she's told me, she couldn't be. Alcoholics don't say no to alcohol nor dilute good beer with tomato juice. Drinking or not drinking isn't the problem. If she'd just listen to me. I love her more than *enough*. She's a great mom. Haley and Jay adore her. Professionally, she's respected for her hard work and creativity.

Through everything, I know Deb believes in me. I want her to know the same. I can't find the right words or actions to show her I believe. Without God, I'd never survive the constant turmoil. At best, she has an idea of a god, a maybe, a possibility. It hurts to say this, but I think she believes God loves me and everyone else, just not her. I don't think she's forgiven herself for committing adultery or for the divorce. I tell her no one is worthy, and then I tell her again. I'm not always patient, surrendering to what she seems to want, name calling, and treating her as *less than*.

One morning, after an argument reached that place of no return, she breaks down.

"I hate who I am. I need something . . . something to shut the noise out. I don't fit this world. I never have. I'm not an alcoholic. I wish I was. I've read every story in the back of the Big Book, looking for one that's like me. There isn't one. I just want to be okay, to walk around living life like everyone else. I'm so tired."

At first, she shoos away my suggestions of Al-Anon and ACOA. Nevertheless, thinking there's no other option, she succumbs, ever the skeptic.

Working a 12-step program and making friends, her life got better, and so did mine. Not that we found the middle or visited normal. The choices remained hot or cold, alive or dead, hurricane or sunny skies. When it was good, it was amazing; when it was bad, it was unbearable. It may not be all her fault. I admit to taking advantage, if she puts her guard down. When she's fighting me, I fight back. When she submits, I think she's weak, taking every advantage. I'm in love with the feisty Irish redhead that not only hits back but often throws the first punch. Women who keep quiet, patting themselves on the back for being good, turn my stomach.

Watching Deb work the program vigorously and in vain is painful. *Serenity* prayer, key word: *serenity!* She loves the word, what it means, how it sounds; she gets lost in the application. She strives, treating *serenity* like any job. At work, she earns promotions, collecting kudos in a massive jar impossible to fill. She went after a new title, public relations director, a position she practiced until they couldn't live without it. Unsatisfied, like an addict, she lives for her next fix, more potent than the last. With no *bigger and better* in view, she quits. And now, we have a shingle hanging on our door: PALMER BUSINESS COMMUNICATIONS.

To Deb, freelance means working around the clock. The sign should read: EXTREMELY TALENTED LUNATIC FOR HIRE. Fueled by fear of failure, alongside her constant enemy "not good enough." From day one, clients knock at our door, wanting press packages, newsletters, résumés.

She hustles to please, saying yes to everything. A note to your wife? Why not? And sadly, the business is booming.

So why wouldn't she go after *serenity* the same way?

With my own addictive tendencies, I get *high by association*. Deb is my *rush*, my cocaine, my amphetamine, my glowing shot of Black Velvet. When we're not in catastrophic mode, our marriage is intoxicating.

We purchased a home, meeting both our styles—a two-story Craftsman with dark woodwork, ten-foot ceilings, leaded glass windows, and a big front porch. Unfortunately, we failed to assess the horrific remodeling by the former owner that needs to be demolished before restorations can begin. The house is stripped of the original chandeliers, doors, kitchen cupboards, and charm. All of these and more need to be made right, put back to the original dream. Now in between striving to be a family, making a living, hunting antique treasures, and frequent fighting, we plan, scheme, and toil over our new home. We're committed to recreating the illusion, or possible delusion, envisioned the first day we walked through the door. I see the overwhelming structural jobs that need immediate assistance: the dirt floor in the basement, tattered shingle roof, and the fence that needs built. Deb sees a library/office with floor-to-ceiling bookshelf and rolling ladder, French doors, and restoration of the hardwood floors hiding under the carpet resembling a three-tone cow.

It's not that I can't say no to Deb or even that I want to. It's more that I end up excited by her vision. Even my dad, an accomplished carpenter whose fingerprints are on hundreds of Yakima Valley homes, is under Deb's foreman spell. So forget the dirt floor in the basement, let's build that library wall. Working with Dad on our home, designing and building together, is rewarding. He may be a little slower now that he's retired, but his skill is as sharp as ever.

With Deb, I'm a great guy, rising to challenges, loving deeply, living fully. I am also a jackass who calls her names, destroys furniture in fits of rage, and screams a toddler's *no* when winning the argument is all that matters. She makes me do things I would never have thought myself capable of, great and terrible. I know the stories of her dad choking her until she gasped his demanded apology. The daddy who used his belt or fists to dole out what she *deserved*, whose angry bellow shriveled her spirit. Yet knowing these things, weighing over 200 pounds, I use my size to bully her. I think she'll cower to my subliminal threats. To the contrary, pressed against the wall, cornered, she responds like a Chihuahua taking on a grizzly bear. I open my mouth, shocked at the words that charge out.

"I'm not going to hit you, but you deserve it!"

Later, I want to puke. In my defense, she uses words to shut me down. I use what I have available.

CHAPTER 37

Cute Shoes
(Deb)

I'M OUT OF CURES: MARRIAGE, motherhood, a love affair, a college degree, a divorce, a career, remarriage, a new profession, get drunk, get sober. They're just Band-Aids, covering a crusty, incurable disease festering in my heart.

No matter what I do, second verse's same as the first. On the last page of my story, I'm the same person as when the story began. I'm not strong like Sandy. He gets back up, more determined, ears plugged as the world screams "Give up!" He stands, brushes off the dust, marching on—the brave, undying soldier. I'm not a good soldier. I want to run, accept the shame of AWOL. I long to be where loved ones don't end up collateral damage to my outbursts, somewhere free from Sandy's stabbing questions.

"What's wrong with you?"

I'm nuts.

"Are you crazy?"

Yep.

"What do you want?"

Peace.

His questions hurt. I've asked them myself as long as I can remember. I've always known I'm different, choosing to wear *odd* with pride. Words scribbled on a scrap of paper hidden in my jewelry box proves my mind's preparation for the future, along with my lack of talent for poetry.

> I'm forever prepared for the inevitable day
> when the white coats appear to drag me away
> to a lovely asylum, where I'll spend my day
> in silence
> pretending to be both deaf and dumb,
> reading classic literature, like Twain,
> Elliot, and Emerson.

My children deserve better than a whacko mom. They always have. They are my big mystery. *Why* I was given a magnificent gift in place of what I really deserve? What was God thinking?

I've tried to do right by them, to be the mom they are entitled to. I've failed, often, placing my needs before theirs. I'm like the boasting pregnant woman whose intentions for a natural birth are sincere until the first pang of birth hits, prompting threats for instant relief. My high ideals for motherhood mock me. The lofty statements of "I would never" have proven to be lies. Lame justifications that they were never hungry, without shelter, or unloved do not erase what I didn't give. I'm proud they're strong and independent. I'll take a little credit for that.

Now sighing, I succumb to my last "I would never."

"Comprehensive Mental Health. How can I help you?"

"My name is Deb Palmer. I was referred by Andrew Collins for an appointment with Dr. Guerro."

"Yes, Ms. Palmer, your evaluation is scheduled for Tuesday at three o'clock."

Tuesday at 2:45 p.m., I ride the elevator up to the psychiatric department at Comprehensive Mental Health (CMH). It feels like I'm wearing a sign reading, "Okay, world, you win. I'm a nutcase."

Here I am, begging at the door. Yet I'm willing because they have the bag of bones I'm barking for—drugs. That's all I want. Please hand over whatever pretty pill makes the world shut up and go away. I'm tired of keeping my finger in the dike of my heart, waiting for God to plug it up.

Sitting in the waiting room of the psychiatric department, my head heavy in my hands, I see a pair of bubblegum-pink heels. They beg attention, not because of the color but the size. I hear my dad's voice in my head, known for his foot fetish, "Look at those clodhoppers!" The mammoth-shoe owner slips a foot out of one shoe, stretches it, then slides it back on in apparent discomfort.

"Ms. Palmer?" I hear from above the shoes. "Please follow me."

I know that she is a he, first clues being the Dudley Do-Right chin, Brutus hands, and yeti feet. What I don't know is if I should pretend not to notice.

"Is that a vintage sweater?" I ask. "It's really cute."

"Yes, thank you," he replies. "Why don't you tell me why you are here?"

Trying not to fixate on the lone nasty whisker on his chin, I grab a Kleenex from the box on the desk. I can't just jump to my request for a send-me-to-the-moon pill. So I spill the messy details bouncing in my head like Mexican jumping beans. He looks at papers on the desk while habitually slipping one foot in and out of his heel. I cover the affair, divorce, lung collapse, quitting smoking, drinking, not drinking, second marriage, my children no longer needing me, my job, Sandy's jobs, quitting work, starting a new business. When I take a quick breath at the end of the "There Was a Little Girl" poem, he breaks in.

"I'm going to write you a prescription for manic depression. I also believe you have an obsessive-compulsive disorder. We'll deal with that after we see how you do on Wellbutrin."

He writes the script, asking questions he'd known the answers to, had he been listening. "Do you smoke? Are you single? Do you have any children?

I just wanted the script, so I could get out of there. He hands me my prize, leaning in with a serious look.

"Next week, I'm sending a letter to all my patients. It's an announcement stating I'll be wearing two earrings instead of one. I think the letter will help with the transition. Do you have any questions?"

"No. Thank you for your time . . . um . . . your shoes are really cute."

I'm glad the hour session ended in twenty minutes. I had what I came for, the pill that will make me okay, fix my marriage, children, and business. *While you're at it, why not trim off a few pounds too?* I'll settle for normal, just make me normal and quick. Tomorrow, we're off to the races. Sandy is hurting. He needs me to be fun, carefree, normal.

CHAPTER 38

Can We Have Breakfast First?
(Sandy)

MY DAD IS THE HERO type, easy to look up to as a child and more so now that I'm a man. He keeps his word, tells no lies, protects, and cares for his family. He's strong, vital, capable—the definition of "a man's man." But one day, I catch him in an unmanly act. He didn't hear me walk into his workshop. Stunned, I watch as he speaks in a cutesy voice, gently brushing while cooing to the butt ugliest cat alive.

"There you go, princess. Does that feel good? No more tangles."

Not long after, the loose fur ball gets knocked up. Now, I own a cat named Slim, after my dad. Seems Deb and the mangy feline whore were in this together, along with Haley and Jay. We put poor old Tubby down when he lost the use of his back legs. He's probably wandering around heaven, lost. That's Deb's gift—persuasion. She may trick me, but the cat's not falling for it. My solace to owning a cat is watching pouty face Slim defy Deb. She insists if we treat it like a dog, it will act like one.

We need comic relief in our home right now. Deb's season, seizing serenity, seems to have lapsed. Last week after work, I found her standing on a chair, nailing sheets over the office windows.

"They won't leave me alone!"

I know who she means, without asking, but I ask anyway.

"What the hell are you talking about?"

Deb's clients soon found that her strict by-appointment-only rule applied in theory, not enforcement. Appear on our doorstep, ask for whatever you please, she'll deliver with a smile. They smell her need to please. Later, she snaps like a rubber band baked in the heat. With sheets over our windows, I nail a *closed* sign to the door, whisking her off on a two-day junking trip. Junking is our fix all. But not this time.

"I have the best idea!"

Oh no.

"Let's rent a space in one of those antique malls. You know, just for fun."

I did know.

Fun just became work. On the way home from our minitrip, we stop in Toppenish, walking away official antique dealers in a mall. Maybe it will still be a fun hobby, if I can keep her ideas harnessed. A week later, Deb closes Palmer Business Communications. The sheets stay over the windows. Phone calls and knocks on the door are ignored. She hides upstairs with headphones on, blasting classical music. She's functioning, taking care of meals, laundry, mom stuff, but she's absent. Weekends we *junk* and arrange our ever-growing rented space in the antique mall. When I asked if she'd go to an AA speakers meeting, I expected a flat no. She not only agrees but seems to embrace a night out, wearing my favorite red high heels. Clint, the speaker, is hilarious. Several hundred AA members and myself roar as he roasts Al-Anon and ACOA members calling them a whining bunch of party poopers. I didn't notice that one person is not laughing. There's a standing ovation at the end with the entire room standing, applauding, except Deb. As we shuffle out of the speaker hall, I place my arm on her shoulder. She stiffens. Alone in the car, she speaks.

"When you stood applauding, along with the rest of the room, you betrayed every child who's been neglected and abused by an alcoholic parent, the wives who dared to hope for a marriage predisposed to die. Really funny that they believed, prayed, begged for help. Truly hilarious that children go off to school every day, believing they did something that caused the screaming. Super hysterical that the very sound of a father's voice makes a child shudder. Yeah, that's so funny I might pee my pants. *You* betrayed them all when you stood up and clapped for that idiot!"

"What is wrong with you?"

My question is followed by silence so thick I wish the yelling would return. Later when I didn't feel under attack, I could admit to myself that she is right. The guy is a buffoon. And worse, the room of alcoholics who collectively have harmed a world of innocent souls laughing at what? The loved ones they've damaged? How many children have I held in my arms as a counselor consoling the unforgivable acts of the alcoholic who hold them captive? Faces of fear and shame. My own face as a child, disgusted, confused, and angry at the vile words spoken by my drunken old granny. Or my own face of sorrow, worried for my mom after too much Thunderbird.

The next morning, Deb apologizes for the outburst.

"I don't know how to be different. I feel so alone. I can't do nothing, hoping it will all go away. I've made an appointment with a psychiatrist. Maybe there's a drug that will keep me . . . make me . . . normal."

My first thoughts are "I can help. You don't need a psychiatrist." I understand she feels unloved and unwanted. When she gave up drinking, she was shut outside her family, especially by her brother, Danny. It should be enough that I love her, as do Haley and Jay.

"I recommend *talk therapy* versus grabbing for medication."

"Really? No, thanks."

She came back from therapy with pills and a wild story I couldn't quite follow: Dr. Guerro looked like a Sasquatch in pink high heels, sending a letter declaring two earrings in place of one. I caught enough of it to know had I met the bigfoot he/she, I'd have thanked God my problems are not as bad and walked out.

The next day, we leave for the dirt cup. At the KOA in Leavenworth, she is already complaining that the pills aren't working.

"Neither of them. Not the one pill last night or the one this morning?"

"Well, when do you think I'll feel different?"

"Just try to relax and have fun. Okay, sweetie?"

She nods, grabbing a tent pole as we set up camp for the night. One of the poles is severely bent, and another is missing. It collapses. Using my head as the center-holding post, I grab the duct tape.

"I can do this! Go sit down."

I made a makeshift new pole, get the tent rigged for the night, unless the wind kicks up. Zipped into our double sleeping bag, I'm ready to sleep. Deb is like an old radio tube, warm and ready to communicate.

"I don't know what I'll do if this medication doesn't work."

"It'll work."

"But what if it doesn't?"

"It will."

Do I believe my own words? How can I? Deb may have severe mood swings, but at least, she's not pondering bra or jockstrap. I don't care what gender this person is or how they got there. Just get it together before you counsel others. Is that too much to ask?

I fell asleep staring at the makeshift pole swaying gently in the breeze. Around 5:00 a.m., I awake, reaching for Deb, but she's escaped our cocoon. I grab my gear, heading for the showers, expecting she's at the picnic table writing or reading. She's not. After my shower, I check the line forming outside the women's showers. No pouty, morning-faced Deb. Back at camp, I light a fire, start the bacon, crack eggs to scramble.

"Good morning!" I hear Deb say from behind me, slapping my butt. "I've been up all night, but that's okay because I feel great. Have you ever sat on a rock in the river in the pitch dark of night? I got so much accomplished. I wrote a poem by flashlight. Do you want to hear it? And I made a list of all the projects we need to do at the house. Oh, are you ready for this, Sandy?"

"What? Ready for what?"

"I think we should start our own antiques business. Not just a mall space, our own."

"Can we have breakfast first?"

I scoop Deb a plate suited for a 300-pound sumo wrestler. What she lacks in body weight, she makes up for in appetite. Juggling the loaded plate along with a metal cup of steaming hot camp coffee, I lean in, expecting she'll take them from me. Instead, she jumps up, knocking the coffee out of my hand.

"No! No! Oh no!" she screams.

"What's wrong?"

"Look at me! It's everywhere!"

Every inch of exposed skin—face, neck, legs—beamed with red splotches like a bad case of chicken pox. I watch as she searches for skin free of red bumps. Then she tosses her head back like a mad scientist, laughing hysterically.

"Great, now I'm crazy and red all over!"

Then she wept.

CHAPTER 39

You Keep Saying That, Are You Sure? (Deb)

WHEN I SAID THE WORDS, I hoped for relief, a sense of closure to my insanity. Instead, the words floated around the room with nowhere to rest.

"My name's Deb. I'm an alcoholic."

As I tell my story, the voice in my head screams, "Shut up!" I want to keep it simple like veni, vidi, vici, only instead of I came, I saw, I conquered—I drank, I quit, I'm fine now. The faces at the table look like our cat, Slim, when I treat her like a dog. I confess to being sober or dry for the past eight years. All eyes glaze over under one giant group frown. Even my quest to score meds turned into a bizarre circus. Why did I get the self-absorbed, confused psychiatrist instead of the normal, stable, old man, glasses on nose, saying stuff like "It's okay, dear. Everything will be fine." And why did my magic bean leave me the color of cherry Kool-Aid, supercharged like a Chatty Cathy doll on speed? Once again, I'm left behind, waving bon voyage to all America as they pop a pill, floating off to chill island.

So here I sit in an AA meeting, attempting to explain the sober-alcoholic clause. Do I care if I meet the base requirements to join their little club? Not really. I loathe the clichés, the constant self ass patting for not doing something stupid yet today, and the guy whining about his ex-wife. Yet I want what they have, well, what a few seem to have found—a God they believe in serenity, hope. There must be a way to get what they have without hanging out with them. All I know is, I don't know diddly, and I have nowhere else to go.

I got a sponsor nicknamed Little Sue, a friend from Al-Anon. She's a cocktail like me—two fingers AA with an Al-Anon mixer, a splash of ACOA, and a little crazy on a toothpick. If you're not familiar with those terms, I'll simplify it for you. It's the trifecta of the disease of alcoholism. AA deals with the alcoholic. Al-Anon deals with all the others harmed by the alcoholic. ACOA is specifically for those who've lived under the chaos of alcoholic parents. Crazy is a bonus for winning the trifecta.

The first time I meet with Little Sue, I'm certain she tries to scare me off. I don't blame her. Who wants to take on the difficult cases? I hope *Difficult Deb* is not my destined nickname.

"We're jumping ahead to step 11 for a moment," she says, sliding the Big Book my way while reciting the step. "Sought through prayer and meditation to improve our conscious contact with God as we understood Him, praying only for knowledge of His will for us and the power to carry that out."

She seems to be waiting for me to respond. I don't hear a question in there, so I keep quiet.

"If I'm to be your sponsor, you'll be looking into the Bible. If that's not okay with you, we won't be a good fit."

I laugh. Lately, I've felt like a cartoon character stalked by Bible thumpers jumping out from every corner. Since we've opened our antiques store in Ellensburg, I'm at the mercy of my customers seven days a week. I'm trapped behind the counter, forced to listen to tales of their ceramic-pig collection, annoying neighbors, upcoming gall-bladder surgery, and God.

One day, a blonde trio approaches the counter, a young mom holding the hand of a toddler dragging an antique doll across the floor. The porcelain doll appears to be the one from the glass case with the $300-price tag and sign reading, "Please do not touch."

"I'm a Christian," says the mom. "Would you take $25 for this doll? My little girl really wants it. We're Christians and can't afford to pay more than that."

I did not say the words begging to spill out. I didn't even say the G-rated version. "Listen, you presumptuous idiot. I don't hold Christians in high regard or think by any means that you are better than anyone else."

I really tried.

"I see she likes the doll, but there's no way I can sell a $300 doll for $25."

Pointing at her child, she continues, "But we can only pay $25. Wouldn't you consider it because we are Christians?"

I remind myself to be kind.

"I'm sorry," I begin, but hearing the lie unleashes my indignation.

"You know what, dear heart? If I could adjust my prices that easily I'd charge Christians double. Why? Because they think they're entitled and better than everybody else. So have a wonderful day, and God bless you!"

I fight the urge to chase her down the sidewalk with *furthermores*. Instead, red faced, I pick the doll up off the floor, finger comb the mussed hair, and return it to the shelf next to the "Please do not touch" sign.

Back at the counter, another woman approaches me. Her hands are empty, so I assume she's overheard the drama and wants to take a shot at me. I feel like I've just slapped the face of Tiny Tim. *God bless us, everyone.* Only in my version, I snag a doll from the weak hands of a deprived little girl.

"I'm a Christian too," she starts.

I'm wondering what's going on. They're circling like the lions in that Bible story. I'm bleeding, and they're moving in for the kill. Before I spring with a defense, she finishes her sentence.

"And I want you to know that we are not all like that woman. I'm so sorry she did that. It was very un-Christian-like."

I like this woman with the kind face. Since that drama, she, Patryk, stops by daily. It seems our store is on her walk route. She listens, even when I spit vile opinions. Best of all, she's not perfect. Sure, imperfection is common, but she's actually aware of the ailment. I've never met a Christian like her. I worked with a guy at People for People who had puffy, sprayed-stiff televangelist hair. He had plenty of time to dampen spirits with news of the fast-approaching end times, but if you were choking on a chicken bone, drowning, or in need of a kind word, he'd hurry on by.

"Christians are either crazy or jerks. You know I'm right, Patryk."

"Well, Deb, I'm a Christian."

"You keep saying that. Are you sure?"

Around the same time, yet another oddball surfaces at the store named Monte. We became fast friends, our bond being a distinct distaste for Christians. He has more rotten things to say about them than me. Yet he speaks of Jesus like someone I might actually like. I got to know Monte when one of my customers told me I should keep an eye on him because he looked like the type that would steal. Although we'd never spoken more than a few sentences of polite customer-clerk exchange, I knew this humble, quiet man was no thief or threat. She, like many others, judged his blond hair traipsing down his back, open shirt, and bull ring in one ear. One conversation with him would reveal the gentlest soul on earth. So I lied to the presumptuous, finger-pointing woman in a voice loud enough for Monte to hear.

"Excuse me? That man is my dearest friend. And the most honest person I know!"

She slithered out the door, justifying her accusations with "I didn't know. I was just trying to help."

Monte approached the counter.

"I apologize for her."

"It's okay. I'm used to it. It happens all the time."

Thus our friendship began. We hang out, sipping tea between customers, bashing Christians, and discussing

Jesus. Soon after, Monte became a store fixture, my next-door business neighbor, Anne, pays me a visit. The sign above her store reads, "Ed's Refrigeration Service," but it is loosely dubbed an antiques store known for dust-covered clutter.

"He's evil," she says, racing into my store just as Monte left out back. "That man with that hair and no shirt. I know things about him."

I try to shine light on her darkness, but she isn't having any of that. I never told Monte about her visit, but we shared many laughs at her expense. Besides dust, she is known around town for her end-of-times sales techniques. Her favorite: placing fake $20 bills on the floor, lurking behind a pile of junk until a customer picks it up then jumping out yelling "Aha!" After giving a lecture on the evils of money, she smiles, handing them a doomsday preparation brochure. Truth is, she's great for our business, sending shaken victims through our door, seeking protection and an explanation.

Looking back, I should not have been surprised that my AA sponsor was in on the *helter-skelter* Christian encounters. I thought I'd be fed the same lingo I'd heard around the tables. No one there speaks of Bible or Jesus. So my coffee date with Little Sue caught me off guard, and even more alarming was my response to her order to read the Bible.

"Okay, I can do that. Makes sense."

Funny thing, I have two new Bibles, one from Patryk and another from Monte. Sadly, it's like reading a foreign language—yada, beget, yada, yada, beget, yada, thou shalt yada yada. I found one part I understood, but I couldn't believe what was happening. It was that creep Lot who wants to protect his sons, so he says, "Hey, take my daughters, and do whatever you want with them."

What? I hate that guy. I am so upset; I call Little Sue moments after reading it. She listens to my paraphrase of the story, cutting me off mid-rant.

"Okay, I don't think you're ready to read the Old Testament alone. You're not really comprehending the context. Please stay in the New Testament for now."

"Is that Lot guy in the New Testament?"

"No. How are you doing with the Big Book? Are you journaling on your fourth step?"

"That's the one that says, 'Made a searching and fearless moral inventory of ourselves.' Right? Well, I've been thinking on it. I haven't written anything down yet."

"Next week, I want you ready to share your inventory with me. Okay?"

"Okay."

CHAPTER 40

Impending Doom Lingers (Sandy)

THE ICY WIND AND SLANTED rain elicits a benign shiver as we walk out the door. Lately, it takes more than bleak weather to dampen our mood. We've just eaten moo goo gai pan and spicy chicken sauté, our Friday-night splurge at the Jade Tree restaurant. Stepping onto the sidewalk, we see an elderly man staggering, pulling away from the helpful arm of his wife like a rebellious two-year-old or a standard drunk.

His wife's look of concern turns to shame as he stumbles, falling onto the sidewalk. I grapple with the guy, getting him to his feet. Deb consoles the woman. Leaning the old sot against a Ford truck, I see the woman grab Deb's arm, pleading a favor, pointing a finger behind me. Deb rolls her eyes at me, following the direction of the finger toward the rear tires of the truck. With wrinkled nose and outstretched arm, she bends down, retrieving a set of smirking false teeth. They must have flown from the drunk's mouth when he fell. The wife weaves over to the truck, revealing her own inebriation. She continues issuing orders with her finger, pointing for Deb to place the teeth in her handbag. Dutifully, Deb plops them into the purse, sighing at the sound of the clicking clasp. We wave good-bye to the couple, nodding off in the back seat of the cab. Then Deb speaks, "Next time? I'm the muscle. You can fetch and carry the dentures!"

Chilled, we race to our car. Deb presses next to me, turns the heat knob, blasting cold air from the heater, content with the expectation of heat.

"That could have been us someday," she whispers.

"I know."

The drive home remains still, pondering the ghost of Christmas future. We could easily be that couple, sad old drunks left to fend for themselves. Children, long gone, bled dry of all hope. Forgiveness expired. Grandchildren kept away safe from the consequences contact with drunken grandparents would certainly gain. There, by the grace of God, goes I, goes us—a gratitude lesson delivered by a couple of lifer alcoholics.

Life is good. I'm doing what I've always wanted—helping youth. With daily doses of kudos from my boss, Joyce, my confidence is healing. She believes in me. When a tough case comes across her desk, she tosses it my way, knowing I'm up to the task. Let someone else handle the potentially problematic child, I'll take a truckload of hooligans. The so-called hopeless, hardcore kids no one else wants, they're mine. No matter what they've done or might do tomorrow, I'm their eager advocate. They're the victims, expected to thrive in a crazy world, ruled by choices and the consequences of those who haphazardly screwed them into existence.

Like John, a seven-year-old who slings cusswords like a construction worker who's just hammered his thumb. I met with John the first time at his school. As we walked across the playground discussing Legos, a boy with bushy hair trips and falls in front of us, spilling a bag of marbles onto the grass. With a politician's ease, John bends down, scoops up a handful of marbles, slipping them into his pocket, nary a pause in chatter. When he takes a breath, I mention the marbles he's fiddling with in his pocket.

"What about the cat eyes, the ones that belong to that other kid?"

"They're mine," he states dryly.

He's one of six children under the reign of a physically and emotionally abusive dad. John is the designated *bad kid*, target for the woe-is-me wrath dealt by the career-welfare dad. John steals. He runs off at least twice a week. He disrespects his teachers. Who wouldn't?

I'd love to slap the parents upside the head. That's why I hang out with them at school, meeting with parents when forced. I can't undo a lifetime of wrongs, suffered and adopted as *how things are done*. My hope and energy goes to the kids whose hearts and minds have not yet closed for eternity. My patience for the parents is tested at tolerance.

A few weeks ago, late at night I got a call from a mom screaming, "Get this kid outta here before I kill him!" The scratchy, high-pitched wail belongs to the mom of another chronic troublemaker, Royce, a great kid who acts out with good reason. Like John, he carries the family's basket of blame. I arrived at his house twelve minutes after the call, unprepared for the jolt of cat pee greeting my nostrils at the door. Entering, I expect a herd of incontinent cats, but none came forward to confess. Royce sits on a wooden chair, head down, stabbing his leg with his right fist, touching thumb to digits on his left hand, as if counting. I bend to sit on the sofa next to his chair, seeing blurs of movement, realizing it's infested with cockroaches. The mom flips on a light, scattering roaches up walls, behind floorboards, under rugs. One runs over the top of my shoe. It was large enough to feel its weight, leaving me wondering if they've been dining on the incontinent cats. Dancing a clumsy jig, holding my breath so as not to gag on the odor, I wave the mom off as politely as I can while directing Royce out the door. Once outside, I take a breathing break while he hops into my van, turning knobs and pushing buttons. For the next hour and a half, we drive a hundred miles, talking, stopping to stretch, eat ice cream, and pee, landing at the Therapeutic Hospital in Tri-Cities. It's a lockdown facility, not ideal, but better than home with no threats, name-calling, or face slaps.

This isn't a job for everyone, but it fits, finally doing what I've always wanted, helping youth, making a difference, a purpose, a reason to exist. The paycheck is a bonus, a needed one but still.

Meanwhile at home, Deb works AA like everything else, pushing, yanking, forcing a fit like the "old square peg in the round hole" cliché. I hope it's helping. She's like the ant pushing a huge crust of bread up a hill. Is she happy? Content? Hell, I don't know! She zips between our business, family, us, and the new mountain to scale, AA. The program is yet another *wannabe* check mark on her to-do list. I wish she'd find rest in something, even faith seems to be a job to master.

Still, life is better than a few months ago when she ran out of solutions. Our marriage is crazy, fun, dangerous, exhilarating, and exhausting. The competitive race of the antiques business fits right into the whirlwind, triggering the addict in us both. Neither of us planned to have a thriving business. We kept one foot out the door, waiting to exit before the business failed. It was a simple, safe business plan. Buy a five-dollar beat-up duck (merchandise), sell it for ten. Buy a ten-dollar better duck, sell it for twenty. Buy a $20 stellar duck, and sell it for $40, and so on until all our ducks stood in a row from cheap to exquisite. As the store grew in popularity, sales warranted hiring help for weekends, leaving us with time to hunt more ducks.

I understand a good bargain, the quality found in antique furniture, and the historical interest. And although I admire Deb's era-specific vignettes, I don't understand the buyers they attract. I maintain a *mantiques* booth in the back of the store where I sell vintage auto parts, fishing and hunting items, poker chips, beer signs. I simply offer great deals on cool stuff. My sales are good, but Deb is a magician. I had this tackle box overflowing with top-of-the-line fishing gear for $12, a steal. One day, I mention my frustration that it had not sold. Deb dumps out all the stuff, places the tackle box next to some garden gloves, planters, and flower seeds, and it sells that day for $24. What planet did these buyers come from? Another time, Dad and I are at the store building a stand to display 300 pounds of architectural pieces. They form a caduceus spared from a demolished medical building in Yakima. I'm balancing the largest piece while Dad measures. I hear the clicking of high heels approaching, turning to see an attractive woman in red lipstick, wearing a 1950s polka-dot dress. Helpless, we watch as she snags Dad's work stool from behind us, pressing it to her chest as if she's been reunited with a ransomed baby.

"Oh my gawd! This is adorable! How much is it?"

At the time, Dad had little exposure to the alien customers. Removing the stool from her arms, he grumbled something about *his work stool*, shooing the clicking high heels away. We spent all day building the stand, placing it in the window at the exact angle specified by Deb. While Dad and I drove the forty minutes home to Yakima, it sold.

We're a pair of junk junkies chasing down the goods on weekends and whenever opportunity allows. Fridays, we often skip town, minutes after I finish up at work. Recently, we headed south toward Pendleton, Oregon. Along the way, we explore *every* backwoods town, quizzing locals for estate sales and auctions. Saturday around midnight, we're headed home, van loaded with finds. Deb's driving while I sleep, meaning exhaustion outweighed the fear of getting lost. I wake, thinking I'd been dreaming about one of the auctions we attended earlier in the day.

"Look! Look what I found in the middle of nowhere," she says, pointing. We're in Umatilla. I saw the auction sign at the exit."

I'm beat up from the junking marathon and need sleep. I admit, her stamina trumps mine. I'm about to tell her to get back on the freeway when I hear the auctioneer.

"Who'll open with $5 on this Hubley Packard sedan toy car from the 1940s?"

"Whoa! Hurry!" I say.

While Deb secures bidding paddles, I race in, arm in the air. Three hours later, we're back on the road, four boxes of junk tied to the top of our van. Sundays, we swear off the madness, planning to slow down. By Friday, we're certain self-control is attainable. And so it goes.

Besides stocking the store, we're furnishing our four-bedroom Craftsman home for pennies. Every stick of furniture in our house has a story, and the tales change as we trade up. We've owned four mohair sofas; each one dubbed by Deb as *the one* until the other *the one* sends the former off to the store. I'm glad she's not as fickle in romance as she is with sofas. One of my favorite keepers is a 1950s range, beaming with chrome and a dash with buttons and knobs worthy of a jet plane, costing a whopping $35. Even Deb's wardrobe is supplied by our business. We both enjoy hearing the compliments like "Great jacket," knowing we scored it for a couple of bucks. It's a gambler's rush, and we are hopelessly addicted.

We're happy. Sober. Yet oddly enough, that familiar feeling of impending doom lingers.

CHAPTER 41

The Black Gunk Clung to My Heart
(Deb)

IF I HAVE TWO JOBS, one easy, the other crap, I grab a shovel. Likewise, tackling AA's notorious fourth step, "Made a searching and fearless moral inventory of ourselves," I jump to the most heart-rending task—Haley and Jay. Page upon page of wrongs, all the broken "I would never" promises recorded in ink on a yellow legal pad.

They deserved the mom I meant to be, not the one I became. No more justifications, claiming good intentions, or disclaimers of "I never meant for them to get hurt." They did get hurt. If all I'm guilty of is treating their father poorly, that's no small thing. Besides, that's not the only wrong.

I slap a period at the end of my mom crimes, sighing relief, knowing no other names will be as tough. Scanning the list, all deserving amends, I choose the runner-up for the *need-to-get-this-over* crown—Wayne.

I fight the urge to scribble alibis, excuses, and reasons for my actions. After all, he played me, groomed me for over a year. He recited a secret script of *what I needed to hear*. I hear my sponsor's voice, "Take care of your side of the street."

What if I'd recoiled from his charms? How might that have changed his life? I wasn't exactly his first cheat and, most likely, not his last. Even so, had I said no, maybe he, too, might have met with his conscience. Whether so or not, my side of the street is filthy. As I write, frantically confessing all, a memory highlights a name, one not on my list—Trudy, Wayne's wife.

I try to push it, her, the memory, away. I fail.

The scene begins with a plebeian phone call from Wayne, whining an apology for not following through with his plan to leave Trudy. That sets me off. I never asked him to leave her, not once. That was all him. But I wanted him to. That's on my side of the street. After the phone call, I drank. When I ran out of all things intoxicating, I slipped on a sweater, noting on the way out the door it's inside out. Wrestling with the fashion faux pas while opening the door of the Cordoba, I turn around, knowing Wayne's brown Plymouth is turning the corner.

"Stop! Wait!" he yells out the window.

I get in the car, fiddling with the key in the ignition until he has time to jump in the passenger side.

"I told her. It's over . . . done. I'm here now. I'm sorry. She wouldn't let me. I finally had to—"

I order him out of the car, hoping he'll stay. He did.

"Let me drive. You're smashed. Where are you going?"

"Get out or buck up, Ollie! I ran out of vodka. I'm going to the liquor store and anywhere else I damn well please!"

The familiar growl of Trudy's red MG interrupts my screams. Like a couple of crooks caught by the sheriff, we watch as she stops two houses down, motor running, waiting for our getaway move. Against Wayne's pleas, I back out. Trudy falls in behind, and we parlay around the neighborhood, a ménage à trois motorcade. Like a glob of gum on my shoe, she turns, slows, or speeds up on my lead. At the red light on the corner of 24th and Nob Hill, Wayne says, "I need to talk with her. Explain. Get her to understand."

In the rearview mirror, I see she's gripping the steering wheel, eyes set on the back of my head. Wayne fidgets like a little boy needing to pee. Before he can open the car door, I turn on the radio, cranking the volume a full turn. Songs floating around in space like seeds from a dandelion suspended midair waiting to be chosen. I listen to an odd variety of stations. Any song could have played. When I heard the song blasting from the radio, I reacted.

Tchaikovsky's *1812 Overture* with full cannons! With the first cannon blast, time moved in single frames, embedding even the slightest fragments of memory forever in my mind—the pattern of the glass on the red light, the child in the back seat of the blue sedan, a plastic bag floating in the wind. I faced Wayne, making sure he didn't miss what came next. Glancing over my shoulder at Trudy, I stand on the gas pedal, sailing through the red light. From the other cars, I see mouths gape, hands gesture, and drivers swerving off the road. Wayne squeaks like a rubber squeeze toy, sending a surge of power through my veins. I'm joyfully overcome with reign, the fate of my oppressors in my hands.

But wait, Trudy has gone off script, racing through the light on my bumper, prepared to follow us to hell.

My hand cramps from writing. Shaking it out, I stand. Staring down at the yellow notepad, I see my side of the street. It's ugly. I don't want to look. How much hurt did it take for a *play-it-safe* woman like Trudy to follow my insanity? Screeching through a busy intersection, a reenactment of the car-chase scene in *The French Connection*, only in hokey Yakima rather than New York City.

The *what ifs* pummel me with shame.

If a different song had rolled out of the radio, might my reaction been less dramatic or more perilous? Initiating a car chase fell into the top five "I would nevers," yet I did. What if Ram Jam's "Black Betty" blazed out when I twisted the radio knob? Or Ted Nugent's "Cat Scratch Fever" or "Born to be Wild"? Would I have crashed into the gas pumps at the minimart, leaping from the car, landing a triple somersault just as the Cordoba explodes into flames? Or how about a Mariachi band? I've been known to listen on occasion. Surely, I'd kept my cool then. No one goes berserk under the influence of oompahs and accordion chords. Maybe I would have polkaed back to Trudy's car and given her a hug. Staring in the mirror, the one revealing who you are capable of being is chilling. What if . . . what if . . . what if Wayne's gun had been within reach? Might I have? Would I? Could I? *I would never* no longer carries credibility.

The chase began with the first cannon shot in the *1812 Overture* and ended with the last. No one was hurt. Thank God. When I think what could have happened, who could have been harmed, a mom, a child, Trudy.

And there it was, the crux of my fourth step. Trudy became a human being with skin, a beating heart, and feelings; a wife, a mother, a fellow woman. She eats, drinks, breathes, loves; loves her children, family; her husband. Oh, God, what does that make me? How could I miss this? She's a warm body, alive, God made like me. I trained like a soldier preparing for war, seeing her as nonhuman. For what? My justifications no longer make sense. My strongest defense—that I was just one in a long line of infidelities for Wayne—makes me feel worse. She suffered at my hand. She is sitting on my side of the street, emotionally battered and bruised from my selfish actions.

By the time I finished writing, a crowd gathered at the curb on my side of the street, all victims of my decision to put myself before others. No justifications, lies, or exaggerations on their part diluted the stark truth of my actions. So much damage, so little I can say or do to make it better.

I call Little Sue, begging for an emergency fifth-step meeting. She meets with me the next afternoon in the park. She listens. I read, finishing with Trudy.

"I need to make amends to Trudy right away. Tell her I'm sorry. Let her know I don't and won't ever again answer Wayne's calls."

Little Sue takes a sip of her soda, face showing no expression.

"He still calls you?"

"Yes. But I hang up. And I ignore the notes he leaves on my car."

"Who will feel better after the apology, you or Trudy?"

"But I need to ask her forgiveness."

"You need?"

The slap of truth, the impeccable mirror.

"Well, what can I do to make amends to her? Write a letter? Send flowers? What if I play like a secret admirer, sending secret notes designed to make Wayne jealous?"

Sue sits in silence.

"Okay, that's stupid. But what can I do? I have to do something!"

I watch and wait as Sue stares at the grass. A friendly cat jumps onto the picnic table, momentarily interrupting Sue. She pets the purring cat before asking another question.

"If you were Trudy, what would make you feel better?"

I knew the answer but kept quiet, and Sue didn't push. If I were Trudy? I'd want a close-up view of the lions ripping my guts out. I'd want to chase me down with a car, gun the motor, smash me like a bug, and then repeatedly drive back and forth over my mass like an insignificant speed bump. If I were Trudy, I'd opt for the naked humiliation parade with the big red, scarlet letter!

And even then, I wouldn't feel satisfied.

All I can do is spare her from ever having to lay eyes on my face. I can't give back what I took, dignity, trust, faith. Maybe by staying away from her, she can take comfort imagining my demise.

We concluded the fifth-step date by burning my scribblings in the firepit. I understood the point.

"It's ashes now. How do you feel?" she asks, wiping soot from her hands.

I wiped the soot off my hands, but the black gunk clung to my heart.

CHAPTER 42

You Love Chinese Food (Sandy)

I WORKED THE STEPS OF AA, the first time, while attending a six-week outpatient treatment facility, strangely alongside Deb's brother. At the time, I didn't know he was the brother of my future wife or that there was a future wife or even if there was a future.

Like-minded, Danny and I both knew we better play nice, if we wanted to convince the courts we're no longer a danger to society. Call it survival. Neither of us wanted Kay, our counselor, to chew on us like the suckers who told the whole truth and nothing but the truth. We took mental notes, watching those poor souls fall victim to her keen ability to fish for the nitty-gritty. Kay's pores oozed truth serum. Once they'd tossed the last morsel of truth, she'd serve them up like chum, hors d'oeuvres for the group to feed on. To withstand, you had to be a master of deception, a gift I'd honed for a lifetime. The trick was to reveal enough details, sating her appetite but not so much as to start a feeding frenzy. If she sensed you were holding back, look out! It's best to confess something outrageous but not too damning, concealing the apocalyptic dirt. For example, I'd admit to cheating on my ex-wife, scandalous but a given for most drunks. But I'd never confess the hatred I felt for myself and the life I'd been given to live.

At the time, I was the manager of a tire shop, a job I felt beneath me. To the group and Kay, I pretended I had it all together. I respected Kay. I may not have bought into her teachings, but later when I wanted a drink, her words kept me sober.

"Alcoholism is a disease, a progressive disease with no cure."

I know the emotions that come with working the inventory steps. I try to be patient with Deb, but she's driving me nuts! Someone please tell her there's no AA cops or teachers slapping hands or handing out prizes. She did a great job writing down her wrongs, enough material for her own set of encyclopedias, but the part about handing it over to God? Not so much. She says so, she wants so, but she's still weeping, beating herself, confessing wrongs to strangers and cornered polite friends. I've told her, as I am sure her sponsor has, "Let go, and let God!" I can't pry her fingers open. No one can. She needs to loosen her grip. The worst part is, now that she's faced and confessed her wrongs, she hates herself and is certain the world agrees. What part of *easy does it* does she not get?

Now like vultures smelling her vulnerability, a flock of weirdo Christians have swooped into our store, cornering Deb, talking up the Bible and Jesus. My bet's on them, prime suspects for filling her head with guilt. One day, Deb came home distraught, after a confrontation with some woman claiming to be a Christian but acting like an entitled, spoiled idiot. You *gotta* love those dimwits who broadcast their Christianity while exercising a heathen will. If I'd been working that day, well, I'm glad for our business that I was not. I'm glad there were witnesses that helped Deb understand she did the right thing by tossing her out. But now, they're hanging out, bringing Deb Bibles and guilt.

It's not my job to protect her. Little Sue is a good sponsor. Deb is doing her best to work the program. I wish she had an ounce of family support. They act like her sobriety is a conspiracy theory, aiming at the obliteration of the McFarland family crest. You'd think I'd learn to listen when Deb warns me about her family. It sounds like an exaggeration but proves 100 percent accurate every time.

We just got back home after a three-day family shenanigans fest—Na-Na's funeral. I would have rather stayed home and stuck sticks in my eyes while sitting in a boiling pot. Then again, no justification seemed worthy of abandoning Deb. Besides, I loved Na-Na too, my only ally in the clan.

The chosen reverend may as well have been a cardboard cutout. Twice, I grabbed Deb's arm, stopping her from stomping out. We knew the reverend had little to go on since he'd never met Na-Na, so having little to say was understandable. But when he made stuff up, portraying her as a stereotypical old lady? Not right. Na-Na deserved better. It was the deadest funeral I'd ever attended, no pun intended.

Afterward, the family gathers at Mac and Dema's. Deb pulls me into the bathroom where the state's arsenal of towels is stored.

"They're going to the Red Lotus to pick up Chinese."

"Okay," I answer, waiting for the list of McFarland instructions I've learned will follow.

"Whatever you do, don't order for yourself. You want whatever they order. And please act happy about it. Do not order anything different. Understand?"

"I don't like Chinese."

"No! You can't do that, please! Just say yes to everything they want and look happy about it. Trust me, you don't want to pay the consequences. Please?"

"Okay."

"And you need to go with to pick up the food."

"What? Why?"

"Trust me, you have to be there to pay. Please, please make sure you hand Dad plenty to cover for all of us. He'll insist you can't pay, but don't listen! Find a way. This is one of those things, okay? Do you understand?"

"Not really."

"Please!"

"Okay, okay. Anything else?"

"Be polite. Stay alert. Be quick and aggressive with your money. Whatever you do, don't complain about Chinese food or do something stupid like order a burger. You love Chinese."

"But I hate Chinese."

"Sandy!"

I'll do whatever she wants. She doesn't need more stress on the day of Na-Na's funeral. In spite of Mac and Danny who do not want me along, I fall in behind them, cash in hand, as they race out the door. Hoping they didn't mean to shut the door in my face, I jog to catch up, diving into the back seat of the car just as Mac steps on the gas. During the fifteen-minute drive to the restaurant, I wonder if they know their plan to ditch me failed. They're whispering and smirking. Feeling like Casper the Ghost, I'm tempted to smack the back of their heads to see if it freaks them out. At the parking lot of the Red Lotus, doors fly open like there's a car bomb detected. I sprint behind them into the restaurant, cash in hand.

Inside, Mac knows the name of all the waitresses. Wong, the owner, greets him like family. I'm ready, arm extended, cash in hand, the phrase "I love Chinese" on my lips. Mac clears his throat, accepts my cash offer, then points to the lounge.

"We'll be right back."

I stand there, looking like a scolded child, feeling as if I'd somehow failed Deb. Do they think the bartender will refuse them service for hanging out with a recovering alcoholic? Not to brag, but I've logged more time in a bar than both of them or at least as much. In my defense, Deb didn't give instructions for this situation.

I sit in a chair with a gold dragon curling off the back. I can see the back of Mac's head and Danny's profile at a table with two generic women. I say generic because, at any given time, there are clones of these women sitting in bars around the world. They're sad, lonely women who seek out men to flatter in exchange for a cocktail and validation that they're not invisible, that they somehow still matter.

Mac's voice carries better than most intercom speakers. In his world of truck-stop cafés, roadside taverns, and smoky lounges known for pouring stiff drinks, he's a welcome celebrity. In a crowd, he's a fun guy, but don't poke his anger behind closed doors. I mostly know Deb's version of Mac. I'm considered the grim reaper at the McFarland's parties, but they have to put up with me on occasion like funerals.

Sitting in the lobby with the children and a designated grandmotherly caretaker, I imagine this is how many children feel hanging on the outside of the *adult-fun circle*. We make alcohol the alluring, *forbidden fruit*. It's no wonder our children chase after it as soon as they can. I'm considering walking out, finding a pay phone to call for Deb to come get me when the cashier interrupts my thoughts.

"Your order is coming right up, sir."

I walk into the lounge under a Chinese dragon and two swords. My near six-foot frame shrinks three feet in façade as I approach the men, commanding them to leave in a pubescent voice. Seemingly ignoring me, they gulp the last of their drinks, each tossing cash on the table, as if privy to a limitless supply. I return to the lobby while they boast goodbyes to the bar babes.

Back at the house, Deb grabs my arm, dragging me down the hall again.

"You paid right?"

"Yeah, but—"

"What? You didn't let Dad give you the money back, did you?"

"No."

"Then what? What's wrong?"

"Nothing."

She doesn't need to know. It would just jam a wedge between us and them, well, a bigger wedge than already exists. After all, this was her life before sobriety. She would have ditched me for the bar too. Now she struggles to feel a part of the family without participating in the family sport, not an easy task. I hate every second of this fiasco. On the upside, I'm closer to Haley and Jay as we hang together outside the drinker's circle. We watch, amused as the others get louder, repetitive, and less witty. To give the impression that the McFarlands are not a loving family would be wrong. Somehow they manage to love and abuse simultaneously, everything ending with hugs and kisses.

If intentions count, then they are model parents. When I return from a quick trip to the bathroom, Haley looks smugly guilty. Jay, the typical little brother that he is, has that "I'm innocent, she did it" face on. I see they both have a Budweiser can concealed under their chairs. Mac grins, winking at them from across the room. Deb's busy working the room, wanting acceptance. She loves her family deeply, and they love her, but there are rules, family expectations, bonds not thicker, but as thick as blood. Unspoken, loudly stated laws or coat of arms—McFarland's work, drink, and love with a vengeance. Take one of the three things out of the equation, and your loyalty is maimed.

Seated at the table, eating nasty Chinese food, Haley looks at me dryly, points to the plastic tarp placed under the designated chairs for her and Jay and asks, "At what age will Grandma Dema trust me to eat at the table without plastic under my chair?"

"Maybe twenty-one for you, but your brother may be tarped for life."

Deb looks our way, both curious and relieved at the sound of our laugher. Danny motions for her to follow him outside. Things have been tense between them since she

233

quit drinking. It's good for them to take some time alone together. She told me on the way here, she hopes that when he sees the improvement in her life, he will consider going to an AA meeting. I kept quiet.

Less than five minutes later, she returns, face scrunched like when she's in pain or worried.

"He doesn't believe I'm sober. He pulled a beer out of his pocket. When I wouldn't drink it, he lit a cigarette and handed it to me . . . said he knew I still drank and smoked. He stuck his finger in my face . . . called me a phony liar."

"I'm sorry."

"He's drunk. I don't think he even knows what he's saying. Losing Na-Na, it's too hard for all of us. She was the good in all things. And not just for us kids, look at mom. Without Na-Na, who will . . . who will . . . be different? We all loved her, even though, maybe even because she stood aside. She never left us, loved us through it all. Now she's gone. Mom is a mess. Taking her out of this family is like turning the lights off."

"It will be okay, sweetie."

"You don't understand. It won't be okay."

The funeral day was excruciating. What followed the next day was worse.

You know that scene in the old black-and-white movie with the horse-drawn hearse, followed by wailing old ladies in black? Well, we're playing that scene in living color, a four-hour scene from Auburn to Brewster, replacing the cool old hearse with three carloads of bickering family members. Na-Na left in the hearse yesterday. I wish I could have ridden with her.

CHAPTER 43

Do You Want to End Up Like This?
(Deb)

JANUARY 21, 1998, A MUNDANE Wednesday for the nurses at Yakima Memorial Hospital. For them, miracles are like lattes, sunshine, a kind word expected, taken for granted.

After hugging the team of nurses, I watch as they walk out of the room, high-spirited in a ho-hum, just another midweek miracle kind of way. How do they do it? I'm jumping around like the bride of Frankenstein, super-charged, wired, fired up with waving jazz hands.

They're going home to eat a ham sandwich and sleep.

Sleep? On the day our grandson, Evan Thomas Garfein, came onto the scene?

I wait as Jon, the dad, holds his son, restraining my urge to beg "Gimme, gimme, gimme!"

I'm grateful beyond human capacity, a zillion prayers have been sent up the heavenly staircase by me, Sandy, the group of oddballs that hang at the store, and about half a dozen customers who made the mistake of asking, "How's it going?"

And God's answer? A healthy birth and delivery of a magnificent baby boy. At last, it's my turn to hold this miracle in my arms. I feel light-headed, faint, overcome with wonder. I find myself praying, begging God to equip me to be the grandmother worthy of this child. Gratitude exudes from my heart, seeing, knowing that this is a second chance, a new beginning. I ask for gumption and courage to be strong and wise. Please, God, let me be like my Na-Na, unselfish, loving, and life-giving. Amen.

Before the *amen* rests, new doubts emerge. Can God handle part B of the miracle? Haley is not ready or willing to be a mom. She's highly capable: smart, caring, kind, responsible, loving, and as a parental bonus, she's gifted with a keen sense of humor. Nonetheless, she lacks motivation and patience, and her degree of stubbornness is off the charts. Once, while learning to drive, she backed into a car. Frustrated, she jumps out, leaving Sandy and me as passengers, stomps her foot, and flatly states, "I'm not doing this!" Experiences like that conjure visions of our grandson standing bowlegged, a heavy load in his diaper crying for assistance as she swipes her hands and resigns as a mom, stating her disclaimer, "Sorry, I don't like babies."

I can't deny God carried her through the labor and birth steps, but she couldn't exactly get up off the table and say "forget it, I'm *outta* here!" I didn't think I could withstand seeing my baby girl in pain, yet I was oddly at peace.

Maybe God?

If he could calm my fears, might he also change Haley's heart? Between labor pains, I witnessed the look of motherhood on her face, searching the eyes of the nurses for assurance her baby was healthy. Again, holding Evan in her arms for the first time, I met Haley, the mother, beaming, checking toes and fingers, soaking in perfection.

The prayers are answered. Our incredible blessing born. Now what? None of us have talked. My silence comes from fear and not knowing what to do, say, or expect. Sandy hasn't said a word, but I know the looks. I've listened to him grumble for years about friends who married, unknowing they would be raising the wife's grandkids. He points them out at the grocery store or a yard sale. He tells their story with the same passion as a prisoner of war tale.

"See that guy, the one holding the box of Pampers. That's Steve. He lived down the block from us. We went to school together. He married some gal Susan, no, Andrea. Anyway, her daughters started popping out babies, then the lazy, unemployed boyfriends moved in. Now Steve pays the bills, even babysits. There's no way I'd ever help raise a bunch of lazy kids, kids . . . not ever!"

Thus, when the word *pregnant* birthed into reality, we stopped talking. What can I say? If ever my daughter needs me, it's now. I'm not deserting her. One brave moment, I told Sandy that I feel like this is a second chance to do what's right. He sat with no expression and gave no response. I've learned this is his way of trying to make things disappear, as if they will all go away if he doesn't react to them. From the start, I've minced no words: "This baby will be a blessing!"

Some days, I'm certain this will be the end of our marriage. Other times, I have that odd peace thing going on. But the need to stand up and fight for my daughter and grandbaby is constant. I'm like a centurion on a mission to slaughter all shame. When I issued the command to my parents, my tone clearly warned them of an attack if they did not follow my order.

"Well, of course, it will be a blessing. Calm down. We love Haley."

They do love Haley, even if pregnant out of wedlock. Yet they're known for serving love up with a huge helping of shame for dessert. I doubt my sister Nancy will ever out-live the traumatizing love they showered on her, all under the good-intention racket. I don't think I will either. No one told me what was going on. She lived with girlfriends in an apartment in Tacoma. They tried to keep us apart, but one day, they messed up. I was watching TV when Nancy's stomach entered the room, two seconds before the rest of her.

Later that night, Danny and I were ordered to wait in the den because they wanted to have a talk with us. I don't know what poor Danny thought. He'd seen her before, but no explanation had been given. In retrospect, I should have known something was up. There were clues: whispers, red faces, and Nancy never being around. Waiting for them, we heard Dad's mighty voice booming from down the hall. Mom showed alone, Dad's absence, a clear statement.

My mother's actions and words don't always match her heart. I'd seen it before. Her face reads easy. When free to act on her heart, there is no mom with more love to give than her. But often, situations replace the heart's desires with fear. As she spoke, I heard the lies. She's wasn't lying to us but to herself, wanting dearly to believe her own words.

The speech went something like this: "Did you notice that Nancy has gained some weight?"

"Giggles." We couldn't help it.

Exhaling, she continues.

"A terrible thing has happened. She got herself pregnant. The man won't marry her. She's eighteen. The choice is up to her. We did *not* interfere. It's her decision. Your father and I didn't say a word. But we certainly are in no position to help. She met with Reverend Unruh. You remember him? He helped her make the right decision. She's decided on her own that it would be best to give the baby up for adoption."

There she sat, speaking as if reading the news on television, red hair curled into an updo, rose lipstick perfectly applied, eyebrows tweezed and arched. Yet her face reads like a behind-the-scenes script of feelings: helplessness, brokenness, sorrow, and *guilt*. If you've ever suffered guilt, the purest form, of which eats you alive or watched someone wither away from it, you know the look. Danny and I just wanted her to quit hurting. Nancy must have been hidden away in a large closet. After the talk, we looked for her, knowing not to ask.

She appeared three days later, Friday night at the Auburn Drive-in Theatre. I was busy learning the art of hickeys in the back seat of some guy's Chevy Impala. The movie *To Sir with Love* scratched over the car speaker.

I had just created my first *hickey* masterpiece when I hear my sister's voice.

"Get out here, right now, Debbie! Look at me! Do you want to end up like this?"

She's bent down, hands parenthesis-style at the sides of her face, peering in the window. She works here, or did, before the whole incognito pregnant scam. Still, it's dark, and no one is watching the movie because they're all giving each other Hoover-strength hickeys. How did she find me? When I wiped the steam off the window, my newfound hickey instructor jumped with a start. There she stood in her faux white fur coat like an angry knocked-up polar bear ready to rip us apart.

Knowing the true motive behind her act of concern, I felt sincere compassion for her. She could care less if I got struck pregnant by a wild hickey. Sadly, she was looking out for herself, not me. Saving little sister might earn her a pinch of favor with Mom and Dad. Knowing the shame she carried and desperately wanted out of, it almost made up for my being the most humiliated, embarrassed teen in all the universe.

I knew, Danny knew, Mom knew Nancy did not have a choice. Saying she did is no different than telling a person standing in a burning building that they can choose to stay if they want. Without saying the words, it was understood that if she kept the baby, they would be disappointed and forever unavailable. Do I believe they would have actually deserted her? Tossed their daughter and grandbaby to the wolves? No.

But what I know, Nancy knows, and Mom knows is this: Accepting help from people who resent giving it is way worse than being eaten by a pack of jagged-toothed wolves. Thus, leaving adoption the only choice. One selection on the menu does not equate choice.

Against the rules, allegedly enforced by the adoption authorities, shortly after the birth, a nurse whispered in Nancy's ear.

"Twin redheaded boys . . . beautiful! Perfect! Twins!"

I guess Mom told me this to heighten the pain of the event so I would not follow suit. The nurse must have believed if Nancy knew, she would change her mind. Years later, Nancy married, and they had two boys. Just once, I asked about the twins if she ever thought about trying to find them.

"I was told to live my life as if this never occurred. And that's what I do."

It's not for me to say what she feels or to blame a life battered by poor choices and alcohol abuse on a single life event. I can only imagine how I would feel.

Now, listen up!

I declare this baby, my grandson, a blessing! The world be warned. Keep your shame machetes at bay. Evan Thomas Garfein will be celebrated, with or without Sandy, my family, the neighbors, or all mankind.

CHAPTER 44

Full Throttle
(Sandy)

PRIDE AND HUMILITY DUKE IT out as I stand in Harvard Square sandwiched between the giant incubators of genius, MIT and Harvard. I'm in Boston to see Nanette receive her well-deserved mechanical-engineering degree from MIT, the crown-of-proud-dad moments.

The battle is between the apex of watching my daughter realize her dream and the abyss of the destruction of my own ambitions. Like Nanette, I was head of my class. The fork in my road surely must be at the corner of Success Avenue/Success Lane. All I had to do was choose. A pilot, an architect, a civil engineer, or all three—no worrisome choices ahead for me. No doubts. I had it all, the intelligence, the will, the means, and more than enough *cocksurety*. But, by golly, my fork had an extra tine. Unlike my daughter, I chose to succumb to the alcoholic gene that would wash away my street to success.

Down the block, I see Stephanie and her boyfriend, Sean, walking toward the square, our agreed meeting place. When Nanette and Barney show, we'll be off to tour historical Boston—the quaint family portrait. I stretch a smile across my face for Stephanie.

"Hey, little one, how ya doin', Sean?"

Stephanie's normally an easy smile. Whether a toddler leaping into my arms, crazy corkscrew curls jiggling, or now a budding woman quizzing me from deep beyond her brown eyes, she brings joy to my heart—a miracle feat considering my mood. I feel as if I've been dragged behind a truck, tarred, feathered, stoned, and now I must act like I'm having the time of my life.

Four days earlier, on Monday, my self-appointed paperwork day, I received a call from Marcia Albright, a stand-in supervisor for the child-services unit. I assume she needs some information on one of my clients. Usually, the information exchanges take place in the hall, almost like passing notes in high school, but this time, she asked me to come to her office. Motioning for me to sit, she shuffles some files across the desk, then back again.

"Sandy, I am sorry, but you are one of the counselors who will not have a job here come September."

For a moment, I think she might be playing a joke. Even though every year at this time there's talk of RIF (reduction in force), I wasn't concerned. During the three and a half years since I'd been hired, I'd become the *golden boy* in child services. I'm the counselor with the heftiest caseload whose paperwork is exemplary, who's given the hard cases because I get the job done. Just ask my boss, Joyce Delgado, the head of child services. She tells everyone how much she appreciates my work, even points to me as an example to the others. I guess, like any sucker who just got hit by a lightning bolt, I'm asking, why me?

But for now, I need to grab Stephanie, hug a bit too tight and hope she doesn't guess my charade. I won't spoil this for them. It's Nanette's time, not mine. I drank away my chance to grab the brass ring, fell off the horse per se. I should be living the future she's starting, but I'm not.

Stephanie's *feelings* antenna scans my face, picking up signals.

"You okay, Dad?"

"Yes, just tired from the flight."

Just looking at her makes me feel better. I'm the luckiest dad ever, knowing both my daughters have bright futures. In her first year at WWU, like her sister, she slam dunks whatever she sets out to do. Guess, she's probably going to marry this pimply faced kid standing next to her. They're high-school sweethearts. He's an okay kid, a jock from a well-to-do family. Not near good enough, but who is?

I take a deep breath, preparing for round two of charades as Nanette and Barney approach. Seeing my ex, I remember her most annoying trait—asking nonstop questions in the peppy spirit of good conversation. People change, right? Maybe she doesn't do that anymore.

"Good morning, Sandy! How are you? How's Deb? The job? Your mom and dad? Did you have a good flight?"

Feigning deafness, I grab Nanette for another slightly too tight hug. I choke back, determined tears hiding my face in her shoulder, praying for composure. My emotions are zinging around like a pinball machine: joy and pride for my baby girl who told me at age four, "I want to graduate from MIT, Daddy;" admiration and respect for her determination and hard work to realize her dream; regret and remorse for my own failures. I order my emotions to behave, releasing her from the hug. Barney is waiting patiently for her answers, assuming I'll get to them after the hug. Good luck with that.

She's just being friendly, but still, I don't want to lie, and I won't spoil Nanette's big moment with my balloon-busting news. Besides, talking about it makes it worse. The anger boils up the "why me?" They all knew I was good at my job. The only difference is that I didn't chummy up with my coworkers. Sorry, I was too busy doing my job to smooch my way to popularity.

Like a good soldier, I take my place next to Nanette, serving as lead and guard between me and Barney. Stephanie and Sean fall in behind, side by side. To strangers' eyes, we look like we belong together. If Deb were here, I'd feel better. We told everyone she needed to take care of our business at home, a partial truth. Honestly, with the loss of my job, we couldn't afford for both of us to go. I wish she were here, oohing and aahing over the architecture, asking me questions about Paul Revere's ride, elbowing me to answer Barney's questions.

Barney and I made great kids; from there, we don't have much in common, at least not anymore. She's a ceaseless reminder of the man I am not. The man I don't want to be. When she looked at me, her heart pitter-pattered for the man I could become. Deb loves me now, as is.

Nanette leads us to the cusp of Boston and Cambridge where Harvard and MIT tower historic intelligence. Knowing my sense of humor, she points out the adult sex store sandwiched between the giants of intellect, sporting leather goods and a size 14 high-heel shoe in the window. While the five of us stand laughing at the anomaly, Nanette's giggle sends me back to a time nearly twenty years ago. If I had to pick a memory to stay stuck in the rest of my life, this is at the top of the list. Nanette, less than two, weighing a whopping thirty-five pounds or so sits in front of me, straddling the gas tank of my Bultaco 175 cycle. She lets out little squeals of joy as we dip down into the ditch. Then, as we surge to the top, her head swings back, turning her squeaks to a hearty full throttle laugh. I love that sound! That moment will always be how I think of her. I see it in everything she does, whether playing sports or acing an exam. Full throttle.

After playing family tourist, I returned to my hotel room. Pretending to be okay is exhausting. I talk with Deb on the phone, just long enough to tell her how much I wish she were here. Later, failing to sleep, I make a familiar choice of locations to unwind—the lounge. Sitting at the bar, drinking grapefruit juice, I fill the barkeeper's ears with stories of how great my life is. Luckily, he was the cardboard cutout type that just listens and never ask questions. I kept the subject on my amazing daughters and off of me.

I want to hang on to the good moments, like my day alone with Nanette antiquing, finding a necklace that promises to send Deb dancing about the room, singing, "It's gorgeous!" The tour of MIT, a night at the Philharmonic Symphony, even the never-ending snore of a ceremony was worth it for the moment my Nanette reached her little hand out to take her degree. The 2,000-plus crowd witnessed a graceful young woman take the walk of scholars.

I saw my little girl, head back, guffawing at the world.

I returned home, exhausted from the highs and lows. If the fat man hogging the armrest next to me on the plane would have asked me about my life, I may have told him it was over. Thankfully, he didn't ask.

CHAPTER 45

The Buffalo and His Brother
(Deb)

ASSUMED NAME TAGS MESS WITH my head. They always have. Titles like wife, mother, divorcee, dangling with unwritten instructions, dripping in expectations. Life flicks by, like the photos in a flip book from out a box of Cracker Jacks. I don't know how I got from point A to point B, a blurred journey, a traveled road, of which there's no recollection.

Like now—Kapow! Kazam!—we're grandparents. How'd that happen? I can speak for both of us when I say that this is not on our *to-do* list. It's not on a *to-don't* list or any list. Like grave plots or funeral plans, we have other priorities. Thinking about that stuff is like dwelling on your digestive system while a delectable chocolate melts in your mouth. As for Sandy? One day, light-heartedly, I mention growing old together. He responds, "Well, I don't plan on getting old, so you'd better not either." I laugh. Then I realize, he's not kidding.

Granted, he may not win the old fart battle, but like the Terminator, he'll keep getting back up claiming, "I'll be back" until beaten by inevitability. After he lost his job at CWCMH, he stood up, returned to college, and earned a Master's Degree, all while working as a para ed and helping me with our busy store. After a stint of graveyard and swing shifts at a drug and alcohol treatment center for teenage felons, he accepted the position as a counselor for primary age students in Naches, a rural bedroom community of Yakima.

At 6:00 a.m., he starts each day making coffee for the AA meeting at the church down the street from our house, leaving the meeting ten minutes early for work. Minutes found are spent renovating our home, sanding floors, scraping popcorn plaster off the ceiling, refinishing woodwork, painting, or hunting treasures for our antique shop. He's happy. I'm happy for him. The hitch is this: The *screw-you-nose-thumbing babe* Sandy fell in love with has changed. It's as if God pinned my eyelids back, forcing me to see the dust bunnies I've swept under the rug. Jay, leaving for college, swept out a pile of regrets from under the bed. The perpetual ticking of the timer ends with a sharp ding— *time's up!* Put away all plans to spend more time, fix things, make up for do-over. The gong has sounded.

Jay is drinking and possibly doing drugs. The out-of-character tattletale being, he is breaking promises.

"Jay, I only ask that I know where you are. If you are going to stay out all night, I need to know. Please."

"No worries, Mom. I'll be home early tonight, I promise."

Around 4:00 a.m., I got out of bed, driving around in the locally named *hole* of Yakima, imagining horrors and praying God would take care of my son. He didn't show until the next afternoon, with a fresh batch of promises. I called Little Sue.

"Let go, and let God," she said.

I did. For nearly thirty minutes.

God plucked Jay from Washington state, out of my arms' reach. I'm proud and happy he's enrolled at ITT Tech in Arizona. But I didn't expect the empty nest to feel like an abduction. I wasn't done. I wanted to make things right, fix the wrongs. The week he left for college, I called my sponsor obsessively. One day, after a heavy sigh, she gave me a task.

"Make yourself a God can."

"What's that?" I asked.

Turns out, it's a coffee can with a slit cut in the lid for a slot. Whenever I'm obsessing about things I can do nothing about, I'm to jot it on a scrap of paper, slip it into the slot and say, "I can't, but God can!" At this rate, I may need more than one as it's filling up fast with folded scraps scribbled with JAY.

Keeping your eyes open, tossing denial to the wind, choosing to live life aware and act responsibly is not an easy thing to do sober and impossible if you're not. By the frequency that people remind me to *let go and let God,* I don't think I'm progressing as fast as some in the program. The clichés sound great. I can even say I mean them when I spit them out, but they don't stick. It's like those silly exercises psychologists have you do, like standing in front of the mirror proclaiming how beautiful you are. Wouldn't that work better without the mirror? The problem is, my denial skills are no longer viable, and even seventy-two zillion AA clichés cannot tame my beast: *progress not perfection; easy does it; it works if you work it; first things first; live and let live.* I'm not saying they don't work, just not for me. At best, they have a fleeting placebo effect. After which, I remember I'm an adulteress, a liar, a wretch, and a coward. There's no sugar-coated cliché for that.

Along with working the program, I've been reading the Bible. My pride of a college degree is not helping me understand this book. Most times, I feel like I might as well be reading a Latin or secret-code version. But then I'll come along a phrase (scripture, I guess you'd call it) that not only rings clear but also brings peace. I even memorized a few to hang on to. My go-to verse is "For God did not give us a spirit of fear but of power and of love and of self-control" (2 Timothy 1:7).

When anxiety pecks at my skull like a hungry vulture, I say the words until the nasty thing flies away. One thing that helps my understanding of the Bible is listening to Christian radio while driving to our store in Ellensburg. I have to laugh at the timing. I will have just read about David dancing around in his undies or Peter's miraculous prison escape, and I click on the radio hearing the same scripture. Even weirder than the radio syncing to my scripture readings is that my customers seem to all be Bible-reading churchgoers who turn every conversation to God. I don't know how it happens. A generic guy in a suit will approach the counter to buy a Victorian jewelry casket for his wife. In less than a minute, the conversation turns from Queen Victoria's persnicketiness to the Queen of Sheba and on to the Bible. And stranger than that is finding myself reciting one of the few scriptures I've memorized to a customer who confided the news that her husband is seriously ill. The scripture just happens to be one she knows, and she thanks me for bringing it to mind. Weird stuff. And it happens every day. It's getting hard to deny that God is, well, hanging around me.

I know I feel different than I ever have. Maybe it's peace. I don't know. I do know I'm different, almost confident, nearly comfortable in my own skin. The name tag grandma or nana, in my case, fits like a snuggly slipper. I have a second chance to do things right. Haley is a good mom, loving and committed. My heart is to come alongside her to help. I'm grateful my worry that she is the *anti-mom* is wrong. I have the perfect nana setup, with them living in our backyard rental house. I take Evan whenever I can. My friends ask if being a grandma makes me feel old. I don't understand it myself, but giggling with my grandboy makes me feel young.

I try to stay clear of Sandy, give him space, but he hovers over Evan like a fairy tale Papa Bear. Evan's nature is pure joy. Who doesn't want to be around that? The other evening, I'm in the basement folding laundry. I didn't hear Haley come in with Evan and leave. Climbing the stairs with a basket of clothes, I see Sandy holding him like a sack of spuds, singing some silly song and dancing a jig like he's Jiminy Cricket. The song had something to do with a buffalo and his brother. Staying quiet, I watch and listen, amazed. When the song ends, I ask, "What are you singing?"

"I wasn't singing," he says.

I'm hopeful.

CHAPTER 46

I'm Done With Kiddiegarden (Sandy)

A YEAR AGO, I'M LYING next to Deb, ready to indulge in some play time, when a tear drops on my chest.

"What's wrong, sweetie?"

"Nothing."

"What do you mean nothing, you're crying."

"I'm sad because we'll never have a baby together. I'd love to play mommy and daddy with you. It's a special time. I wish we could have shared it. Wouldn't you like to have a baby together?"

Ladies and gentleman, the mood has left the room, the planet, the universe. Dead, gone, kaput! Since we've both had procedures rendering us sterile, I respond, confident my true feelings are safe.

"Sure."

Six months later, Deb announced we're having a baby, via Haley! How did a phantasmal, buzz-killer conversation reap a bouncing baby boy? Am I the victim of a spell? A hex?

I don't want a baby. I like things as they are. No! I won't be *that guy* raising his wife's grandkids. Not happening.

To my surprise and relief, Haley stepped up to the mom plate. I was certain she'd stomp her foot at first base, yell foul, and walk off, expecting me and Deb to finish the game. I respect Deb for wanting to stand by her daughter. She sees this as a second chance to do things right. That's all fine and dandy as long as I am not expected to be the *sucker* grandpa, holding a pile of bills and changing diapers.

The other day, Deb is in the basement folding clothes when Haley drops the baby by for some *Na-Na time.* I figure the little guy might start fussing when she left, so I walk over to his carrier. He smiles at me like I am a giant sugar teat. For some reason, the kid likes me. When I take him out of his carrier because he seems uncomfortable, he looks me in the eye and laughs, an invitation to play. For a baby, he's kind of cool. It must be Deb's persistent commands proclaiming, "This baby will be a blessing!"

I guess it won't kill me to hang out with him once in a while, even change a few diapers, as long as it's on my terms. We can take naps together, have a few laughs. But if they expect me to be responsible, I'm done. Things are finally going my way. Come hell, high water or babies, I'm not giving up my life. I get paid to play with kindergartners and first graders. After years dealing with gangbangers, felon parents, or worse, my problems have switched from finding a semi-automatic pistol on the van to little Miss Sierra's independence issues.

The first weeks of school, I cruise and observe returning first graders and kindergarten recruits. One square-peg cutie with orange frizzy hair dons a subliminal T-shirt reading, "Attention Counselors, I am a behavior problem." Within hours, Sierra becomes the number one name dropped by teachers and staff.

"Sierra, sit down. Sierra, come back. Sierra, stay put."

Three days into the first week, Sierra ups her game, moving me from observation to red alert. Ten minutes before lunch, she saunters over to the playground door, collects her pink quilted parka with the fake fur hood and purple Barney backpack from the row of hooks. Returning to her desk, she packs up crayons and papers and, as if late for a prestigious appointment, heads for the exit.

"Sierra, you need to come sit down. We'll be going to lunch soon," I say, pointing to her empty desk.

For Sierra, the trial membership has ended. She'd made her decision. Looking my way in a strikingly adult manner, she replies, "I'm going home. I don't like it here. I'm done with *kiddiegarden*."

"I see, but look outside, Sierra," I say, as she looks out the window. "There's no bus to take you home. Why don't you stay and have lunch with me in the lunchroom? Today is Cheese Zombie day. I'm hungry. Are you?"

After a momentary contemplative delay, she returns to her desk. Seated with arms across her chest and pink sparkly shoes swinging to and fro, she waits for Miss Stevens to announce, "Please line up to wash hands." Lunch is when I do my finest work. I never bother to check the lunchroom patrol rotation schedule because I always eat with the kids. I prefer the deafening squeals of the short squad over the drowsy drone in the teacher's lounge. The cafeteria is my laboratory where trust is earned. Upon entering, tiny fingers point and yell, "*Mr. Pommer* with the mole." I'm a celebrity of sorts, rather like Barney or Big Bird; only instead of yellow feathers or purple fur, it's a mole. The button-like mole protrudes from the center of my forehead. Like magic when pressed, my tongue shoots out of my mouth, causing mass giggles and clamoring to please "do it again."

With Sierra at my side, I inform the crowd that the magical mole is out of order today. She tags along, aping my moves, as I slide a plastic tray across the stainless-steel table, accepting a zombie and a carton of chocolate milk from the lunch ladies. She follows me to a sparse table, sitting across from me but not making eye contact. As she bites into the cheesy warm dough, I proceed with care.

"Cheese Zombies are my favorite. What do you think?"

"Okay," she answers, diving for another bite.

"You don't like school?"

"No."

"Why not?"

"I like it at home better."

"What would you do at home?"

"I'd play with my toys."

"Yeah. I like to play with toys too. Did you know I have boxes of Legos in my office? Big ones, little ones, I even have a box of all pink ones."

"I want to go home."

"I know. But if you go now, you'll miss recess. I thought we could play four square with some of the other kids. What do you think?"

Once Sierra got involved playing with other kids, convincing her to stay until the next recess was easy. She just needed a reason to stay and put up with the classroom busy work. Some of my little guys with tough home lives need a little more than Sierra's easy fix. My specialty is called play therapy; my tools are Legos, picture books, puppets, and the infamous magical mole.

I look forward to Tuesdays and Thursdays at school. I'm hoping soon the position will become full-time. Sundays and Mondays, I work at the store, giving Deb a break. Wednesdays, I hate. We invested in a fourplex located in my childhood stomping grounds. It may not have been the (S)Nob Hill region of Yakima, but back then, it was a hearty, healthy place to grow up. Today, it's gangland, known for drive-by shootings, drugs, and graffiti. Deb and I agreed to invest in property; from there, we disagreed.

"How can I be a landlord of a place I would never live in? If you do this, I won't be involved. I will concentrate on our other business."

It's been a great investment. It's making money. It's just not as easy as at first. Wednesdays (and other times I won't admit) I haul off garbage from overloaded dumpsters, spray for cockroaches, fill fist-sized holes in the drywall, paint over graffiti, and the worst job, beg tenants to pay their rent. It's crazy. I carefully screen potential renters, selecting honest, vulnerable people who need a hand up, like single parents or recovering alcoholics. The kind of people I know will appreciate the help and the person who trusted and took a chance on them. I watch them move in, proud to have played a part in their journey to a better life. All is hunky-dory until the next month's rent is due. That's when my down-and-outer, who just needs a chance, turns into an actor, a liar, a schemer, and an ace-system user. The sweet twenty-something mom moves her drug-dealer boyfriend in; the single dad quits going to work, stays home watching

The Price is Right, drinking cases of Budweiser beer; and the white-haired bun-topped grandmother disappears leaving her gangbanger son and homies a place to flop and trash. I believed I could be a kind, understanding landlord, earning respect and fair treatment. Instead, around the first of every month, I knock on doors that have voices behind them but never a soul to answer. Resorting to tricks, I wait, cornering them late at night or on a day they don't expect me, only to hear sad tales and promises. Wanting to believe and not having anything more than threats, I extend the rent a week, then two, until I have no choice but to hope they will do as promised and pay double next month. Inevitably, owing months of back rent, they disappear in the middle of the night, leaving the onetime pristine apartment needing new carpet, drywall, and appliances.

It drives Deb crazy.

"I love that about you. You want to see the good in people. But I hate watching them treat you like this."

"You mean, I'm a sap."

"Well, there's that too."

CHAPTER 47

Our Communications Officer (Deb)

THE FRONT DOOR SLAMS, FOLLOWED by the thud of a chair hitting the hardwood floor. Sadly, of late, door slams, furniture tantrums, and fluent blue words are the norm.

"What's wrong?" I ask, lifting the chair to its upright position.

"They told me to leave . . . never come back! They won't listen to me. They just want to throw drugs at me and wave goodbye."

I know better than to ask questions. Sandy needs to unravel organically. My heart sinks as he shares what happened at the medical clinic. I understand his side, but I also know how he's been lately and suspect the people at the clinic may have feared for their lives.

The havoc began three months ago in the midst of moving 3,600 square feet of antiques across the street to a 2,400-square-foot building. With a perpetual "I'm fine," Sandy ignored his twenty-five-year-old back injury. By the time the move was over, his occasional severe pain turned constant and unbearable. Throughout the night, he paces, unable to sit or recline for more than moments at a time. The good news? He's finally doing something about the chronic pain he's lived with for a quarter century. The bad news? He needs a GP referral before the surgery can take place, and he has zero patience left to handle it. The surgery appointment is all set for April. The referral is only needed to appease the insurance gods.

Sitting in Dr. Bronson's office in Spokane, getting a referral seemed a cinch. The problems began when Sandy told the doctor at the clinic he didn't want painkillers because he's an alcoholic. The doctor's flippant, dismissing response leaves me to wonder if he has his own issues, a consumer or a codependent by-product. It doesn't matter. The fact is, he tossed Sandy out of the office, sending a letter banning us (yes, me too) from the property. When I asked Sandy how he managed to get us banned from a medical clinic, he said, "I don't know." Later, he dropped a few hints.

"I asked him if he fell off a turnip truck."

In his defense, the doctor had no understanding of alcoholism or consideration that Sandy has been zombified by pain and no sleep for months. Still, what doctor is going to let a patient yell at him?

I let him rant. The next day, he made an appointment with a new doctor. There's nothing I can do but pray. When you're living 24/7 in level 10 pain, you have one desire: to be free of it. All my good intentioned "Can I get you? Are you hungry? What can I do for you?" questions feel like a pointy finger, poking the spot that hurts.

I miss the gentle soul I've taken for granted. He comes home from work exhausted, excruciatingly aware that relief is not in range. I don't know how he manages standing or kneeling all day working with children. He's working in Naches and Moxee as well, finally attaining full-time by combining jobs in two school districts. He refuses to take sick leave, saying he won't feel any less pain at home. By the time I get home from the store, he's raging at the thought of spending another sleepless night.

I miss his laugh. The last time was months ago. I walked in the door after work, arms loaded with vintage clothing needing to be laundered and steamed. Sandy was on the sofa, tears streaming down his face, body shaking as he attempted to quiet his laughter. He holds a finger to his lips, motioning for me to be still, and look at Evan who is on the telephone.

"He's been talking to that telemarketer for five minutes," he whispers. "They asked to speak to the person in charge of our long-distance service, so I handed the phone to our communications officer."

At age two, Evan loves to talk, long, bubbly conversations that have no beginning or end. As if trained in telemarketing combat, he's holding the caller hostage. He keeps jabbering in his own made-up language that no one can decipher because Evan carries the only translation in his head.

Whenever I watch Sandy with our grandson, I fall in love with him all over again. A pair of toddlers, one small, one large, exploring whatever is in front of them. Whether tossing wooden spools down the stairs or building avant-garde structures out of scraps of this and that, they are in the land of Peter Pan, sailing on a sea of joy. Their world is not easy for me to enter. I've spoiled their fun more than once, thinking structure will improve the project or rules will enhance the game. I admire Sandy's ability to let a child be—think up wild stuff, act it out, taste it, see it, be it. It's what he refers to as play therapy. It's a magical world where a child is more than enough, just as is. My heart bursts with pride to be the grandma next to this grandpa. Again, something proclaiming to label me as old makes me feel beautiful.

Not wanting Evan to see Sandy in pain, we've kept the visits short. Understandably, Sandy wants to be left alone. I'm doing my best to give him space. I've grown curious about church. I even made a list of potential tryouts based on recommendations from people in the program that I'm surprised like church. I'm not up to walking into a church, hearing a collective gasp at the audacity of me showing up. I want to check it out incognito, if that's possible. Besides, I don't have patience for people who've lived a sheltered life. You know, the ones that always have an umbrella, extra toilet paper, and tons of advice on subjects they know nothing about. If they find out the things I've done, their brains will explode. At the top of the list is the Vineyard Christian Church. Little Sue says it's good but warns, "Some who went there never returned to AA." That's kind of scary, but it can't hurt to check it out. I'm hoping Sandy will go too.

CHAPTER 48

Obsessive Compulsive God Disorder (Sandy)

FACE DOWN ON A GURNEY prepped for surgery, I surrender to the anesthesia with three prayers: First, that I would not wake up a cripple; second, that I would not wake up at all if it meant living with this pain; third, that God's will be done in correlation with the first two disclaimers.

Four hours later, I wake up thinking I'm dreaming because the pain is weighing in between two and three. Did I need the morphine drip glistening glory from the hanging plastic bag whispering, "Press my button, big boy?" Who cares! I've earned the right to push the heaven button. Thank you, God! I survived. I'm not in pain, and I can wiggle my toes. For years, random people have hunted me down, force-feeding me nightmarish tales of epic back surgery failures. Had it not been for my daughters, I would not have taken the chance. I was granted a speedy surgery date because Stephanie happens to work in Dr. Bronson's clinic. She's been campaigning for me to get surgery for years. Nanette researched the knife-wielding surgeon, noted as the best in the Northwest. Basically, they tag teamed me.

I spend the first night in the hospital. The next morning, after checking his work and hearing my claim of level two pain, the doctor releases me, not for travel but to stay with Deb across the street in a closet-sized room let out by Sacred Heart. When the nurse leans in, preparing to unplug Mother Morphine, I press the button for one last boost because I could. If all goes well, tomorrow I'll be checked and released to travel the 200 miles back to Yakima. Nothing can spoil my mood, lying in bed next to my sweetie, floating on morphine, celebrating victory over a life of pain.

That is until Deb's lemon-yellow flip phone rings.

"Hi, Dad. No . . . no, we're in Spokane. Remember? Sandy's back surgery? What? Mom? What happened? Oh no, Dad, no, I can't come right away. Sandy can't travel until tomorrow. Okay, I know. Okay. All right. Call me later."

Good old McFarland drama swooping down to kill my buzz. I should have asked for a doggy bag of morphine. Dema is in the hospital, but I doubt that it's serious. I like Dema; she's full of life, never idle. But never underestimate her power as the known, but never spoken, family matriarch. Next to Dema, the godfather is a weenie. Even now in a hospital bed 300 miles away, she's floating above us like a dark cloud. Deb, who was catering to my every need, is now on the phone, covering shifts at the store so she can race to her mom's side.

It's guilt. Last summer, she led a brother-sister SWAT-team intervention on Dema. What a disaster that was. She prepped Danny to *stay strong, no matter what*. Then, before the first tear fully formed in her mom's eye, she broke, apologizing for even thinking she might be an alcoholic. That's the kind of power Dema holds. Amusingly, to me at least, it was too late to take back the call Deb made to Dema's doctor, defining "one drink a day" as a sixteen-ounce tumbler, refreshed as needed until bedtime. Three days after the hapless intervention, a social worker came knocking at Dema's door. Deb's information leak to the doctor, comes with a life-long warranty of consequence. Dema did quit drinking, but now every conversation with her daughter includes clarification that she was not, is not, and never will be an alcoholic along with the addendum: "Having to sit there with that social worker was the most humiliating thing I have ever experienced."

To the McFarland's, oozing open-sore leprosy is less disgusting than sobriety. And now, Deb and I are both to blame for diluting the purity of the alcohol levels in the family gene pool. She still greets us with her sincere hugs and gracious inviting smile but not without stating her new mantra.

"I only quit drinking because I do not want to go back to the hospital with pancreatitis, not because I'm an alcoholic. My doctor agrees. He admits you can have pancreatitis without being an alcoholic."

The last line always paints a picture, for me, of Dema holding the doctor captive, performing the Irish version of Chinese torture until he gives and says what she needed to hear. It didn't take me long to learn. Don't argue with her unless you like long bloody battles predestined to lose.

When Deb gets off the phone, I try to console her, but she's not having it.

"You don't understand. My mom doesn't go anywhere without making sure Dad has a guard. She doesn't trust him to be on his own. If Dad is home alone, Mom is in dire trouble."

Like I said, it's guilt. A few months back, Deb gets a whim to go to church. I don't need church for spirituality. Been there, done that. AA is the only place I've ever felt God show up. I thought Deb was happy going to meetings, but typically, nothing is ever enough for her. I wish she'd leave me out of it. Every Sunday after service, she goes on about how great it was. It's the worse sales job ever, face streaked with mascara, eyes red and swollen, claiming, "It was incredible!"

Sounds fun, right?

I admit, since this church thing started, she's different. For one thing, she's given up some control and is not as hard on herself. But how does every conversation end up having something to do with God? Can someone be obsessed with God? OCGD (Obsessive Compulsive God Disorder). Yep, that's it. One Sunday, the preacher gave a sermon on grace. Deb comes home bouncing off the walls. I kept my mouth shut, but it wasn't easy. She acted like Webster just invented the word *grace*. Nearly every meeting topic covers grace in some form. Why didn't she *get it* then? There's more grace in a dumpy back-alley AA meeting than all the churches I've been to combined. That's where I learned of grace. It's not like I haven't shared about grace with her. But then I'm not Pastor *Whatshisface*.

"Sandy! You should have been there. Pastor Wayne spoke of grace. We're not forgiven because we deserve it. Thank you, Jesus! I don't want what I deserve. I want what

I can never earn—*grace*! Do you get it? We're forgiven, even though, in spite of! Isn't that cool?"

"Yeah, cool."

"Do you want to come with me next week?"

"No."

CHAPTER 49

What if, Could Happen, Surely Next Time (Deb)

"Mom, you know I love you, right? You're a good mom. I'm so sorry for not being around much the last few years, for calling your doctor. I only did it because I was worried. Forgive me, Mom. I'm proud of you for buying Charlton Heston's VHS tape of the Bible. I'm sorry I laughed. It wasn't funny. You were seeking God. I was a jerk. I'm sorry for everything. I love you. You know that, right Mom? Okay, well, it's time to call Dad and brush my teeth. I'll be back soon."

How did the pile of unsaid words grow so tall? Since learning my first word, syllables fly out of my mouth with no thought, a steady stream of jabber. Yet now I sit atop a mountain of the unsaid, hoping their belated arrival will penetrate my mother's heart. I have no way of knowing. She cannot respond because she's zoned out on pain medication. It feels like she's purposely checked out, shut down, given up. When I arrived at the hospital, she was in extreme pain but coherent enough to say, "Don't let your dad come in here." I thought it was because she didn't have her lipstick on. She's like that. Later, Dad spun justifications for not going in her room. When he asked if she'd said anything about him, suspicions arose. Over the years, I've watched her forgive Dad for every variety of unforgivable acts—lies, infidelity, black eyes, bruises, and fat lips. Through it all, she never gave up on him, keeping guard so he would not misbehave. What could he have possibly done that freed mom from charge over his behavior causing this mental checkout before her body's reservation time?

She has a team of doctors, one for each organ it seems. They come in and out of her room singing their line in "The Skeleton" song—*the neck bone connected to the head bone*, and so on. Doctor Fu, the lead singer of the routine, shakes his head and saying, "I put one fire out, and another starts." Meanwhile, poor Mom gets wheeled in and out of her room, undergoing experimental procedures. They even installed a screen near her heart that acts like a sieve for clots. When the doctor explained it to me, he lit up like a kid blabbering plans for building a contraption out of Legos.

While Mom undergoes various lab-rat procedures, I sit in the waiting room with an array of others facing similar circumstances with their loved ones. Monica arrives every day, around one o'clock, after working the morning shift at the dry cleaners in Renton. She sits with her son when he's not by his wife's side and takes his place when he needs a break from the darkness of cancer. Andrea strolls in and out, along with other extended family members. Their dad, a ninety-eight-year-old pastor, is in transition from earth to heaven. When I met Andrea, our conversation fast-forwarded from Seattle rain to prayer. Now, each time we meet, we bow our heads together, as if under order. With one foot dangling off this world, her dad is exiting life first class. Watching the family be at peace as they honor his voyage feels like a heartwarming black-and-white movie, only better because this is real life, as it should be. They know he is ready, even eager to leave. The mystery is that his body doesn't know to give up. Every day, the family gathers and waits. What seemed certain to be hours turned to days. It feels both bizarre and natural witnessing their peace.

I'm here three to four days each week, leaving Sandy to manage whatever I can't handle on the phone. We've promoted our part-time employee to manager and hired a second to fill in. Through financial stress and an absentee wife, Sandy doles out hugs and words of encouragement.

"Just do whatever you need to do, sweetie. Don't worry."

I need to be with my mom. No thanks to yet another life lesson regarding time—you can never have back. I want to be here, and I know it helps my sisters and brother to know she is not alone. Danny owns and runs Hometown Motors, a busy used-car lot whose clientele want to deal directly with the redhead known for practical jokes and a fair deal. Candy, the eldest sister, travels all over the world with her job and is here at the hospital as much as possible. And Nancy is in California with zero resources to travel. I'm not here for them or Mom who hasn't opened her eyes or spoken a word in weeks. I'm here for me.

I sit by her bed, legs to the side, because the room is cramped with hissing machines, dangling tubes and wires.

I read the Bible aloud, pray, and whisper *sorrys* and *love yous* in Mom's ear. The doctors stumble in, scratch their heads, and say things like "Let's try this or that procedure." When I ask why this or that is happening, they name one of the dozens of medications she's been taking for years, explaining it has, over time, caused this or that organ to shut down. The latest "might as well try this" is an intimidating kidney-dialysis machine that straddles the doorway, being too large for the room. Every day, I watch Mom's blood travel down a tube, enter the giant machine, exit through another tube, and reenter her helpless body. One intuitive nurse noticed I was a little bothered by this procedure. Maybe the hands covering my eyes, knees pulled up under my chin, and white face gave me away. Sympathetic to my concerns, she attempted to humanize the alien machine.

"Just think of it as a blood washing machine. The bad blood goes in, gets purified, and returns to your mom, fresh and laundered."

It didn't help.

Mom has been able to muster a voice three times to say one thing: "Please don't let them put me on that breathing machine again." After breaking the promise three times, we meet with Dr. Fu who admits he's running out of ideas. He has a few more experiments he could try but none that he feels would help. Mom had run the gamut of medical tortures for all of April. It was now May 1. Dr. Fu suggests it might be time to take her off all life-support machines, with expectations of her passing within a few hours to possibly several days. After prayerful family discussion, the appointment to unplug the machine is scheduled for the next day.

Candy and I agree to say goodbye to Mom together. Danny, broken and lost, said his goodbyes that night. Dad said he couldn't do it and left. I thought I'd stay another night in the hospital lobby chair, but soon after the plan was in place, I decide it best to get a shower and a better night's rest at Dad's house in Auburn. Disappointed but not surprised, he's not home when I arrive. Grateful for the key he gave me back when this began, I let myself in. Cody, their much-adored standard poodle, greets me at the door, nearly knocking me over with a push to my chest.

"Cody, where's Dad?"

I don't need the tattletale look of judgment to know. Anyone knowing Dad, even casually, could blast out the answer to that question. "He's at the casino." The Muckleshoot Casino opened its doors in April 1995, a 100-yard walk from Dad's front yard. With the swoosh of the sliding automatic doors, calls of "Hey, Mac, how's it going?" sing out from waitresses, proprietors, gamblers, and janitors. Plopping a casino next door to Dad is like a free beer sign to the alcoholic, a pill mill to the addict, a candy store to the starving, or a brothel to the satyr. The demise takes time, wearing clever disguises like *what if, could happen, surely next time.* Escalating wins—$500, $3,000, $10,000, and $22,000—soothe the calls from creditors, extending death-sentence pardons over a period of six years. Hope for the next big win lends reason to rise out of bed, ignore the twelve messages from the bank, and put one foot in front of the other toward the friendly neighborhood casino. Dad thinks the fast-approaching foreclosure on the house is a secret. Danny told me about it after he asked him for a loan. He denied the loan not only because of the gambling issue but also due to the disrespect he's shown Mom.

I owe her an apology. I really thought she was nuts. For fifty years of marriage, she kept him on a leash, insisting if she loosened her grip, he'd run off like a crazed dog after a squirrel. She'd say things like "I can't leave your dad home alone." She gave him an allowance and kept the credit cards hidden, claiming he'd spend every cent on women and gambling. Now I see. The leash snapped, and the squirrels are in trouble. He's not only lived up to her expectations but excelled to the top of his class.

Danny is disgusted with the women hitting Dad up for money. I agree. They flirt, implying maybe I'll sleep with you to gain favors for loans. It scares me knowing women choose this lifestyle. They lurk in the corners of casinos, searching for toothless old guys like him, ready to pounce. One gal lured him away from his bingo machine, just long enough for her boyfriend to empty out the remaining credit. Is it just me? Or does a life of flipping burgers at McDonald's sound more glamorous than rolling *Grandpa Pervert* for chump change? Out of all the women who've scammed my dad, there's only one that showed some integrity. She, a rather large woman, banged on his front door, demanding cash. When refused, she punched him in the nose and emptied his pockets. At least, she didn't feign attraction and lie. She figured he deserved it for waving wads of money around the casino, boasting about living next door in the brown house on the corner.

I spend the night napping. When he comes home around 7:00 a.m., I am wide awake. How does a seventy-seven-year-old man dragging an oxygen tank behind him keep going like this? What bothers me is when well-meaning friends ask, "How is your dad holding up through all this?" They're picturing a fragile, old white-haired, soft-spoken, child-loving, granpa-ish dear of a man. They expect me to respond with "Oh, he's hanging in there." Is the truth a choice? "Oh, poor soul, he's consoling himself with pornography, gambling, and loose women."

I stay in bed another twenty minutes until I hear Dad snoring from his recliner. I'm not meeting with Candy until 9:00 a.m., but I shower quickly and leave, not wanting to linger in the house now vacant of what made it a home. I don't know how to partake in a day that will most likely end with my mother's death. Feeling numb and incapable of focus, I pray with all I have left, my gut.

"Lord, I beg you, please let us know Mom is going to be okay. That she will be at peace."

Sneaking by Dad, I grab my keys off the end table and leave. At the convenience store on the corner by the casino, I grab a coffee, sit on the curb, and call Sandy. He's my person, the one who hears all. Sometimes I wonder if it's harder for him living the regurgitated version of this mess.

At the hospital, I check in with my waiting-room friends, giving an update on Mom. I learn that the old pastor is rejoicing in heaven, and we say our goodbyes with a last prayer. I'm grateful for the time and hope we shared. Just as we finish praying, I see Candy walk through the doors. She carries the same kind of beauty as Mom. Today, I worked on my appearance, a little makeup, pressed clothing, real shoes. Candy has that effect on me. So did (does) Mom.

I see the pain in her face, but no one else would. We gravitate to the comfort machine, selecting a chocolate bar and a cup of make-believe cocoa. Sitting together quietly nibbling at our chocolate, we wait for the occupational therapist to finish working with Mom. She knows, we know it's ludicrous working on her muscles today. She won't need them. If she wants to put a check mark next to Dema McFarland so she can get paid, okay. The irony is not unseen but rather unworthy of valuable energy.

God gets full credit for my relationship with Candy. Before Mom's illness, we were estranged and distant by choice. We were always cordial in public, polite and forever avoiding a private meeting. After letting God into my life, I felt different around her and her family, whereas before, I felt less than, judged, looked down upon. With Mom's illness, the pettiness fell away. I was able to tell her I was sorry for how I'd treated her. She forgave me. Today, we sit knitted together by our faith in God.

We hang out with Mom, telling stories, laughing, holding her hand. When the 2:00 p.m. deadline nears, we're asked to leave the room until all life-support apparatus has been unplugged and removed. Dr. Fu meets with us, reiterating what we'd been told; it could take hours or days. Once back in the room with Mom, we pray. I don't know how long we stood there, awkwardly watching her like a pot of water soon to bubble into a boil before deciding to gather more comfort food. At the cafeteria entrance, we realize our purses are back in Mom's room.

We open the door without a glance her way. I grab my bag, toss it over my shoulder, and while reaching for Candy's bag, we both stop as if tapped on the shoulder, turning toward the bed. We share a quick look of confirmation, stunned by the unbelievable, undeniable scene before us. Mom's brown eyes that have not been open for weeks are fixated behind us. We turn, searching for what she sees and delights in with amazing anticipation, empowering her to lift her head off the pillow. Again, we share a look, confirming this time that we see nothing. Entranced by the possibilities mirrored in her eyes, we corral the bed, daughters one on each side, mesmerized. We try to enter the moment by calling to her, quickly aware she's not where we are and vice versa. Her eyes and smile proclaim she is experiencing something beyond our understanding. Time has no measure as we watch Mom embrace what she could see and we could not. At last, we take a final look, straining to see the invisible life-giving form, seeing only a blank hospital wall. When we look back, her eyes are closed, and we know without question she is no longer in the room. Her body left behind like a still-life painting.

We call for a nurse who checks her vitals, announcing the time of death. The nurse encourages us to stay as long as we like. I've never been any place more empty than that moment in that room. Candy and I agree there is no reason to stay.

How perfectly he answered the prayer that we would know Mom will be okay. How privileged we are to witness her journey from this world to his. How unimaginable that our powerful, omnipotent God answered our prayer so sweetly. I needed one last nudge toward him; this gift of sight feels like I was catapulted into his arms.

CHAPTER 50

Canine Heal Thyself
(Sandy)

IF I TREATED DEB LIKE her dad does, she'd rise up in all her womanhood glory, emasculate, squash, and fillet my ego; then repeat. I don't get it. The woman I married would have walked away from Mac's daily fiascos before he could gum a meal. She's changed. Her church buddies would say for the better. I'm not so sure.

I want to be Deb's rock, but at times, I feel like I'm cheerleading while she bangs her head against the wall. I honestly thought Dema would recover. At least, I did until Deb convinced me to go with her to the hospital, a weekend that felt like a month. We drove over Saturday, meeting with the family around noon. For hours, we sat around in the waiting room, family-reunion style. There was laughing, hugging, catching up on everything, but no mention of Dema. I enjoyed looking around the lobby, picking out the characters Deb has described over the phone, strangers turned fast friends through the bond of illness.

"Do you want to see her?" Deb asks.

What a stupid question. Who wants to visit any sick person? No offense to Dema, but hospital visits are not fun.

"Sure, let's go."

I think Deb's poor sense of direction led us into the wrong room. It wouldn't be a first. Then I recognize the signature red hair. I've never seen Dema without lipstick and perfected hair, but it was more than that. Deb gabs away. I'm not sure to whom. Guilt punches me in the gut. No one has overreacted; Dema is dying. Deb looks at me like I should say something. Normally, I ignore that look, but in this circumstance, it's not much to ask that I play along and speak to her mom's unresponsive shell.

"Hey, Dema, sorry . . . I'm sorry you're sick."

I want to help. Sharing tears is all I have to offer, and those are not voluntary. Deb sits on the edge of the bed, pointing for me to take the chair. She places her hands on Dema's legs, closing her eyes. I get it now. This is what she's been doing for nearly a month—sitting, watching, waiting for death. Soon, Candy joins us, and I slip out with the excuse there's not room for all of us. It was true. With all the machinery, the tiny room is cramped. We spend the day playing the hospital-room version of musical chairs with Danny, Candy, and Dennis, Deb's niece and nephew, and even the great niece and nephew. I skip my turn, choosing instead to hang with the little guys, making myself useful. As soon as I suggest Barbie take a swim in the lobby fountain, they like me. Their mom? Not so much. By the end of the day, Barbie had drowned, barely surviving, the makeshift CPR with a stick and a straw. It's the highlight of my day. When it's time to leave, I'm relieved, thinking the worst is over. I'm wrong.

Walking through the door of Deb's family home, albeit the land of crazy, always came with love, hugs, and laughter. When Mac opens the door, I'm braced, ready for Cody, the hundred-pound untrained standard poodle. I was not prepared for the olfactory punch in the nose that nearly knocks me over. Normally, Dema has Cody decked out in a satin ribbon, puffy hairdo, and painted toenails. This is the ghetto version, like the before and after photos of meth heads. Instead of missing teeth and acne, Cody has poop caked on his butt and fur matted with slobber.

Like everything else in the land of McFarland's, Cody comes with rules. I admit, he's been my most challenging McFarland subject and the source of many squabbles. This time, I want to get it right and please Deb. The lesson is simple enough: No matter what the dog does, I must smile and pretend like I like him. I've been warned; not liking the dog is worse than my unforgivable sin of sobriety.

It's not the dog's fault. He has no rules. How bizarre is that? The dog is the only life-form free from the exorbitant list of rules. Mac stays at the casino all night, then sleeps all day, often through Cody's whines to be let outside. It's hard on Deb seeing her family home like this. Dema may have packed it with stuff like towels, but it was always clean. Now, whenever something needs to be done, Mac plays the *old-man* card. It seems he only has the strength to gamble and carouse with *sleazeball* women. What I don't get is why Deb falls for it.

Seated on the love seat, we take turns gently pushing the dog off our laps and out of our faces. His breath rivals the problem under his tail.

"Hey, Cody, you're such a sweet dog," Deb says, pushing him away from her face.

Rejected, Cody lunges at me, paws pushing into my groin, panting toxic fumes straight up my nostrils. I do my best to follow Deb's lead.

"Hey, ouch, oh gawd, what have you been eating? Get down . . . ouch . . . now! Uh, you're a good dog."

Saving Deb from her turn, I whisper sweet lies in Cody's ears, one hand over my nose, the other clamped around the dog's front legs.

"Dad, is Cody still having dysentery?" Deb asks. "Are you still feeding him ice cream?"

"Cody won't eat ice cream anymore. The Rocky Road I put in his bowl two days ago is still there."

For the first time, I'm impressed with the dog; canine heals thyself. Good job, Cody! Now if you can learn to bathe and groom yourself, there's hope. Mac falls asleep to the tune of his daughter's suggestions for calling the vet, getting more sleep, and the scariest words ever, *move to Yakima and live with us.*

Mac snores. Deb scrapes crusted poop piles off the floor, washes food-caked dishes, and prepares a roast for dinner. I sit, waiting for this all to be over, pushing the dog away like a giant hairy yo-yo rolled in dung. Mac's cheeks fill with air, making him look like a puffer fish as the snores blow out the toothless cave and repeat. In the moment, I don't know who I resent most, Mac, the dog, or Deb for putting up with it.

In the morning, I wake at my usual 5:00 a.m. time. Mac is not in his recliner, so he must be serving time at the casino. I'm relieved. Last night, he threatened to make me his favorite breakfast, oyster stew. I asked Deb, "What's in it?"

"Dad's version is simply oysters floating in a bowl of hot milk with lots of pepper." Gags.

Cody jumps me on my way down the hall, placing a paw on either side of my shoulders, eager to share his gnarly morning breath. With no witnesses, I skip the positive affirmations and let him outside. Instead of running off to take care of business, he stands there staring at me. I hear Deb stirring. I doubt she slept much. I savor my shower, seizing the only probable time of peace this day will bring. Later, we're meeting Deb's sister and brother-in-law for church.

"Thanks a lot," Deb says, sticking her head in the bathroom door.

"For what?" I ask, thinking it's for sacrificing my time to be by her side.

"You left Cody outside to howl and bark!"

"I hate that dog! He stinks, and he's spoiled."

"Shhhh!"

"There's no one here."

After a lengthy fight about whether or not "being there" for Deb includes liking the dog, we drive to the tiny church in Orting. Of course, we arrive before Deb's sister. Candy is always late, but it's never her fault. She showed for our wedding thirty minutes after the *I dos*, claiming it was my directions. Their church holds no more than fifty in its rustic steepled structure. The problem is, how do you remain unnoticed when you're sitting in a congregation of twenty, including pastors, wives, and cousins. All heads turn as we walk through the door like new vegetarians starving for fresh meat. Candy and Dennis arrive just as the service begins. Worship is emotional for me as well as Deb. I lose the spiritual feelings when a woman walks to the front saying she has a prophetic word. I try to clear my head, worried she'll find something in there inappropriate for church. Thank God, she doesn't call me out about how much I hate the dog and just want to go home.

I haven't been much support for Deb through this. In my defense, the McFarlands have a flair for exaggeration. Until I saw Dema myself, I thought they might be cranking up the drama a bit. Even the tales of Mac's escapades seemed out of proportion. Never again will I doubt the miracle of crazy abounding in this family. For me, the hardest part is listening to Mac's constant attempts to justify slapstick antics as sound and logical. Yesterday in the hospital lobby, he held me hostage, hoping I would cave, becoming the one person to agree with him about some gal he's been seeing.

"Danny, Deb, and Candy think she is after my money, but she is a sweet girl who needs support for her son. A single mom."

This is the man who treated his children like monotonous burdens, personal debts he must pay because he married a breeder. Now he's a shining candidate for giving advice to single moms. While he's telling me all this, Deb walks up and remains quiet. How scary is that? I duck every time Mac blurts stupidity, certain Deb will toss something at him and miss. Instead, she gives him a hug?

The weekend did finally end. I had my doubts. Deb stayed home two days then returned to be by her mother's side. One week later, I receive two hysterical calls from Deb. I had to strain to understand the words through her sobs.

Call one: "They're taking mom off life support tomorrow morning."

The next day, call two: "I watched Mom leave with Jesus! You should have seen her face. She was so happy. God did that for me and Candy. He answered our prayer. Can you believe it? Oh, I wish you could have been there. It's the most amazing gift. It's a privilege to have witnessed this. I know she's okay, better than okay, happy. You know how scared I was for her. Well, not anymore."

I can't deny God gave Deb proof that her mom is in heaven. Letting Deb and her sister peek into heaven momentarily is the only way they could heal the deep hurts leading up to their mom's death. What I didn't know then is how much this memory would be needed in the days ahead.

CHAPTER 51

After All, I Denied Him More Than Once (Deb)

As a child, I tricked the world into believing I was different by choice. Hidden deep in my soul, I kept a secret; I longed to be normal. Our photograph was not the one in the new wallet representing the American dream but rather the one representing the behind-closed-doors family. Mom worked hard, painting the illusion of normal on our faces whenever we walked out the door.

Normal. That's what I want for my mother's funeral. It's what she would want: a pastor in a suit to say nice things, a church with family and friends sharing great stories and tears. Personally, I hate funerals. Whatever delusion supports the logic of this bizarre event, I don't understand. We pay to have our loved one pumped full of chemicals, painted and coiffed like a wax-museum doll. We gently place their head on a satin pillow, crisscrossing their hands across their lap. Then it gets really weird. We drag the body to the church and parade by the coffin, exclaiming how peaceful, at rest, and serene they look. No one speaks up saying the truth.

"Whoa! Who did this?" Makeup does not hide dead! Thank God, our family agreed Mom would have chosen a closed casket. Still, we stuffed her body in an expensive satin-lined box and dragged her to church. From there, finding normal is challenging.

Over the years, my parents moved up the ladder of the fraternal order: elks to moose to eagles. In these orders, with each rung, the drinking progresses. By the time the top rung is climbed, many have either hopped on the sobriety wagon or died of liver failure. The last man standing represents Darwin's theory for the survival of the fittest. As such, most or all Mom's friends have already been pumped, boxed, and dragged to church years ago. Knowing this, we kept the arrangements simple.

Nevertheless, a normal service was doomed from the start. With the family seated to the side behind a curtain, less than ten people were left in the pews. The pastor, who'd never met Mom, stands and fumbles with the sound equipment. Wrapping his fingers around the microphone Vegas-style, channeling Elvis, he sings "Love Me Tender." The curtain serves as a veil for the eyes but not the ears. As he impersonates the "King," I remind myself that we all agreed to this. The pastor rewrote the songs to include Jesus, yet somehow the idea played better in our heads than live here in Viva La Funeral. Once again, the McFarlands fail at normal.

With Haley at my side, prepared to stand in if I fell apart, I read a short eulogy to the few in the pews. Then it was back to "Viva Las Vegas" or maybe "Heartbreak Hotel."

At some point, the pastor asked if anyone would like to say a few words. A woman stood and called out, "Dema was a beautiful woman." After the funeral, Dad boasts about the huge crowd and all the nice things people had to say. I wonder which one of us is bonkers, deciding we both must be.

Our family without Mom is all wrong, like yanking the rose bush out of the garden expecting the dandelions to carry on. Dad without Mom? Just as she predicted, a leashless dog gone mad! With Mom too busy dying to keep guard, he's collected an entourage of bimbos. They beg loans, leaving him holding a bad check to be cashed *as soon as*. They must have a grand chuckle, patting themselves on the back for sweet talking Dad yet again. Besides the loan scams, he's been robbed three times. The last one has left the family pointing fingers at each other. It is suspicious that whoever did this knew about Mom's secret cupboard. But Dad's boastings of location and goods leave me picturing the clientele at the Muckleshoot Casino decked out in Mom's finest squash-blossom necklace.

Dad is an anomaly. Sometimes, our phone conversations play in my head like an *Abbott and Costello* rerun, only less funny.

"Dad, what happened? You're hurt?"

"I'm okay. It's just my face."

"What happened?"

"My oxygen tank blew up."

"Oh no! How?"

"I don't know how. I was on the pot, smoking a cigarette, but I've done that plenty of times, and it didn't blow up."

"Dad! You promised not to smoke with the oxygen. How bad are you hurt? Did you call your doctor?"

"My nose hurts the worst. Blisters are popping up all over my face. I'm not calling that damn clinic. I'm tired of them not listening to me."

I'd hoped Dad would settle down with Mom's death. He has not. His *pornogenarian* quest continues. I want him to feel love, not criticism. Somedays I succeed in not judging, others I fail. I stay with him two or three days a week, cleaning and listening to his latest tales of woe. The foreclosure moves forward, dispassionately waiting for the old toothless guy in the striped overalls to slip scaling the casino cliffs. His failed attempts at big casino wins and Danny's loan refusal have led to plan C. Certain the Muckleshoot tribe wants his house on the corner, Dad meets with the tribal council to discuss cash. Seems apropos that the casino would own his house. He returned from the meeting, offended. I don't think anyone is betting on Dad to be around long.

I know it's his fault, but it's hard to respect professions that exist solely to prey on the weaknesses of others. Days when I'm stingy with grace, I imagine wheeling Dad on a gurney through the front doors of the casino, dog and oxygen tank attached, screaming, "You just won the jackpot. Dad's inheritance, home, spare change, and dog. Have fun taking care of him. Have a blessed day."

Not jumping down Dad's throat is my biggest challenge. I fail often, always when he tries to justify horrendous acts. The worst being the time he beat my sister Nancy. If that happened today, the doctor would not have kept quiet based on Mom's promise; it would never happen again. I can forgive the act; it's the attempts to excuse it that snatch forgiveness from my heart.

"What was I supposed to do? The school called saying if she missed one more day she wouldn't graduate. She told me to f——off. She wouldn't get up."

Strangely, it wasn't until seven years later that the trauma surfaced for me. In the middle of the first *Rocky* movie, I raced out of the theater, heart pounding, gasping for air. Seeing Rocky Balboa's face after being pummeled by Apollo Creed jerked me back to that day. The shock came when I remembered Nancy's face, swollen to triple its size, much worse than Rocky's mug. The day it happened, Mom met me at the door after school. She warned me that Nancy was hurt. I found her in her room, lying in bed with the lights off. When I asked what happened, she left out the curse word but spared no detail as to the violence. According to Nancy, Dad snapped, jumping on top of her, his knees on either side of her shoulders, slugging her face, yelling, "Say 'Uncle!'" Do grown-ups even say that?

I left Nancy without saying a word. Mom was locked in her room. I found Dad asleep in his recliner. As sick as it sounds, I fell at his feet, overwhelmed with pity for him. Imagine how he felt? Many years later, I confess the feelings I had to Sandy. He said my reaction, called a trauma bond, is not unusual for the situation and does not mean I'm a horrible person.

I have forgiven him. I do forgive him. I even attended an intense workshop at our church called "Surrendered Hearts," reaping much healing. It was there I formally forgave many, Dad included. In every case, forgiveness stuck except Dad. I continue to forgive him daily. Talking with him daily, either by phone or in person. I fail each day. The best I can do for now is not act on my resentments. When he upsets me, I pray before speaking, usually a primitive silent prayer like "Jesus, help me!" When I do that, the strangest things happen. Sometimes he stops talking as if slapped by an angel. Other times, I find myself speaking to him with words and manners outside of my character, diffusing the conversation. There've even been times when the phone went dead midsentence or someone knocked on his door causing him to hang up before I could react. I'm worried the only way I'll ever be able to forgive him and have it stick is if when he dies. He may be a *tough old bird*, as the doctors refer to him, but his lifestyle keeps him dangerously close to the grave.

I live for Sundays. Walking into the church with Evan never fails to renew my strength. Like dominoes falling, the logical sequence of God's grace and power line up in my mind. I'm not the woman I used to be. God changed me. If God can change me, he can do anything. Therefore, I need not worry, not even for my dad.

I like the woman holding her grandson's hand, walking toward the pre-K classroom, giggling at the cardboard cutout of Jesus hiding behind the plant. I like me, the me with God. That's a miracle. If you'd asked me a few years ago if I wanted to sign up for a life where church day is the best day of the week and hanging with my grandson is the cherry on top? After a good laugh, I'd have disappeared. My life today is funny, but it's no joke. It's like one of the opposite-day episodes Haley and Jay loved watching on Nickelodeon. I go to church more than once a week, read the Bible most days, and pray. Today, my biggest fear is that my life will go back to normal. I know that can't happen. I've given my life to Jesus, and my old self is no longer.

Still, it doesn't hurt to repeat the life-saving words, relive the miracle of birth. That's why whenever Dr. Stanley asks for an altar call on CNN radio as I'm driving home from work, I repeat the words. I can't imagine God will be upset with me for surrendering my life too many times. After all, I denied him more than once.

I've quit asking Sandy to come to church with us. My friends warned me that pushing too much might keep him away. Instead, they pray with me. It's just hard because I know he would love it. He thinks God only shows up at AA meetings. I want to share the place that gives me life with the man I love with all my heart.

Sometimes I wonder if AA stunts his spiritual growth. They share a good-intentioned gang mentality, held together with slogans, restricted and chained to what works. I'm a hypocrite for even thinking this because it was the program of Alcoholics Anonymous that softened my own heart toward God. Anyway, my case for the church is not looking good. Sandy has moved one of his AA buds into our backyard rental house. All I know is his name is Ray; he has fourteen years' sobriety, and he's earned Sandy's respect. He talks about him like he's one of the twelve disciples of the AA God.

"Ray will do whatever it takes to stay sober. Even if it hurts him. He'll go to any lengths. Remember, he's the guy I told you about that went to prison when he really didn't have to because it was the right thing to do."

I don' know how I feel about *Saint Ray* living in our backyard. To be honest, I prefer *Invisible* Ray. The prior renters were rarely seen or heard. Ray is friendly, a little loud and apparently incapable of allowing my preference for ignored status.

Honestly, I'm more excited about our other new addition, Gabe, a 110-pound golden lab mix with more character than the Three Stooges, Charlie Chaplin, and Mother Theresa combined. I met Gabe at a party held at Sandy's ex-wife's house. Our eyes met from across the room. He quickly returned to begging for scraps, but I fell in love. He was older, wise, suave. Truth be told, he snubbed me, turning tail when I revealed empty hands. Three days after the party, Stephanie calls, asking if we would want Gabe. She said he was causing problems at her mom's, barking when left home, irritating the neighbors. Bonnie, the ex, planned to take him to the pound.

That night, I approached Sandy with the big question. "Remember Gabe?"

"Who?"

"Gabe, the great dog we met at Stephanie's certification party. The one that kept finding ways out of the locked room to glean the guests for scraps. Big, gorgeous, brown-eyed lab mix."

"The one that barked when my mom stopped feeding him? Okay, yeah."

"Well, Bonnie is going to send him to the pound. Stephanie called to see if we could save him. Take him in."

"Why doesn't Barney want him?"

"He barks all day while she is at work, and the neighbors are complaining."

"So what would be different here? We have closer neighbors than she does?"

"That's just it. He doesn't have to stay home. He is the perfect store dog. Remember Eartha Kitty? She was great advertising for that antique store in Bellingham. Everyone remembers the store because of the cat."

"Yeah, when a giant barking dog scares the socks off our customers, they'll remember to never come back!"

"I know I can train him to greet customers and not bark. Obviously, if he had to stay home by himself, we'd have to find him a different home. Can we just give him a try? After all, I was able to train Bonnie's ex-husband, don't you think I can handle her ex-dog?"

"Ha ha, funny. I don't know. He's old. Do we want to go through that again?"

CHAPTER 52

Don't Let the Dog Trick Me, Got It (Sandy)

WE DODGED A BULLET. BETTER said, we dodged a nuclear bomb named Mac! Deb wanted to move him into our house. She asked permission. I could have said no. But I said yes. We even made plans. The office will be gutted and transformed into a bedroom. In my defense, she posed polar statements that only a two-year-old has rights to deny.

"You understand it is the right thing to do? To honor my father, be a loving example for him."

I squeaked out *yes*. The fallout from the blast surfaced.

"Thank you. I know it's a huge sacrifice. This is the only way Dad won't have to be separated from Cody."

"The dog too? But I hate that dog!"

For the next week, I carried the burden of my future, picturing life with Mac and Cody ruling my home. I spoke with my sponsor, hoping he'd give me permission to renege my promise based on the dog-from-hell clause. He did not.

I prayed for God to not let this happen. Then I prayed for God's will to be done, ready to accept life on his terms.

The following weeks continued as usual with Deb splitting her time between home in Yakima, business in Ellensburg, and Mac in Auburn. Then one day, it fell apart or came together. I'm not sure which. Deb came back the same day she'd left for her three-day caretaking with Mac.

"I'm not going back to Dad's, not on a regular basis. I realize he just wants me to clean up his messes so he can stay out all night like some college kid in a dorm. I'm not angry with him. Instead, I feel released. He's made it clear he does not want to live with us or any family member. I need to let him do what he needs to do. Trust God is taking care of him."

Her words feel like a warm, soothing shower of relief. She seems okay. I know she's disappointed in Mac. She's been waiting for Mac to change into the man she thinks he should be, the dad she wants him to be.

Not long after Deb's epiphany, Mac surprised us all, driving over Chinook Pass on a Sunday morning dressed in his best Roy Rogers–style church attire. Only Jesus himself could have excited Deb more. I knew which gears were turning in her mind, jumping from Dad attending church to Saint Mac of the Muckleshoot Casino in two seconds flat. Before leaving for the service, Deb peeks around the corner behind her dad, motioning for me to follow her upstairs. I sneak away, leaving four-year-old Evan to answer Mac's question, "How many girlfriends do you have?"

"Can you believe this? He drove all the way here to go to church. You don't understand. He is going to love our church. When he sees that we have a band, he'll be blown away."

When they return home, Deb's spirits have deflated. Later, she says he liked the band, but he had embarrassed her, something about flirting with the worship leader, telling her what a beautiful voice she had, and suggesting she might be good enough to sing in a real band. Exasperated, Deb added, "He asked her if she ever threw in a nonreligious song."

I managed not to laugh.

I escaped suicide by standard poodle. I knew Mac would never want to live with us, but fear of *what if* ruled my nerves. I may have been granted an end run play with Mac, but somehow, we are once again dog owners. When Deb called Stephanie to decline the dog based on his elder status, she laughed.

"Gabe is only two years old."

I thought I was off the hook when we agreed the dog was too old. Who would have thought a young dog, a golden lab-chow mix, could be so laid back and wise to the finer things in life like naps? I feel duped, but it won't happen again. Deb promised we'd find a new home for the dog if he flunks greeting 101. According to her, after three days with Gabe at the store, he's ready to open his own shop. I'm the one who needs instructions.

"When you get to the store, first thing, get his tie out of the store room. Are you listening?"

"Yeah."

"He loves it. Trust me. Then leave the front door open as we always do, but keep the back door closed. He knows he can go out the back door, but he won't take one step over the front threshold. You won't believe how quickly he learned."

"What if a squirrel walks by?"

"Would you listen, please? When a customer walks in, he'll get up and go greet them."

"He won't bark?"

"Only at the UPS guy. We're working on that. After he greets them, he'll come ask you for a treat. Only give him one, and only if he greets them. Oh, also, don't let him trick you into giving him one per person. It's one per group. Okay?"

"I should write that down. Don't let the dog trick me. Got it."

The dog is great, smarter than most. Still, I'm not buying the executive greeter, employee-of-the-month hype. It didn't help that on my day to work with him, the first thing he does is jump in the driver's seat of my truck. As Deb waves us off to work like tots on their first day of school, I ask.

"Shall I drive, or did you teach him that also?"

Driving the Yakima River Canyon Road, I nearly forget my passenger. But when the rolling river is in view from the road, Gabe nudges my arm and whines. He might be an okay dog, tagging along on fishing trips. I'm not fluent in *dogese* as Deb seems to be, but even I understand the snorts mean "Hey, let's get out of the vehicle and play in the water."

Forgiving a bad bout of gas, he's an okay car-pool buddy. Once at the store, he follows me into the store room, just as Deb said he would. Amused, I hold up his necktie, as I'd been instructed. He approaches, tail wagging. Skeptical, I hold the tie open, and to my amazement, he sticks his head through the pre-tied loop. He's one up on me with the tie since I've always balked at the idea. Strutting off, head held high, like he's late for a board meeting, Gabe positions himself in front of the door. Leary, I open it as instructed and command him to take a nap. He obeys. Naps and fishing may well be our bond.

I'm flipping on the last light switch when the first customer walks through the door. I'm braced, ready to call an ambulance if she keels over from fright when greeted by a giant barking dog. Instead, he gets up, saunters over to the lady, tail swaying gently, giving and receiving a warm welcome. He walks to the counter, gives me a commanding look, waiting for me to pay up with a treat for a job well done. Momentarily, I suspect Deb is hiding around the corner with a remote-control device. This continued all day with every customer, man, woman, or child. He did have two forgivable barking episodes: When the UPS guy rushed in startling him awake and at me when I could not get down off a fourteen-foot ladder to pay him his treat fast enough.

Sheepishly, I admit, Deb is right.

Gabe quickly became our poster boy, his photo on business cards, ads, even flyers for those wanting a souvenir of the big yellow dog. It really appears as if this dog loves his job. I even tested the tie attraction, purposely forgetting to get it off the hook the next time I worked with him. He stood at the store-room door, staring at me, looking like you'd imagine if a dog could tap his foot or paw. When I did not respond, he snorted, followed by a one-bark command meaning, "Ahem, did you forget something?"

I don't know if I'm as enamored with Gabe as Deb is, but he's proving to be worth his annoyances i.e., stretching out over the entire truck seat on the way home, huge head in my lap, snoring and occasionally spewing lethal gas. He is fast becoming a draw to our store, tagging us as the *antique store with the big yellow dog in a tie.* There's only two things that make me regret having this dog, and they both have to do with Deb's big mouth. One, she makes it known to all that I didn't think he would make a good store dog. And two, she has a new story that she tells to whomever will stand still.

"Have I told you where we got Gabe? He belonged to Sandy's ex-wife. She was going to take him to the pound! I thought hmmm, the husband worked out, why not give the dog a shot." (Insert out-of-control laughter at one's own joke.) Why does she think that is so funny? Meantime, life is shaping up. When trouble knocks, we work it out, move on. I'm glad it's less complicated between us as our family progresses. Nanette, married three years now, gave birth last spring to our second grandson, my biological first, Matthew James McFerran. Although his birth cooperated with her life itinerary, I chuckle knowing the lessons coming; babies won't abide by mommy engineer's blueprints. Even so, she's the most well-read mom on earth, tackling motherhood the same as her studies at MIT. Her mom style is best described as concierge, rather than mother hen. As a child, whether at school or home, Nanette would speak up for her sister, instructing teachers or sitters as to the idiosyncrasies of Stephanie's likes and dislikes. Mostly, she mandated, "Just put ketchup on it, and she'll eat it."

It's great the Palmer name will carry on, but honestly, that's not my thing. What value is a name floating on if the kid doesn't know who I am. That's what's important to me. I want this brown-eyed, super-sized baby to know me.

Another change is Deb's attitude toward our new backyard tenant, Ray. Even before Ray offered to paint our two-story home in exchange for rent, she had grown fond of him. Now, his name links in conversation with the words *blessing, godsend, answer to prayer*. Our two-tone, drab-brown, chippy-paint home was one task Deb and I were not up to, both of us being lousy painters. I admit, her prayers to have the house painted and Ray, a professional painter, dropping into our rental might be beyond coincidence.

Deb's prejudiced views of the cookie cutter AA guy are being challenged. It's not fair to say she's anti-AA. On the contrary, she is humbly grateful for the program and for those who take it seriously. However, her patience bleeds out over those in the program who are long on talking, short on walking it out. In her words, "If they perform the slightest act of service, they go on and on flying a banner across the sky, writing home to mommy, banging cymbals. 'Hello, world, please take note, I took out the garbage, poured coffee, held the door for the person behind me.'"

Ray is good exposure for Deb, modeling the principles without the self-back patting. He's solid. In Deb's words, "Ray is capable of doing a good deed without a parade and a clown to scoop poop behind him."

With our life bursting with blessings, I decided we should do some service together as a couple. Months ago, maybe closer to a year, Deb stopped asking me to go to church. But this time, I surprised her, offering to go with her to serve dinner to the homeless on Thanksgiving Day. The dinner is at the church, but that's not like partaking in the whole "we're all holier than thou" Sunday celebration.

The church building is amazing—oak beams, stained-glass windows, twenty-foot-tall oak sliding partition doors, and one hundred rooms. I expected to find a group of elderly women cooking and swapping kitchen war stories. Instead, I am greeted by a smiling late thirties male reeking with really-nice-guy character.

"Hey, you must be Sandy. Nice to meet you. I'm Wayne."

Had I not known the name, Wayne Purdom, it would prove I never listen since he's mentioned at least once a week. Back when she was running a vigorous campaign for my church attendance, she called him a *man's man*. She is not an expert on this topic, so it didn't mean much.

When I commented on the architecture, Wayne took off his apron, deserting a sink full of spuds waiting to be peeled, and took me on a guided tour of the building. I nearly forgot he's a pastor. After the tour, ten or so of us cooked and served dinner for thirty people. It was fun, and I didn't feel out of place. The weirdest part of all is that Deb didn't say anything about it, not during or after, not one "I told you so" or "Now will you go to church?" I'll say this, if I was going to attend church, this one might be okay.

CHAPTER 53

You Know I Was an Altar Boy
(Deb)

My PARENTS BOUGHT THE FIRST house in Forest Villa, a housing development in Auburn, built on the Muckleshoot Indian Reservation. It was a great place to grow up. Every day, we traipsed through maidenhair ferns to hang out in our hand-built forts under evergreens forever dripping from rain. I can still smell the dew and rich soil. When we tired of the woods, we'd play in the half-built homes or torment the realtors attending open-house presentations meant for buyers, not bored children with dirty shoes. Our house sat on the corner with a streetlight. Mom used to keep track of us after dark. One day, a team of bulldozers came to mow down the neighborhood forts in the woods. A Piggly Wiggly grocery store with a huge parking lot replaced them. Later, the Piggly Wiggly became a QVC, an AM/PM minimart popped up on the corner, and the Muckleshoot Casino arrived in all its glory across the street.

Who would have guessed what was coming? After paying nearly two mortgages, Dad let the bank take back the house, a consequence of placing all hope in a casino. My sister Candy and I reluctantly, against what we felt God was asking, invited Dad to live in our homes.

He said no.

"I still have a life to live."

Candy researched suitable retirement-home options, to which he responded, "Hell no! I won't live with a bunch of old people."

Dad clutched onto one hope—a big casino win, allowing him to live Hugh Hefner-style in his own bachelor pad. We placed our bets on God, praying as fervently as the pie-eyed people pushing the slot-machine buttons, only our gaze was focused above.

The big win Dad banked on never happened. Without a dime to get his own place, he moved on to plan B—move in with Danny. According to my brother, Dad imagined they'd be the hottest father-son team on the prowl for women. The first morning, Danny went off to work; Dad, the oxygen hose, and Cody tangled, causing a tumble, resulting in a broken hip and an extended stay in the hospital.

Days before Dad would be released to a nursing home, Candy ran into an old friend who happened to work at the Old Soldiers Home in Orting, a facility thirty minutes from her house. We both knew this had to be God's answer. Problem is, the home had no openings. With no other plan, I got permission to take Dad out of the hospital for a tour of the grounds, as long as he was back by early evening. Dad remained unimpressed while I drove around the circular courtyard a dozen times, trying to convince him to get out and look around.

"Look, Dad, a tank. Let's walk around. You have your walker. We don't have to go far. Oh, and look, there's someone waving us over. I'll ask him where to go for a tour. You know, Dad, they have live music here every Saturday night. They bring in bands from all over."

The gentleman greets us with a big smile. I adore him instantly. If I were to pick a supermodel to represent the perfect elderly man, this would be him. He's dressed fashionably, looking quite dapper with plaid tam and suspenders, soft-spoken, kind, and he calls me sweetheart with no slime attached. Eddy explains that the official tour guide doesn't work on Sundays but offers to give us a tour, even though he's just a resident.

"I'll take good care of you and your dad. Let me get him a wheelchair, so we can go wherever we want. Okay, sweetheart?"

Dad refused the wheelchair, but Eddy and I pretend not to hear. It was a rare sunny day in Western Washington. We stroll through the halls, the cafeteria, and down to the lake where men are fishing.

"You'd be able to fish every day, Dad. You love fishing. How long has it been since you fished?"

For me, it was the most specific answer to prayer anyone could hope for. They offer bingo and even allow gambling for canteen goods. Dad could swap stories with other old soldiers, fish, play bingo, and party on Saturday night with a full band.

How *good* is that?

For Dad, it was the only choice left.

"Dad, if they have an opening, would you be okay here?"

With no beds available, Dad gambled and agreed.

Two days later and one day before Dad would be released, Candy receives a call from her friend, and with some spiritual manipulation of red tape, Dad is given the opening. My first visit to see him, I ask about Eddy, learning he had passed away the day after our tour.

It wasn't ideal. To our surprise, most of the vets were Vietnam era, not Korean War. They weren't interested in Dad's stories and vice versa. Dad's single-mom friend could not afford the trip from Auburn to Orting, unless Dad paid for a spendy cab. Cody could not live at the home but could visit, as long as he behaved. Danny brought him for visits anyway. With those complaints, there were benefits too. Dad was granted a motorized scooter, and he was allowed to come and go as he pleased.

Occasionally, he'd take off on his scooter with a two-hour oxygen supply, hang at the Firehouse Tavern, and then have to make the ride back, gasping for air. One morning, Haley and I sat waiting for him, wondering where he was. When he returned, winded, he explained.

"I felt like having a bloody Mary. That ride to the tavern can be a little risky. They need to fix the potholes. I nearly toppled over into traffic. Sorry, I was late."

"Dad!"

"What?"

"Never mind [sigh]."

Weariness closed my eyes and ears, leading me to give up. Hope opened them, leading me to let go. I found hope hiding in conversations that never happened before, a still, small voice whispering behind my dad's words.

"Maybe I could have done better with Danny. Oh, and you girls too. I tried."

"I know Dad."

"And your mother, I should have . . . I shouldn't have . . . I hurt her the day I took her to the hospital. I lost my temper because I couldn't get her in the car. That's why she was angry with me."

I don't know how long we sat in silence while I digested the words, explaining what happened the day Mom was admitted to the hospital. It was a truth feared, filed away in my mind under *please don't be real.* The confession woke up the anger hiding deep in my heart. I prayed for one drop of mercy and grace to surface. Finally, I spoke.

"You must have noticed how much I've changed. Right? I'm at peace today. I have God's love to thank for that. And he loves you."

Dad jumps in before I can finish.

"Did I ever tell you about the time the holy rollers stayed at our house when I was a kid? They were whooping it up in our barn. Mom fed them and bedded them down."

"Yes, Dad, I have heard that story. I guess what I want to ask is if you have ever thought about what Jesus did for you and me, for all of us. For God so loved the world, he sent his Son to earth."

"You know I was an altar boy?"

"I do know that, Dad, but do you know that Jesus died for our sins, and because of his sacrifice our heavenly Father wants to forgive us for our sins? Dad, have you ever—"

"I think I was twelve years old."

"When you?"

"When I was an altar boy."

"Did you learn about Jesus then?"

"They have church here at the soldier's home every Sunday. I went a couple of times."

"Dad, that's great!"

"But I'm not going back. The music is awful. One old guy named Frank scratching out three lousy songs."

"Oh, I'm sorry to hear that. I know Candy or Danny would love to take you to their church."

"That's okay. I started having my own service. Last Sunday, I left Frank and the others and went back to my room. I cranked up my stereo cassette player with Hank Williams, Conway Twitty, and Dolly Parton. It wasn't five minutes before my room had a bigger congregation than Frank could ever pull in. We had our own church. You know what I mean? Debbie?"

I didn't know nor understand. Whatever God and Dad had going, it was between them. I had worked up courage to share Christ, pray with my dad, and walk him through forgiveness. It may not have looked like I thought it should, but I knew in my heart God was working something in my dad.

I know that my Bible studies and prayer have helped me to understand God's will, but as far as knowing how he is going to make something happen? I am rarely right. Just when I'm ready to place a worn-out prayer on the line between giving up and letting go, he moves on it. Like one seemingly ordinary Sunday morning: "Sweetie, wait up. I think I'll go with today."

"Go where?"

"What do you mean? Aren't you and Evan going to church today?"

"Well yeah, you want to go?"

"Yes, let's go," he says, grabbing the keys.

Two years of prayers, mine and a dozen women from church standing by my side, reminding me to quit whining and nagging at Sandy, teaching me to pray silently in faith. Then when I least expect it, God answers the prayer. When I looked away from the pot, it bubbled to a full boil. I admit, at first, I tended the pot like a crazed chef. Progress not perfection, right? I let go of the controls faster than ever before, returning to prayer. It's a good thing I turned to faith because Sandy's beginnings at church were not at all as I'd pictured.

"Isn't the music great?" I asked midway through the first song.

"It's loud."

And when Wayne's message was especially dynamic, I asked, "What do you think?"

"I can't really hear. I can't focus."

After service, a fellow asked Sandy if he could pray with him. I would have chosen someone else, more of a *man's man*. Later, I asked how it went.

"Are you okay with the prayer you got?"

And he replied with tears in his eyes.

"Yeah, it was great."

The months that followed were not easy for Sandy. He'd go every week, but once there, it was as if he was being poked and prodded by invisible sharp-toothed gremlins. Most Sundays, he'd pace or stand in the back during the message and worship.

"Are you okay?" I'd ask.

"No! I don't want to be here. I'm not okay. I don't belong."

I can't exactly say when the torment stopped, but it did.

CHAPTER 54

What Are You Going to do Differently?
(Sandy)

MY PICKUP OVERFLOWS WITH GARBAGE, yet at least one more load remains scattered around the overstuffed dumpster. When did the fourplex become the neighborhood dump site? For all that, hauling trash twice a week is not as bad as my next chore. With three days left before May rent is due, I'm banging on doors, begging for April's rent.

Pockets empty, I tie the tarp down over a beat-up sofa, a three-legged chair, and fourteen plastic bags reeking of juicy garbage and loaded Pampers. On the drive to the dump, I continue the ongoing head argument, I never win nor lose. The fourplex is a decent investment, but I didn't sign up to be the grand pooh-bah of trash or the classic bad guy, Snidely Whiplash.

At home, before I can shower and take a breath, Deb greets me at the door, upset.

"You just missed some guy. He asked for you. He said Ray is loaded. He's lying, playing the AA hero, stirring up drama. He talked about him like he's a threat."

"Who was it?" I asked.

"I'm sorry, I don't know if he said his name. I was rattled. He wore a baseball cap, probably my age, not tall but taller than me. I told him he was mistaken and that he shouldn't be blabbing rumors without all the facts."

I agree with Deb. Ray wouldn't toss fourteen years of sobriety out the door. He's going through some marriage stuff; that's why he moved into our little house, but he's not the type who only stays sober on a sunny day. No way. After calming Deb down with assurances of Ray's well-being, I pry for more details about the messenger. I learn the guy was wearing a green shirt, not grass green but olive, and he drove a silver generic car. Tip: Don't bother calling Deb to testify if you ever need an eyewitness.

The next day, I'm mowing the lawn, a challenge with Gabe. He stands in the way, looking at me like "That's noisy. What are you doing?" I have to stop, tell him to get out of the way, wait while he moves two feet, mow up to him, and repeat. Sick of the game, I yell at him, just as a truck pulls into the alley. It's Ray's estranged wife, Kim, and David, a long-time sober friend of mine. Gabe barks twice, then approaches, on alert for food.

"Hey, David, how's it going?" I ask as he rolls down the window. "Hi, Kim."

"Have you seen Ray?"

"No, not for a while."

"He's loaded. We're looking for him."

I listen to David and Kim, sharing sightings and stories of Ray's supposed adventures. It's not that I think they're making stuff up, but certainly they must be victims of rampant rumors. Ray hasn't been around much lately, but that doesn't mean he's avoiding me because he's loaded.

Two more days passed with no sign of Ray. At AA meetings around town, whispers of Ray's crack use and pawn-shop activity run amok. We keep watch for him, anticipating his return and rumor-killing explanation. Finally, while in the garage tinkering with a broken Victrola, I hear Ray's 1967 popsicle-orange Chevy Stepside pickup pull up next to the rental. Rag in hand, wiping WD-40 from my hands, I race out to catch him.

"HooRay! [My pet name for him] Hey, can I talk to you a sec?"

He was nearly inside the house. Closing the screen door, he walks toward me.

"Sure."

"You need to show your face in a meeting. People are passing rumors that you've run off and got loaded. Even David and Kim believe it. They stopped by to warn us."

Following a clumsy silence, he looks me in the eye, responding as if he'd rehearsed for this moment.

"They're right. I did get loaded."

"It's true?"

"Yeah. But I'm done now."

On cue, Gabe lightens the mood, sniffing and frisking Ray for a T-bone. He's enamored with his buddy Ray who frequently tosses him steak scraps from the porch. I give them a moment of ear scratching and tail wagging before moving on.

"Are you sure you're done?"

"Yeah, I'm done."

"What are you going to do differently?"

Indignant, he responds, "Not use."

"Well, you were going to meetings, in service, reading the book, what's going to be different?"

He walks away, mumbling.

The next morning, he steps into the garage, quietly watching me clean the workbench. Not knowing what to say, I wait for him to speak.

"Hey, friend. I need help."

That's what I needed to hear. "We admitted we were powerless over alcohol—that our lives had become unmanageable." The first step. The one that opens the door to hope. Together, we travel back fourteen years, opening the Big Book as if for the first time, attending daily meetings, and a few more for good measure. Within a couple of weeks, Ray is back, busy painting houses and mowing lawns. All is well. The days stack up. I have the honor of presenting his thirty-day sober coin.

Shortly after the one-month celebration, Ray went back out with a vengeance, disappearing for days, surfacing to crash, shower, and go back out. Tales of his whereabouts and doings swelled Tsunami-style. What we witnessed with our own eyes from our kitchen window broke Deb's heart.

"He's so skinny. He doesn't even seem like the same person. Where's the boisterous, big-hearted guy blasting *good morning*? He's so dark and sullen. He hides under that hoodie, diverting eyes and soul."

And when she couldn't see him from the window, fear took over.

"Oh, dear God. Sandy, do you think he's okay over there? What if he's OD'd? Will you please go check on him?"

The routine becomes: bang on the door, call out his name, and repeat until he rouses from a grave sleep, grumbling expletives. Then report to Deb he's okay. On occasion, he let me in the door, slouching in a chair, moaning when asked my single-focus question.

"What are you going to do differently?"

His possessions disappeared one by one, gobbled up, Pac-Man-style. Three vehicles became two, the last standing being his labor of love, Chevy truck. One day, he handed me the title to keep it safe from himself. With little to pack, he moved out of our rental, and soon thereafter, the drugs outshined the beautiful orange truck. Standing at the kitchen sink staring at the empty rental is not much different than before. Ray may be out of our view but not our minds or hearts.

"Sandy, I don't understand. Do you think he's trying to kill himself? He's going to die."

"I know. I don't get it either. It makes no sense. He loves his little girl more than anything, but he's going to die if he keeps this up."

"We can't just let him kill himself. What can we do?"

"We keep praying."

Over time, our prayers dwindled from ones with lots of details "keep him safe, send an army of believers, open his ears, soften his heart, heal his addiction, send him to jail" and so on to one simple plea. "Please, Father, drench Ray with your grace. Help him to know your love for him."

People all over town and across the state pray for Ray, the great guy who gives freely to others. In our own circle, his name is lifted in prayer at church, home groups, and in private. News of his whereabouts and exploits resemble those of abominable snowman sightings—frequent, far-out, and false. When we heard he was living in a campground in the canyon, we took a drive, searching every campsite for signs of him. We want to tell him we care, that we love him. We don't find him but may have spotted a Yeti.

He does jail time in Monroe and Spokane, along with time in a treatment center and more jail back in Yakima. The prayers never cease. I admit, though with no visible hope, the *amens* feel stagnant. Then one day, Ray knocks at the door with a humble heart, asking how he can make amends for the grief we'd suffered. Without knowing it, he met all amend requirements by sharing his revelation on God's amazing grace. Any other proclamation would have been heard with doubt. God's grace is and was his and our only hope. Ray, standing before us, speaking about grace, is no less a miracle than watching a paraplegic grow limbs.

That same month, April, we are blessed with our third grandson, Ty James Howard. Blond like mom but blue-eyed instead of brown. Stephanie never said she wanted to be a mom. It didn't need to be said. Family is her heartbeat. I admire her life and even approve of her choice of husband, Tim. Deb should take note; he is a *man's man*. He hunts, rides rodeo bulls, and can hold a conversation about stuff that matters, like racing or fishing. They're not like many young couples who find themselves married with children, asking, "Uh, now what, honey?" Instead, they have it all mapped out, sacrificing today's wants for tomorrow's. For now, they live in a mobile home on ten acres in a wooded area near Deer Park. When money allows, they'll build a home.

We wait a week before visiting to see our new grandson, Ty, granting first grabs to competing relatives. This way, we can say "our turn, hands off" without feeling guilty. The mobile home looks like a bomb went off in a baby boutique. Stephanie looks tired enough to have been in the blast, but at the same time, she's exploding with the joy of motherhood. Tim looks plain tired. Holding Ty, knowing my baby girl is a mom is surreal. Sitting with Deb talking *grandparentese* is beyond bizarre. How can it be? Deb says it makes her feel young. I don't know about that, but it's all good. Yes, it's very good.

Driving home, we pass the town of George, infamous to Washingtonians for its name and apropos greasy diner, Martha's Inn. It's also the last pit stop for twenty miles.

"Hey, honey, how far to the next restroom?"

"We just passed George. There's a rest stop at Vantage hill about twenty miles but—"

"But what?"

"It's one of the ones you won't use because of the stainless-steel seats."

"You mean, the toilets designed by a sadistic woman hater who gets his thrills laughing at the thought of women having to sit on an ice-cold steel toilet seat? I'll wait until Ellensburg."

Laughing, I barely hear my phone ringing. Deb finds it for me, answers, and hands it over to me, whispering, "It's your sister."

"Hey, San, it's Robin. Daddy had a stroke."

Pow! Sucker punched!

"Will you pick up Dad's car from Don? Can you meet us at the hospital on Whidbey Island? It's not good, San. It looks really bad."

It's as if I'm standing next to myself on the phone, watching a home video. I hear the words. I know they are real, but I reject them. It is not *really bad*. It's just another ministroke, slightly more serious than the last one. He's going to be okay. Robin's upset and rightfully so. Dad is the family plumb bob. He keeps us upright and stable. Seeing him ill is too much to handle, then add in Mom whose dementia peaks with small dramas, and it's over the top.

I don't remember the rest of the trip home to Yakima. As asked, I meet with Don and drive Dad's car home. I don't think I slept. I leave for Whidbey Island the next morning before daylight. I spend the six-hour drive analyzing the details leading up to Dad's ordeal and going over Robin's account. Mom and Dad were set to go with us to Spokane to meet their newest great-grandson. Looking back, I see how strange it was that he canceled last minute. He doesn't do that. Out of the blue, he calls Robin, asking if she'd take them to Anacortes. Of course, she agrees because she'll do anything for them. She turned on her heel, gathered up Don, and off they went. The trip to Anacortes for the Tulip Festival has always been Mom and Dad's thing. They went every year until Mom's dementia prevented her leaving the house to buy bread, let alone go on a trip. Besides the memories made with Mom, he grew up in that area, holding on to treasured times with his dad. I'm guessing once he talked Mom into going to Spokane, he opted for Anacortes. The scene Robin described on the phone is incomprehensible. Dad collapsing? Landing on the floor in a restaurant? Poor Robin, keeping Mom calm while they wait for an ambulance.

I arrive at the hospital early afternoon, rush in as if time matters, asking for Flavius Palmer's room number at the desk. I hear Mom and Robin's voices as I walk down the hall. Seeing me, they fall silent. Taking a deep breath as I walk into the room, I prepare for seeing our hero, ill, uncomfortable, pale, sickly. I was not ready to see him laid out flat with tubes and monitors, unable to rest or lay still, moaning and writhing in pain. Another deep breath moves me closer, hoping to speak. Robin steers me from his left side over to the right.

"Dad, it's Sandy. I'm here, Dad."

He stirs, making a guttural noise. Looking at him, I know he's not going to be okay. Robin assures me that he knows I'm here. I don't know how long we stand there in a stupor before stepping into the hall to talk. This time, as Robin repeats the doctor's words, I hear and believe a massive stroke, no function on his left side, best-case scenario he might stabilize. Spending the rest of his life with one side of his body dead and the other wreaking pain? That's not the best of anything!

Back in the room, Mom chatters plans that will never be. She talks about what she'll cook and how he will have to listen and do as the doctor says. She hasn't taken care of Dad for some time now, but she doesn't know that. I'm grateful for Robin because she knows how to calm Mom's fears, bring comfort, and say stuff like "It will be okay, Mommy." I don't have that kind of tolerance right now. I care, and I know Mom needs help, but I don't have what Robin has, and I don't know how to manufacture it.

The next two days, we hop between motel, hospital, and diners. Finally, the doctor tells us what we can see for ourselves: No sign of improvement. We made arrangements for Dad to be taken back to Yakima in the morning. After the ferry ride back to Mukilteo, we speed ahead, not wanting to tail behind Dad in the ambulance.

That night, back in Yakima, Deb and I visit the care facility where Dad had been admitted earlier. Walking down the hall, we see a familiar figure pacing outside Dad's room. It's my brother, Mark.

"Sandy," he says, shaking his head. "I didn't know he was this bad."

It was a time-machine moment—two brothers, scared of losing the man they love and respect more than any other. The man, ever the protector. The man with the right answers. The invincible, taken-for-granted hero who doesn't get sick and will never go away. Neither of us is strong with words, but we hold on to each other, sharing sorrow, fear, and tears. Then together, we walk through the door of Dad's room where he lay, broken. Helpless, we stand, unable to do what Palmers do—fix things.

I know Mark is feeling like me, wanting to go, wanting to stay, not able to leave, not able to stay. Finally, we say our goodbyes in the hall and leave. Out in the parking lot, Deb asks if I want to go to life group. I don't have a better idea, so I agree. After all, being with others might be a good distraction. I've been going to church several months now, and the people are okay. Our timing is perfect, arriving right after chitchat, just as the worship music begins. I don't remember my thoughts or feelings during worship or the discussion. For all I know they talked about spuds and prunes. At the end, they ask if anyone needs prayer. I'd certainly never asked for prayer, but I figure if there is ever a time, this is it.

"My daddy is dying," I said, surprised hearing the words come out in a childlike voice and manner.

The room stills. Soft-spoken people gather around me, placing warm hands gently on my shoulders. I don't remember many of the words prayed, a few *healing, comfort, peace.* I do remember feeling God's presence. And with the amen, I feel hope.

The next morning while getting ready for work in Naches, the phone rings.

Dad is gone. So much for prayer.

CHAPTER 55

In Spite of Us
(Deb)

No one deserves forgiveness less than me. I thumbed my nose at the thought. I didn't need nor want it. He offered it. I refused. He offered it again. I said, "No, thank you." He left forgiveness in front of me, ready for the asking. I ignored it.

One day, broken and filled with despair, his offer was the only choice left. Rightfully afraid, fearing I'd get what I deserve, I asked that my sins be forgiven. Jesus did not thumb his divine nose at me. He didn't make me grovel and beg. He asked for nothing in return. He invited me to stand before our Father, fully clean, forgiven and loved. Then, as if an eternal gift, changing my course from hell to heaven is not enough, he promised I'd never be alone, granting ever-present help in times of trouble, a gift given on the spot to me in my as-is condition, no small print or hidden clause stating I must fulfill a list of renovations on my soul prior to receiving it—the full-salvation deal given while knee-deep in sin.

After that, forgiving others should be a snap. Right? That's what I thought. I joined a small group workshop, focused on deep-root forgiveness called "Surrendered Hearts." In obedience and God's word in my mind and heart, I made my list of vows and bitter-root judgments that needed to be nailed to the cross.

"For if you forgive other people when they sin against you, your heavenly Father will also forgive you. But if you do not forgive others their sins, your Father will not forgive your sins" (Matthew 6:14).

Having already done the fifth step in AA, most resentments, judgments, and unforgiveness acquired since we're in pupal stage. Even so, some were found buried deep in my clenched heart, released only after the women in the group joined me in prayer. Then there was one left in the form of a person, my dad. Obedience, my motive to forgive, got the words out. Forgiving is not a feeling; it's an action, a command. With the others, I felt a breaking away and closure. No matter how many times I said the words, I felt nothing.

"I forgive you, Dad. I forgive you. I forgive!"

I meant it. Or at least, I wanted to. It just wouldn't stick. A phone call or visit with Dad churned up the ugliness in my soul. Have I really forgiven him, if he still angers and hurts me, ranting on, trying to justify the unjustifiable? As soon as he starts making excuses for losing his temper with Mom or my sister Nancy, my words of forgiveness fall flat and feel silly like a dieter convincing myself a celery stick is a brownie.

When Sandy's dad died, a childish voice rose up inside me. It was jealousy. Sandy and his siblings had the dad in the white hat, the one riding the white horse, swooshing in to protect his family at all costs, the one who showed them love, respect, and tenderness. Why did we get stuck with the dad in the hillbilly hat, riding an angry black horse, rushing in with threats and fists?

Listening to the eulogy Sandy wrote about his dad, hearing Mark and Robin speak of the *rock*, the *pillar*, the *hero* hurt. I felt shame, like the body I'd tossed into the sea with cement shoes had surfaced. What terrible person would resent the Palmer children for having a kind and loving dad? Am I two years old? They deserved a loving father. All children do.

I spent years bouncing between forgiving Dad and repenting for not. Somewhere in this process, I asked God for wisdom. Why? Why can't I forgive? I want to. I need to. One day, when at rest, the answer swooshed in as if riding in on a white horse: Love. I need to love my dad *as is*. Thus far, my eyes saw only who he was not. He was not the idealized dad picture I had in my head. Could I take a good look at Dad in reality and love him? Alone, I could not.

Through much prayer and practice, a miracle sprouted. I don't know when it matured, only when it could be seen. Like most days, I was listening to Dad go on about the drama in his life. As usual, the conversation turned to justifications for hurting his wife and children, pointing fingers at us for his actions. Prayer being my survival tool, I kept quiet, asking God for forbearance. Unlike the other times, something was different, new, not with Dad but me. My heart ached. Compassion tickled my soul like a father's hand gently sweeping his daughter's hair from her face. I felt love for my dad. Here I'd been watching, waiting for God to change my dad. Yet Dad is as always with no sugar-coating, and I love him. God tricked me in the best of ways. God is the same. Dad is the same. I am changed.

The aftermath of Flavius's death is similar to that when my mother passed. We siblings were left keepers of our father, whereas Sandy, Mark, and Robin were left chasing their mom through *the land of dementia*. Possibly, Laurel's Alzheimer's worsened with the loss but more likely without Flavius; we were all forced to open our eyes.

Laurel is active in her disease, no laid-back, drowsy, go with the flow, can't remember much anyway for her. She works it like a job. Even worse yet, she self-medicates with large doses of beer, wine, and whiskey. She's always been creative and able to work with what she's been given, whether designing and sewing clothes for herself, sisters, and four children or creating master chef soup from refrigerator plunder. In *dementia land*, she's no less resourceful. Not able to drive and not wanting to hear the word *no* from loved ones, she calls a cab driver. For a hefty price, they'll pick up a case of beer from the local grocer, deliver it to your door with a smile and a hand out for a tip. The only thing worse than dementia is adding alcohol to it. Just when you think you've arrived at crazy, it takes a fast detour uphill. Laurel, forever awake and lively, begins making frequent calls to the police, reporting illusory shootings, break-ins, and noises. The fears of the night depended on whatever she watched earlier in a movie or on the news.

Clearly, unless the drinking stopped, a catastrophic crisis was at bay. Thus, plans evolved for Laurel to attend a local drug and alcohol treatment facility. Since it is a voluntary program, getting her there would be tricky. Keeping her in a dry, unlocked facility where you are free to go, if you choose took a miracle. And so, God provided miracles. Laurel reluctantly agreed to go to treatment. At the ranch, against everything she'd been told by family and staff, she came to believe she'd moved into an apartment complex. Later, when needed, her mind told her she was not allowed to leave. Upon completion of the twenty-eight-day program, her children moved her into a retirement home, a lovely facility with minimal care, privacy, and a do-as-you-please policy. Prayers increased with concerns she'd make fast friends with a new cabbie willing to bring a bottle and a smile for a nice tip. Once again, a still small voice planted a seed in her mind that alcohol was not allowed on the premises.

Even with a fragile memory, when taken on outings, having a beer was on the top of her list of *to-dos*. Once at a nearby restaurant, I interceded her attempt to order a beer, saying, "No, Laurel, you cannot have a beer." After lunch, the waiter approached the table, addressing me in a snarky tone. "Is it okay with you if she has some dessert?"

During that same lunch date, she shared graphic details of a liposuction surgery she'd underwent some time ago. She spared no details, including the intense pain when they stuck the thin hollow tube into her abdomen, moving it back and forth. That night, I mentioned it to Sandy.

"I didn't know your mom had a liposuction procedure. When was that?"

"What?

"Your mom's liposuction. It sounds awful."

"She's never had anything like that done. But the other day when I stopped by to check on her, she had the television on the health station, watching some medical procedure. That's probably how she got it in her head."

She is susceptible to suggestion, especially negative. We all look for outings with a minimal stimulus, anything to bring her peace. Every Sunday, Sandy calls Laurel, reminding her to get ready for church, only to find her in robe, wondering why he's stopped by. Once he's won the debate for what day it is, he reprograms the TV, proving once again it is not a giant radio. Then and only then will she get dressed for church. Albeit a hassle, seeing her sit through the service at peace is well worth it.

I'm grateful for our church family. Just as with me, they've shown great love with Sandy. His first few months attending were rocky. He walked through the doors, happy and content, yet by midworship, he's grumbling. Sandy's hearing deficit often leaves him believing only I hear his complaints.

"I can't stay here! I don't belong."

I suspect, by the glances our way, bountiful anonymous prayers were sent above.

The night that became Sandy's dad's last on earth, I wanted to help. By then, I knew I had no power to do so. Certain he'd refuse but hopeful I'd be wrong, I asked if he'd go to my home group with me. Agreeing it might be better to be around other people, he said yes. It was a small group, most knowing the situation. They gave him space; let him be with the Lord. When the group leader asked for prayer requests, Sandy responded. As the body of Christ, we prayed for him, loved on him, and cried with him. In that communal bath of the Holy Spirit, I rested, knowing that my husband is more importantly my brother in Christ.

The next morning, Flavius died from a massive stroke. That was not our prayer, hope or plan. It was God's. It's not easy to understand why God doesn't choose what seems to be the easy way, heal Flavius, secure the faith of us all, especially Sandy. If God is God, then God is in every sense God. That means trusting he knows what he's doing. Although Sandy trusts God in much, taking his dad pushed the line. He'll work through this in his stubborn, self-abusive way, but it hurts to see him struggle. I can't fix him, but I know Someone who can.

Speaking of God's ability to right wrongs, change the unchangeable, and fix the incurable, Ray is above ground. He left us all shaking our heads, wondering how he could *take such a licking and keep on ticking.* God, not Timex, kept him safe. It's funny, how after God moves mountains, we try to convince ourselves we knew it all along. I confess, I thought Ray was a goner. One day, he's this effervescent guy, taking time to make someone smile, the next, a sullen shadow, wearing a hoodie three times too large. You learn a lot about a person, watching from your kitchen window. I know we share love and respect for my husband; that he adores his daughter; that he's an honest man who keeps his word; that he's a heck of a nice guy with a big heart for others. From the same window, I watched the extrovert, shrink fifty pounds in size and twice that in spirit. It was like watching an apple dry out in the sun, shriveling, darkening, dying.

Ray was the proverbial lost sheep who wandered off alone, found by God dangling on the cliff edge. The day

Ray shared with us how God's grace lifted him up and out of death served to cement our own faith. Through all the doubts, God was actively working to answer our prayers.

Likewise, God stayed with my Sandy, whether he's was angry or not. Sandy did not quit God or church when prayer did not get the result he had wanted. He sat next to me in the pew every Sunday, like it or not. He even continued going with me to home group, complaining all the way there and back. I admit my prayers turned to pleas for patience.

Then one day, he surprised me.

August 29, 2005, Hurricane Katrina struck the Gulf Coast, a storm, catastrophic in itself with an aftermath equally devastating. Come November, Sandy announces he's taking his vacation from Naches school district to join a small team from our church of four adults and three youth on a mission trip to New Orleans. As he spoke, I realized it had been awhile since I'd seen his smile.

God knew what Sandy needed—to be about his father's work. So while Sandy hammered away rebuilding homes destroyed by the hurricane, God rebuilt his faith. He returned from this first mission trip, minus the grudge, overflowing with stories of new life.

"The main job we worked on should have been condemned before the flood. At first, I thought *what the hey?* But when I met the single mother of three children and heard the story—"

It was a rickety tract house, built at least eighty years ago in the hardest hit Ninth Ward. To the young mom, the dilapidated family home was worth more than any castle. It was a matter of family roots, and more practically, with no mortgage, it was survival. Without it, they'd be homeless, with no means to pay rent or take on a mortgage.

"When my crew and I got there, it had already been gutted by another team. My guys were unskilled, so I got to teach them."

More kudos to God for not only giving Sandy something to build but also tossing in a few God-loving strong back guys needing to be taught. Who but God would know to put that cherry on top?

"Oh, and I should tell you, I paid a prostitute," he says, grinning like an idiot.

"What?" I ask, feigning outrage but confident there's more to the story.

And there was.

Taking a short break from work, the all-male crew of five loaded into a van. With the mission soon over, they wanted a glimpse of the sights on Bourbon Street and a taste of the famous New Orleans's cuisine. Back at the mission station, a volunteer cook had recommended the restaurant, Café DuMonde, on Decatur Street in the French Quarter. Short on time and bored with driving in circles, they agree to ask for directions from the first person who looks like a local. They reject three groups of obvious tourists before spotting a young woman in a miniskirt and extratall heels. Riding shotgun, Sandy initiates the conversation.

"Excuse me, miss?"

Approaching the van, she leans into the window, smiling, and invitingly friendly.

"Hello."

"Could you help us? We need directions to Café DuMonde. It's around here close somewhere."

"I could."

"Okay?"

"The thing is, I'm working."

"Oh . . . oh! She's working," he says to the guys in the back who might be deaf.

"So I'd need to be paid."

Sandy reaches into his pocket, handing her a $5 bill.

"Of course. Here you go."

"It's straight ahead, two blocks on the right, sweethearts."

The best story happened while Sandy was walking from the sleeping tent to the mess hall. In God's glorious way of sneaking miracles into everyday situations, a fellow worker with numerous missions under his tool belt strikes up a conversation. Somehow, God being a suspect, the conversation turns to Sandy, and he shares that he recently lost his dad.

"May I pray for you, right now?" the man asks.

Thrown by the spontaneity of the request, he agrees to prayer.

"I don't remember the words of the prayer, only that afterward, I felt at peace for the first time since losing Dad."

Sandy returned to Louisiana twice, each time with more stories and signs of healing. In September 2008, after Hurricane Ike swept across Texas, he packed his tools and flew to Galveston.

"I am at peace when building and helping others. Using the skills I learned from my dad, that's when I feel close to him and even closer to God."

It sounds cliché, but I have to say, "God is good!" In spite of us.

EPILOGUE

Deb and Sandy

TWENTY-FIVE YEARS LATER.

The waves rise and fall, the tides ebb and flow while the cool sand soothes our bare feet. Peering over its vast expanse, feeling small in the most glorious sense, it seems nothing has changed since we walked this beach as honeymooners, a quarter century ago. Yet beaches do change; they move like curtains in a breeze, shifting year to year, decade to decade.

Walking along the foggy shore, reminiscing the cherished moments peppered with the shameful ones, we share an epiphany: We are like the sandy shore, changed one grain at a time, eroded and rebuilt over time, new, transformed.

Deb: "Twenty-five years, can you believe it?"
Sandy: "No, sweetie. I can't."
Deb: "I didn't think we'd make it very long, did you?"
Sandy: "What? Of course, I did! I knew we'd be together forever! You didn't?"

Deb: "I'm sorry. No, I didn't. Forever was a fairy-tale word. But you know I love you, and that I believe in forever now, right?"

Sandy: "Yes, I do."

Deb: "Look at that silly seagull. Remember Gabe tip-toeing behind them thinking he was so sneaky?"

Sandy: "The seagulls loved messing with him, leading him on to think he might have a chance. [Laughing] Oh . . . and he was scared by the tide, remember? He thought it was chasing him. The king of water dogs, afraid of the ocean. But he loved to swim in the river."

Deb: "I miss him so much."

Sandy: "Me too, thirteen years is not a bad run for a big old honky lab."

Deb: "How far do you want to walk down the beach?"

Sandy: "Not that far. How long have we been out here? Forty minutes?"

Deb: "We used to walk for three hours, eat trucker-sized stacks of pancakes, go back to our room, have sex, and take a short nap."

Sandy: "That was a quarter century ago. The sex is even better now, and the naps are longer! What more could we want?"

Deb: "Pancakes. We don't get to eat pancakes anymore."

Sandy: "You really didn't think we'd stay together? Back when we got married?"

Deb: "Well, think about it. My heart had a tapeworm gobbling up what love I found, leaving me to chase after whatever would make me feel okay.

Nothing could fill that black hole. I was destined to destruct."

Sandy: "Yeah, that's true."

Deb: "And, dear, if you try real hard, you might also remember a man rather stuck on himself, convinced he could fix me. Would you have placed a bet on that couple surviving the real life that was waiting to unfold?"

Sandy: "How much of a bet?"

Deb: "Seriously, Sandy. Back then, I expected you to be my god. You're hot stuff, dear, but you could have never filled that order. You had faith but—"

Sandy: "But what?"

Deb: "Well, it was selective? Answer this, do you think your faith today is bigger than when we met?"

Sandy: "Hmph, okay, I get your point. It's like measuring the ocean with a ruler. How would we have ever gotten through the losses?"

Deb: "I know. I often think about the grace we were shown just when we needed it."

Sandy: "Dad's death, at the time, I didn't understand. I kept asking why."

Deb: "I think my hardest was losing my little brother, Danny, at age fifty-two."

Sandy: "I don't know, sweetie. What about that time leading up to your dad's death?"

Deb: "Yeah, that was really hard. That's what I mean. You showed your mom kindness, patience, and love through all her troubles, right up to the day she passed. Where did that come from?"

Sandy: "God loving me first. Changing, softening my heart. I think we thought our faith meant living the rest of our days on easy street."

Deb: "Yes, we did. Now I find comfort knowing, no matter what, God is in charge, that all is well through the trials and times when we're living out the consequences of our past."

Sandy: "Yeah. It's hard to understand when it hits. Like when budget cuts sliced my position in Naches. I felt like I was being punished, forced into an early retirement. It was a challenge trusting, waiting in faith, knowing God's will is better than mine. I still miss my job sometimes."

Deb: "I know. But look at you now. You're a blessing to the church with your building skills. You enjoy that and always do well when you're needed You're an answer to prayer for many."

Sandy: "I don't' know about that. Grab that sand dollar by your foot. Is it a good one?"

Deb: "It's perfect, see?"

Sandy: "Nice."

Deb: "We have so much to be grateful for. All our children are wonderful and doing well."

Sandy: "And look at us? Just imagine, if back when we met, I'd have said, 'Hey, darling, let's get hitched, stay sober, find God, and have a pack of grandsons?' What do you say? Sound like fun?"

Deb: "That's easy. I'd have said 'Adios, amigo' and ran. What if I'd asked you that? What would you have said?"

Sandy: "You run slow. I would have walked away and never looked back. How about now, knowing what you know today, would you say yes if I proposed?"

Deb: "Absolutely! I'd even sign the papers in permanent ink this time. What about you, knowing who we'd become today?"

Sandy: "In a heartbeat, especially knowing the life God has planned for us."

Deb: "I know. I spent most my life searching for love in all the wrong places."

Sandy: [Singing in twangy-cowboy mode] "Looking for love in all the wrong places, looking for—"

Deb: "Stop! That's awful. Be serious, goofball."

Sandy: "It's crazy how clueless we are as to what will bring peace and contentment to our lives. He knows and wants us to have what's good. His grace is amazing."

Deb: [Singing in twangy-cowgirl mode] "Amazing grace how sweet—"

Sandy: "Now that's bad! Stop now, my ears. You about ready to head back to the room?"

Deb: "Sure."

Sandy: "Okay, let's pray."

"Thank you, Father. We love you with all our heart. We are humbled by the changes you've made in us. And grateful, oh so grateful. Please help us to keep changing every day, striving to be in perfect alignment with your will. Forgive us for our daily failures. Purify our hearts and transform our thoughts. Thank you for always providing for our needs and more. Thank you for our relationship, for blessing our marriage. We do not deserve all you've done for us. We pray that each day, our lives will better give glory to you."

DEB AND SANDY PALMER reside in the Pacific Northwest where they celebrate a blessed marriage, sobriety, family, and a spirit-filled church.

Deb has published an array of fiction and nonfiction articles in numerous print magazines, online journals, and anthologies. In addition, she writes an inspirational blog "In Spite of Us" known for gut-wrenching truth and humor with a message. Check out her stories here: http://debpalmerauthor.com/

Sandy, a former primary-school counselor, admits he is retired when it suits him. He is a cheerful servant, not only as a volunteer handyman for a 107-year-old church with over one hundred rooms but also as a carpenter on missions needing homes rebuilt after natural disasters. Besides sharing authorship of this book, Sandy partners with Deb in their antiques business.

CPSIA information can be obtained
at www.ICGtesting.com
Printed in the USA
BVHW031607140119
537772BV00003B/258/P